D1420618

JOHN SUCHET

MOZART

THE MAN REVEALED

CLASSIC *f*M

JOHN SUCHET

MOZART

THE MAN REVEALED

First published 2016 by
Elliott and Thompson Limited
27 John Street, London WC1N 2BX
www.eandtbooks.com

ISBN: 978-1-78396-293-8

9 8 7 6 5 4 3 2

A catalogue record for this book is available from the British Library.

Designed by James Collins

Printed and bound in Italy by Printer Trento.

This book is dedicated to the memory of James Black.

Lover of Mozart's music and chronicler of his life.

CONTENTS

PREFACE

Mozart the man is easy to understand. Mozart the genius is impossible to comprehend.

The story of his life is well known. Austrian-born, with a tyrant of a father who drove him relentlessly, an unhappy marriage to a spendthrift woman, a childlike character ill at ease amid the pomp and aristocratic splendour of the Viennese court, poisoned by his great rival Salieri, which led to an early death that robbed the world of its most instinctive musical genius.

Only the last is true. In this era of mass entertainment, it is possible the most prevalent image we have of Mozart is that portrayed in the hugely successful film *Amadeus*. Like the plot of the film, and the play from which it was adapted, the character is largely fictitious, or at least grossly exaggerated.

One element, though, rings totally true. That smile stretching from ear to ear, that uncontrollable laugh, that permanent sense of happiness, of being comfortable with himself and at ease with his genius – all that permeated his being.

Musical history is replete with tortured souls, tormented geniuses. Among them is one who can lay claim to be the greatest of them all, given how much he achieved in such a short life. And even if that is disputed, one fact cannot be: despite repeated disappointment at his failure to gain regular paid employment, despite money problems in the final three years of his life, Mozart is surely the happiest composer who ever lived.

Listening to Mozart's music induces a sense of well-being, a feeling that all is well with the world. Whatever is happening outside the concert hall or opera house, if a human being can create such beauty, then there will always be hope for humanity.

Mozart was giving us the benefits of a gift with which he was imbued. He knew it. He did not know where it came from, or why he alone possessed it, but he knew it and he continued to use it. We owe him a limitless debt of gratitude, as will our children, grandchildren, great-grandchildren, and every generation that follows them.

Everything Mozart created exists for us to enjoy. It was a brief life, but we should be eternally grateful that he lived at all.

PROLOGUE

On 5 September 1842, a year behind schedule – something of an embarrassment – a monument to Wolfgang Amadeus Mozart was unveiled in the centre of the city of his birth, Salzburg. It had been planned for the year before, the fiftieth anniversary of his death, but had been postponed when a Roman mosaic floor was uncovered during excavation work.

As well as a lasting memorial to Salzburg's most famous son, the monument was also intended as an act of reconciliation. Mozart, like his father Leopold, had come to loathe Salzburg, the archbishop-prince who ruled over it, and indeed its people.

The feeling was entirely mutual, and when Wolfgang left Salzburg for Vienna, never to return, there was something of a collective sigh of relief that this difficult, disobedient – although admittedly highly talented – musician had finally left.

The monument was a form of belated apology. Mozart should have been better treated by his home town, as people from far and wide had been saying ever since his death. Now Salzburg would be able to point to the huge, imposing monument by a celebrated German sculptor.

The site had been carefully chosen. Mozart's wife Constanze had recently moved to a new apartment in the Michaelsplatz. It was decided the statue would be erected there, and the square renamed Mozartplatz. Constanze would be able to gaze out of her apartment window onto the statue of her husband.

She would not have recognised the larger-than-life-size figure: handsome and serious face, cloak over the shoulder gathered at the waist like a toga, pen in hand. This was not a representation, but a deification.[*]

Two thousand people gathered for the unveiling, many coming from distant parts of the world. Mozart's two sons, Karl and Wolfgang, were

Left

The statue of Mozart in Salzburg's Mozartplatz.

---

[*] There were marked similarities to the statue of Beethoven unveiled in his home city of Bonn three years later. Albeit by a different sculptor, it showed a godlike figure, toga thrown over the shoulder, and a pen in the right hand.

there. But their mother was not. During that year's delay, she had died at 3.45 a.m. on 6 March 1842, at the age of eighty. She had outlived her husband by more than fifty years.

The other centrally important woman in Mozart's life was not there either. Like Constanze, she would not have recognised the Mozart she knew, her laughing, mischievous brother, in the dignified and imposing figure staring into the distance.

But even if she had been there, Nannerl would not have been able to see the statue. In her final years she slowly became blind. The attractive young girl, 'a regular beauty'[1] whose musical abilities – along with those of her younger brother – had stunned Europe and who had been labelled 'a prodigy of nature', was described in her final years as 'a decay of nature'.

Maria Anna Mozart, known throughout her life as Nannerl, had outlived her famous brother by almost forty years, dying thirteen years before the unveiling of the statue at the age of seventy-eight.

One woman was at the unveiling, and she was a totally unexpected guest. In the midst of the ceremony, a very tall, thin and eccentric-looking woman interrupted proceedings by declaiming, '*Ich bin die erste Pamina!*' ('I am the first Pamina!')

The woman was the celebrated Austrian soprano Anna Gottlieb. More than half a century earlier, when she was just twelve years of age, Mozart had cast her in the role of Barbarina, the gardener's daughter, in *The Marriage of Figaro*.

Five years later, when she was still only seventeen, her voice was so beautiful that Mozart gave her the all-important role of the steadfastly loyal Pamina, the embodiment of innocence and beauty, in the great creation of his final year, *The Magic Flute*.

At the time of the unveiling of the statue, Anna was the last singer still alive who had known Mozart.

1

The Handsomest Couple in Salzburg

Mozart was born on 27 January 1756 in the city of Salzburg. At the time of his birth it was a wealthy city state sitting between Bavaria and Austria, and independent of both. It had grown rich and important on the back of its abundant natural product, salt, which gave it its name, *Salz-Burg* – 'Salt Castle'.

Technically it was part of the Holy Roman Empire of the German Nation, and so loosely speaking was part of Germany.* Mozart himself was in no doubt. Throughout his life he referred to himself as German by birth and a German composer.

From its earliest years Salzburg had an abbey, and by the eighteenth century a cathedral had stood there for a thousand years. The most powerful man in Salzburg was the archbishop, who was not only the most senior religious figure but also a prince of the Holy Roman Empire, answerable only to the Pope and the Holy Roman Emperor in Vienna.

The prince-archbishop, and the canons under him, ran the city of Salzburg, and they ran it according to strict Roman Catholic principles. A *Law*

---

* Salzburg has had a chequered history, due largely to the shifting borders of Continental Europe during the Napoleonic wars. It was annexed to Austria after the Battle of Austerlitz in 1805. It was briefly transferred to the Kingdom of Bavaria as punishment for the Austrian defeat at Wagram in 1809. In 1815, at the Congress of Vienna, the city was definitively returned to Austria, the bicentenary of which was celebrated in 2015–16.

on Morals, issued by the archbishop in 1736, a mere twenty years before Mozart was born, decreed:

> *Men are not to leave their beds without wearing shirt and trousers, nor women without wearing shirt and petticoat. Trousers must be waist high, fastened in front. Women's skirts must cover half the calf; shirts and bodices must be made wide enough as to overlap and lace properly. Absolutely forbidden is the irritating, bestial and fiendish habit occurring in the public baths, where men and women bathe together almost naked and then dry each other off.*

The prince-archbishop's court was by far the biggest employer, controlling the lives of a huge number of people, from lawyers, soldiers and local industrialists, down to secretaries, valets and maidservants.

And musicians. Salzburg was a cultured city, maintaining a large court orchestra and choir, and giving employment to a number of composers. In all, around a hundred musicians were employed by the court.

Traditionally the archbishop of Salzburg held himself aloof from the people of the city, allowing his canons to extort money from them. For centuries there had been palpable resentment directed from the city, and from outlying villages in the diocese, towards the wealth that existed within the cathedral.

There was thus quiet satisfaction when, in 1753, a new archbishop was appointed – a cultured man, with affection towards his people, and a great love of music. Archbishop Siegmund Schrattenbach made it his aim to put Salzburg at the forefront of music within the states of the Holy Roman Empire.

This was an enormous stroke of good fortune for one man in particular, who some years earlier had left his home in Augsburg in Bavaria to escape a career in the priesthood, and headed for Salzburg to pursue his vocation in music. After attending university in Salzburg he secured a position at court as a violinist and violin teacher.

With prodigious musical talent, and a regular income, it was not long before he married. Following the appointment of the new archbishop, he became a court composer, and soon after that deputy kapellmeister. He was rising fast in his chosen profession and the future looked rosy. He and his wife were in a position to start a family.

His name was Johann Georg Leopold Mozart.

⌐

History has not been kind to the father of the boy genius, and it is not hard to see why. Contemporaries described him variously as acerbic and

difficult, aloof and domineering. He controlled the lives of those closest to him in every detail. His wife was barely allowed to make a decision for herself, and his children would find that their every move was decided for them well into adulthood.

It seems that Leopold Mozart's contrary character was formed early in life. Born in Augsburg, he was the eldest of nine children, and found himself left increasingly to his own devices by a mother who had too many demands on her time to pay him much attention.

At the age of seventeen, just four months after his father's sudden death, he took himself out of school. If this upset his mother, he was to make matters much worse by announcing he had no desire to take up the family business of bookbinding, or to follow his mother's second wish by entering the Jesuit priesthood.

An estrangement became a rift when Leopold decided to leave Augsburg altogether and head for Salzburg, intending to turn his natural talent for music into a career. He enrolled at Salzburg university, where his headstrong character really showed itself.

In September 1739, at the age of nineteen, he was expelled for 'want of application and poor attendance'; in effect, for truancy. But what really

shocked the university authorities was his calm acceptance of his fate. The rector reported:

> *A few days before the examination he was called before the Dean and informed that henceforth he would no longer be numbered among the students. Having heard this sentence, he offered no appeals, accepted the sentence, and departed as if indifferent: therefore he was not called for further examination.*[2]

'*As if indifferent ...*' You can just picture the look on his youthful face that caused the rector to write these words. Maybe it was a slight curl of the lip, the beginnings of a sardonic smile. There must have been something in his expression that struck the academic panel, and made it worth noting. If one is tempted to admire Leopold's independent spirit, such admiration must surely be tempered by his display of youthful arrogance.

It was a quality that stayed with him in later life. Those academics would not be the last to feel the force of Leopold's character. But there was method behind Leopold's seeming indifference to the end of his student career. He immediately obtained employment as a musician, and as early as the following year published his first compositions, a set of six trio sonatas.

Meanwhile Leopold's relationship with his mother only got worse. He informed her that he had met a young woman in Salzburg and intended to marry her. This was, as it were, the final straw. If Leopold married a Salzburg girl, it was unlikely he would ever return to live in Augsburg. His mother disapproved so totally that she disinherited him.

The rift was never healed. As far as we know, Leopold's mother never met her daughter-in-law. Even more extraordinary, when her two highly talented grandchildren were brought by their parents to Augsburg, where they gave three public concerts, she did not come to see them perform.

Consider this. Wolfgang Mozart, boy genius, comes to Augsburg at the age of six to demonstrate his extraordinary musical skills – which are already known and marvelled at – and his own grandmother refuses to leave her house to come and see him.

When a break occurs between mother and child, whatever brave words the son may choose to put on it, however successfully he may suppress it, the guilt can linger and fester. I believe this is what happened with Leopold. He was in any case a difficult character. The fact that the schism was never healed is likely to have made him an even more irascible and unpredictable individual.

Unlike Leopold, the woman he chose to marry, the woman who would give birth to the greatest of musical geniuses, remains a somewhat shadowy

Left
Johann Georg Leopold Mozart, c. 1765, thought to be by Pietro Antonio Lorenzoni.

figure. As we shall see, in the many letters that Leopold would write to her during travels with their son, she rarely rates a mention.

Anna Maria Pertl* was born in the village of St Gilgen, on the banks of the Wolfgangsee in the Salzkammergut mountains, one of the most beautiful regions of Austria.

What could have been an idyllic childhood was anything but. Anna Maria's father, who was forty-five when he married, had suffered a near-fatal illness five years before she was born. His health continued to decline and she was only three years old when he died.

He left the family destitute. As his health worsened he had borrowed more and more money, and at his death his debts totalled more than four times his annual salary as a minor local official. His effects were confiscated and Anna Maria, together with her mother and elder sister, had to move from the calm of a lakeside village to the bustle of Salzburg, where they lived on charity.

It seems that both his daughters had inherited his ill health. Anna Maria's elder sister died soon after the move, and Anna Maria herself was described in charity records as 'constantly ailing' and 'the constantly ill bedridden daughter'.

Her fragile health was clearly not helped by having to look after her widowed mother. What she could not yet know was that her father had possibly passed on one truly great gift. Although he had not pursued music as a profession, he was a highly gifted musician. It might not have manifested itself in his daughter, but it most certainly would in her own children.

It is not known how Anna Maria came to meet a young violinist at court by the name of Leopold Mozart, but after what appears to have been a fairly lengthy engagement – 'All good things take time!'[3] Leopold wrote to his wife on their twenty-fifth wedding anniversary – they married on 21 November 1747. Leopold had just turned twenty-eight; his wife was thirteen months younger.

Leopold had, as he wrote later in the same letter, and with a rare touch of humour, 'joined the Order of Patched Trousers'. He had reason to celebrate his marriage. His wife was, by all accounts, docile and obedient which, given Leopold's natural proclivity for decision-making and brooking no disagreement, made for a contented union.

---

* Mozart biographers seem evenly divided over whether his mother was Anna Maria or Maria Anna. The portrait of her that hangs in Mozart's birth house in Salzburg is labelled Anna Maria. Also, since her daughter was christened Maria Anna, and one of the children's cousins too, I shall refer to her throughout as Anna Maria.

Leopold and his wife Anna Maria were soon considered the handsomest couple in Salzburg. Their portraits, painted when they were in middle age, show fine sensitive faces. There appears to be a touch of self-assurance, arrogance even, in the portrait of Leopold, with his half-lidded eyes and slightly curled lip, and Anna Maria's pose perhaps presents a stronger character than we suspect to be the case.

Yet if those faces had been shown etched in some pain, it would have been understandable. Exactly nine months after their marriage a son was born, named Leopold after his father. The infant lived for less than six months.

Anna Maria was already pregnant again when he died, and gave birth to a daughter, Maria Anna, four months later. The child lived for just six days. Anna Maria was soon pregnant once more, and less than a year later gave birth to another daughter, again named Maria Anna. This infant lived for a little over two months.

Three children lost in the space of seventeen months, and the couple had not yet been married three years.

It is hardly surprising that when another daughter was born exactly a year after they had lost their third child, Leopold and Anna Maria lived in a state of high anxiety, celebrating each day that the child survived as a miracle.

Once again – and one can imagine this decision being made only after much soul-searching – they named their daughter Maria Anna, like her two deceased sisters. The third Maria Anna, known as Nannerl, was to live for seventy-eight years and three months.

But the couple's heartbreak was not yet over. A son Johann Karl, born sixteen months after Maria Anna, lived for just three months, and a daughter Maria Crescentia, born in the following year, died at seven weeks.

Six children in a little less than six years, and only one who had lived to see a first birthday. It is impossible to know, when Anna Maria fell pregnant yet again, whether she was elated or in despair. Infant mortality was high in the mid-eighteenth century, and there will have been many families in Salzburg who lost as many, or more, children than the Mozarts. But still the toll of seven pregnancies in such a short period of time must surely have debilitated Anna Maria both physically and emotionally.

I imagine an exhausted woman, now thirty-five years of age – middle aged, in fact – resigned to almost constant child-bearing, followed by the infinite sadness of seeing tiny coffins bearing each child away. Now a seventh child was on the way.

Anna Maria gave birth to a son at eight o'clock on the evening of 27 January 1756. It was not an easy delivery. The placenta failed to emerge naturally and Leopold reported that it had to be removed forcibly. As a result Anna Maria became extremely weak; she was at high risk of fatal infection, and for a time it was not known if she would survive.

A child who was more than a day old without being baptised was believed to be in danger of hellfire, and so the infant was baptised at ten thirty the following morning. He was given the names Johannes Chrisostomus Wolfgangus Theophilus. The first two names were for the saint, St John Chrysostom, on whose name day the child had been born; Wolfgangus was for his maternal grandfather; Theophilus was the Greek version of Gottlieb, 'Beloved of God', the name of his godfather.

From the start he was called by his third name, Wolfgang, or more often its diminutive, Wolferl. In later life he himself preferred the Latin version of his fourth name, Amadeus, though he was more inclined to use Amadè, or Amadé, or even (when in Italy) Amadeo.

Wolfgang Amadeus Mozart was his parents' seventh, and final, child. He and his elder sister Nannerl were the only two to survive into adulthood. But his was not to be a long life. Nannerl would outlive her younger brother by almost thirty-eight years.

Above
Kitchen of the Mozarts' home on Getreidegasse.

As soon as they were married, Leopold and his wife had moved into an apartment on the third floor of a building at 9 Getreidegasse ('Grain Lane').[*] The building was owned by the Hagenauers, a family that dealt in groceries and spices on the ground floor and one imagines the infant Wolfgang and his sister growing up with the pungent aroma of these products under their noses.

It was a fortuitous move. The Hagenauers became firm friends of their tenants, the Mozarts. Johann Lorenz Hagenauer was also a banker and music lover. Not only did he encourage Leopold to take his young son on

---

[*] The whole building was acquired by the Salzburg Mozarteum Foundation in 1917, and is today a museum devoted to Mozart.

Right

The family home
at 9 Getreidegasse;
Mozart's Geburtshaus
(birthplace) is now
a museum.

tours of Europe, but in effect bankrolled them by issuing credit in cities along the way.

The building was in the old town in the centre of Salzburg. The Getreidegasse was the commercial heart of the city. It was home to court offices, bakers, grocers, goldsmiths, hotels and taverns. It was the most heavily populated street in the whole of Salzburg.

The boy Mozart thus spent his formative years in the heart of the city, surrounded by its noise and bustle. He remained a city boy all his life, and when many years later he moved to Vienna, he never lived beyond the close suburbs, preferring always to be as near to the centre of the city as possible.

The Mozart apartment, while not large, was able to accommodate a family of four. There was also room for a clavier, a small keyboard instrument. Had more of the children survived, it's likely the family would soon have had to move out. As it was, they remained there for twenty-six years, until the seventeen-year-old Wolfgang's fame and resultant earnings allowed them to move to a larger home.

The apartment in the Getreidegasse frequently echoed to the sound of music. Leopold and his professional friends would play together, and Leopold was able to supplement his income by giving private violin lessons there.

He was a very successful teacher. In the year Wolfgang was born he had published a book entitled *Versuch einer gründlichen Violinschule* ('A Treatise on the Fundamental Principles of Violin Playing'). It was reprinted twice in German, and was then translated into Dutch and French.

Leopold Mozart was firmly established as one of Salzburg's leading musicians, and it would not be long before he was appointed deputy kapellmeister (deputy head of music at court), a senior position second only to the kapellmeister himself.

Given his professional reputation, it must have come as a welcome surprise to Leopold when he realised his eldest child Nannerl was showing signs of an interest in music. Maybe she sang for him; maybe she picked out notes on the clavier.

He will no doubt have surmised that, given his own natural musical talent, supplemented by that of his father-in-law before his untimely death, his children might display some aptitude for music. Little could he have known just to what an extent that would prove to be true.

Trusting his instincts, he began to teach Nannerl the clavier when she was around seven years of age. She took to it immediately, surprising and delighting her father. He probably did not pay much attention at first when his young son, just three years of age, began to watch these lessons intently. When they were over the boy would pick out notes, playing simple chords and smiling at the pleasing sound.

To aid Nannerl's progress, Leopold compiled a book of pieces for harpsichord by composers of the day, including a number of anonymous ones, almost certainly by Leopold himself. Mostly the pieces were minuets, but he arranged them in such a way that they became increasingly difficult, the rhythms more complex, ever wider jumps, tricky ornamentation, advancing to hands crossing over.

The book, which Leopold called *Notenbuch für Nannerl* ('Book of Notes for Nannerl'), was exactly what Wolfgang needed, as playing thirds up and down the keyboard began to bore him. He started playing the pieces in Nannerl's book.

Leopold began to pay attention. He could clearly see that Wolfgang was gifted. He started to teach his young son some minuets, then some more difficult pieces. Recalling this later in life, Nannerl said Wolfgang could learn a minuet in just half an hour, and a more difficult piece in an hour. He would then play them with the utmost delicacy, faultlessly, and in exact time, she said. This might normally be expected in a highly talented young musician at least ten years older than Wolfgang.

Realising that his son was more than just usually talented, Leopold began to teach him the organ, and then the violin, at the age of four. The boy took to them naturally, particularly the violin. But his father was something of a taskmaster, and Wolfgang had to work hard to gain his approval.

On one extraordinary occasion, two of Leopold's colleagues came to the apartment in the Getreidegasse to run through some new string trios with him. Little Wolfgang, aged six, nagged his father to allow him to play second violin. Leopold was adamant he could not. He was a child, nowhere near competent enough. Wolfgang insisted he could do it. Again his father refused. Wolfgang cried tears of frustration and left the room.

The second violinist, one Johann Andreas Schachtner, suggested to Leopold he let the boy play alongside him. It couldn't do any harm. Leopold relented, on condition Wolfgang followed Schachtner's lead.

'I was astonished to realise,' Schachtner recalled, 'that I was soon entirely superfluous.'[4] He put down his violin and allowed Wolfgang to continue. The boy successfully navigated all six trios, reading from sight.

Wolfgang, emboldened, asked his father to let him play the first violin part. This meant Leopold relinquishing the lead to his young son. Schachtner related how Wolfgang, given his small hands, had to resort to 'wrong and irregular positions',[5] but he and Leopold were stunned to admit he carried it off without any serious mistakes.

We are indebted to Schachtner for recalling another occasion, which happened at about the same time, and was of even more significance than the string trios run-through.

He and Leopold returned to the apartment after Thursday service to find the small boy sitting at the table, pen in hand, blotches of ink on a piece of paper. They watched him dipping the pen to the bottom of the inkwell, which caused drops of ink to spill onto the paper. Wolfgang wiped the blotches away with the palm of his hand, and continued writing. They asked him what he was doing.

'I am writing a clavier concerto. The first movement is nearly ready,' the boy replied.

Leopold laughed at his son's bravado, pointing out that nothing could be read under the ink smears. But then he began to look more closely. Soon, according to Schachtner, he was shedding tears of wonderment and joy.

'Look, Schachtner, how correctly and properly it is written. But it is too difficult. No one could play this.'

'That's why it's a concerto,' Wolfgang said. 'You must practise very hard to be able to play it.'[6]

Then, to the men's utter amazement, Wolfgang demonstrated what he meant on the keyboard.

He soon put it aside, though, as if instinctively he knew that he should start with less ambitious compositions. He composed several small pieces for clavier, which his father wrote down in Nannerl's book. Several pages went missing in the intervening centuries. Two pieces have survived. Soon after his fifth birthday, Wolfgang composed an Andante and Allegro in C major for clavier (κ. 1a and 1b).* They are his first known compositions.

Leopold Mozart was now in no doubt. He had a son with a musical talent neither he, nor anyone, had ever encountered before. The question confronting him: how should he handle it?

---

* According to the numbers assigned to Mozart's compositions by Ludwig von Köchel in his catalogue of 1862.

2

THE LITTLE
WIZARD

The short answer: show it off and make money out of it. In early
January 1762 Leopold took his two children to the capital city of
Bavaria, Munich. Nannerl was ten, her brother approaching his sixth birthday.

Leopold Mozart has, in the intervening centuries, taken much criticism
from biographers of his son for setting out on travels when his children were
so young, with the explicit aim of showing off their musical talent. Today
we might call him a 'tiger dad' and accuse him of 'hot-housing' the children.

On one level the criticism is justified. Neither child ever attended
school. For a daughter in the mid-eighteenth century this was probably not
exceptional. But Wolfgang never attended school either. His father taught
him entirely at home, in subjects as wide-ranging as mathematics, reading,
writing, literature, languages, history, geography, dancing, even moral and
religious training. Excellent musician Leopold might have been, but one has
to wonder whether he was skilled enough in these disciplines to educate his
son adequately in them all.

From Leopold's point of view, though, his behaviour was entirely justifi-
able. He realised he had two young children of exceptional talent. Nannerl
was well ahead of her age in musical performance. She could sight-read,
improvise on a given melody, take it through several keys, and compose accompanying bass lines. As for Wolfgang, he was so much more skilled than
his sister that he put her in the shade.

This, in fact, was of some concern to Leopold. What if it was a temporary gift? Given that he had started so young, what was to say that his talent

might not end as abruptly, or at least decline and wither? Wolfgang might reach a level of brilliance, but not improve from there. If he were not to progress in the next ten years, say, his prodigious talent at the age of sixteen would be a lot less impressive than at the tender age of six.

And so, keen to make the most of his children's talent while it lasted, Leopold left for Munich with Nannerl and Wolfgang, leaving his wife behind. It was to be a brief trip – no longer than three weeks – and it is probable that Leopold did not need to ask the archbishop for leave of absence from musical duties at court.

Very little is known about what happened in Munich, other than the fact that Leopold must have had an impressive letter of introduction in his pocket, since he was able to gain an audience with the elector of Bavaria, Maximilian III Joseph, and present his highly gifted children before him.

We can also be sure that the prince, himself a talented composer and player of the viola da gamba, was impressed, because the aristocracy of the city took the lead from their ruler and invited the two Mozart children to perform in their salons.

Leopold returned home to Salzburg in early February, flushed with the success of the trip, inordinately proud of his children, and already planning his next move. Leopold was beginning to realise that his children could become a seriously successful source of income.

He immediately began working on another trip, and lobbied at the highest level to achieve it. This time he was setting his sights high. The ultimate goal within the Habsburg empire, the seat of the Holy Roman Emperor, the capital city of the empire as well as the capital city of music: Vienna. It is also more than likely word had filtered back from Munich to Salzburg that the Mozart children really were quite exceptional.

Leopold achieved his goal, and more. The music-loving Archbishop Schrattenbach approved Leopold's leave of absence. More than that, he agreed to sponsor the trip, at least in part, and keep Leopold on his full court salary while he was away. With that commitment in his back pocket, so to speak, Leopold was able to persuade his landlord, Johann Lorenz Hagenauer, to provide more financial assistance. Hagenauer lent Leopold money and allowed him to draw money on the Hagenauer business account while he was away. Hagenauer, as well as being Leopold's landlord, was effectively his banker as well.

Conditions were thus perfect for the Mozart family to try their fortune in the sophisticated capital city of Vienna, with its plethora of wealthy aristocrats and patrons of the arts.

'Family' is the operative word. Leopold was not going to do this by halves. This time he would take his wife with him as well: they all left

Left

Archbishop Schrattenbach, 1755, by Franz Xaver König.

Salzburg on 18 September 1762. Finances were secure enough to take a servant with them, though that is probably too lowly a word. Joseph Richard Eslinger was a bassoonist and copyist, but his job was to look after the family's clothing and baggage, make sure all the music was kept in order, and generally run errands for them.

It might be imagined that Leopold was over-brimming with confidence, secure in the knowledge that his young son – still only six years and eight months of age – would stun the musically sophisticated Viennese with his extraordinary talent.

Quite the opposite. Leopold was a natural worrier and something of a born pessimist. Soon after arriving in the capital, he wrote to Hagenauer, 'If only I knew how it will finally turn out.'

⁓

The journey from Salzburg to Vienna took almost three weeks. The Mozarts were in no hurry. There were plenty of people to impress along the way, with musical performances that would act as rehearsals for the big city. There was also always the possibility that such performances would bring financial reward.

The most direct route to Vienna would have taken them east, but instead they travelled north to Passau, on the Bavarian border with Austria. Leopold's aim was to show off his children's talents to the prince-bishop, Count Joseph Maria Thun-Hohenstein.

There, on the very first stop of the trip, he was reminded that things could be anything but straightforward. A local aristocrat, used to issuing orders and expecting tasks to be performed at his pleasure, might issue an invitation to an itinerant musician. It could be a vague invitation, with no set date or time. The musician had no choice but to wait, running up the cost of board and lodging in the meantime.

That was exactly what happened to the Mozart family in Passau. The count kept them waiting for five days, before summoning Wolfgang to play, but not his sister. To compound the disappointment the boy was rewarded with a measly four gulden, which Leopold complained left him with a net loss of 80 gulden.

Leopold's initial optimism was tempered by reality as the family boarded a boat in Passau to travel down the Danube to Linz, the bustling and busy capital of Upper Austria that straddled the mighty river. But things began to look up.

On the boat Leopold fell into discussion with a certain Count Herberstein, who knew the city well and was soon to become the first Bishop of Linz. He told Leopold exactly who he should get in touch with when they arrived.

This paid dividends. In Linz, under the sponsorship of a senior member of the aristocracy, Wolfgang and Nannerl gave their first public concert. Several visiting Viennese noblemen were in the audience, including one, Count Pálffy, who had the ear of Archduke Joseph, son of Empress Maria Theresa no less (and later co-ruler with her, before becoming emperor in his own right).

Count Pálffy, a delighted Leopold reported, 'listened with astonishment' to the two children, and on his return to Vienna duly spoke 'with great excitement' to his friend the archduke, who in turn – just as Leopold had hoped – passed it on to his mother, the empress. She, without any doubt, will have mentioned it to her husband, the emperor.

Leopold had good cause for optimism. Word of his children's musical prowess had reached the very top. No doubt emboldened, he decided not to head straight for Vienna but instead to leave the boat at the little town of Ybbs – let word spread, let a sense of excitement and anticipation build up.

There Wolfgang played the organ in the Franciscan Church. He played it so well, Leopold wrote in a letter back to Hagenauer in Salzburg, that 'the Franciscans rushed to the choir stalls and were almost struck dead with amazement'. You can understand why. This was a boy not yet seven years of age playing a mighty organ.

The Mozart family arrived in Vienna on 6 October, almost three weeks after leaving home. At the quayside, reality struck. The Mozart name might have reached the imperial royal family in the Hofburg Palace, but it was unknown to custom officials on the banks of the Danube.

The Mozarts were told to open their luggage for inspection. Perhaps Leopold gave his son a knowing look; perhaps it was Wolfgang's own initiative. The boy took his violin out of its case and played a minuet. The senior customs officer, enchanted by the impromptu recital, allowed the family to proceed without opening their bags.

They stayed first in temporary accommodation on the Fleischmarkt, then moved into lodgings on the Tiefer Graben. It was not the height of comfort. Leopold reported that they had a single room on the first floor, 'a thousand feet long and one foot wide'. It was partitioned in two, with Leopold and Wolfgang sharing one bed in the sleeping area, Anna Maria and Nannerl sharing the other. Leopold was irritable, and complained the children would not stop wriggling.

Word had most definitely arrived in Vienna ahead of them, and it had spread at the highest level. Leopold took himself off to the opera four days after arriving in the capital (to see Gluck's *Orfeo*) and overheard another of Maria Theresa's sons spreading the word from his opera box that 'there is a boy in Vienna who plays the clavier admirably'.

This son was Archduke Leopold, who in time would succeed his brother Joseph as emperor. We know, therefore, that even before the Mozarts arrived in Vienna, the extraordinary talent of young Wolfgang was talked about by the emperor, empress and two future emperors.

And it permeated down. The senior aristocrat who had arranged the recital in Linz had returned to Vienna and spoken immediately to the highly influential director of opera. Count Herberstein, Leopold's companion on the boat, had done his part too to spread the word in Vienna.

Leopold was most certainly not exaggerating when he wrote to Hagenauer in Salzburg, 'As soon as it became known that we were in Vienna, the order arrived that we should present ourselves at court.'

On Wednesday, 13 October, the family took a carriage to Schönbrunn Palace, the emperor's summer residence west of the city. To say they had arrived, in more senses than one, would be an understatement.

One can picture Anna Maria and the two children looking agog as the imperial carriage, which had been sent to collect them, drew up to the grand, imposing and beautiful baroque palace, recently improved and remodelled on orders from Empress Maria Theresa. Leopold, I imagine, sat quietly, expressionless, jaw probably set, wondering if everything was about to go as planned. Was it possible that his son could have an off day?

"Leopold had good cause for optimism. Word of his children's musical prowess had reached the very top."

He need not have worried. The account of the occasion, as detailed by Leopold in letters to Salzburg, has achieved legendary status. It is the first real evidence we have of young Wolfgang's extraordinary talent at the keyboard. It also gives us our first true insight into his character, into what kind of child he was.

The family was ushered into the royal presence. Empress Maria and her husband Emperor Franz sat in two luxuriously upholstered chairs. Also present was their youngest daughter, Maria Antonia, just three months older than Wolfgang, who in a few short decades would enter history as Queen Marie Antoinette of France. There were also other family members in the room, as well as some senior figures such as ladies in waiting.

It began conventionally enough – other than the fact that this was a boy aged six and a half, and inordinately small for his age. Wolfgang climbed onto the stool, little legs dangling, and played on the clavier. To his father's relief he did not disappoint.

'People could hardly believe their ears and eyes at [Wolfgang's] performance,' reported one of the ladies of the court.[7]

Emperor Franz himself, taking control, decided on a little mischief. Little Wolfgang was to be put to the test. 'I can see that you play with all your fingers, which is what you are used to doing. But what if the keyboard were covered? Could you pick out a tune then with even one finger?'[8]

Wolfgang squealed with delight. It was just the kind of trick that appealed to him. A piece of cloth was found, and laid along the length of the keyboard to cover the keys. The black keys being raised will have held the cloth slightly above the white keys, so that no indentation to mark the separation between the keys would have been apparent. Wolfgang would have to play completely blind, which unsurprisingly caused him no problem at all.

First he picked out a tune with one finger. Then, with no difficulty, he played with all his fingers, probably looking up into the air with a mischievous grin, maybe cheekily directed at the emperor himself.

Emperor Franz, spellbound, dubbed him *Hexenmeister* ('little wizard'). The empress, too, was unstinting in her praise, because little Wolfgang jumped down from the piano stool, ran over to her, leapt up onto her lap, put his arms round her neck and showered her with kisses.

Never had the empress of the Habsburg empire been treated with such familiarity by anyone outside her immediate family, and then by a child she had never met before.

There was more familiarity that caused much amusement. At one point Wolfgang, careering round the room as a child would, slipped on the marble floor. Maria Antonia, the future Queen Marie Antoinette, helped him to his feet. 'You are very kind,' he said to her. 'One day I will marry you.'[9]

The emperor then informed everyone that Herr Mozart was author of an indispensable guide to playing the violin, and ordered his daughter-in-law, who was learning violin, to play for Leopold.

One can imagine Leopold swelling with pride at this unexpected encomium. Not only had his young son impressed the royal family beyond measure, but his own talents were being praised too.

It was a thoroughly satisfied Leopold Mozart who took his family back to the humble lodgings they shared on the Tiefer Graben – rather below what a family of musicians who had entertained the emperor and empress might be used to.

The whole visit to Schönbrunn had lasted three hours, which included a personal guided tour for Wolfgang of the empress's private apartments, carried out by the royal children who were excited to have a new young friend.

If word had reached the royal palace before the Mozarts' arrival in Vienna, it now raced through the ranks of the nobility like a forest fire. So many requests were there for Wolfgang to perform in aristocratic palaces and salons that Leopold had to write home to the prince-elector in Salzburg asking for an extended leave of absence.

Since one of those requests was for a second visit to Schönbrunn palace, the extension was a formality. That particular request from the very top

Above

Mozart and his sister play for Empress Maria Theresa.

brought with it 100 ducats, a very welcome addition to Leopold's finances.

There was more. Other aristocrats gave Leopold a variety of gifts and – much more welcome – money. By the time the family had been in Vienna for a month, Leopold had sent home to be banked the sum of 120 ducats, which was more than two full years' worth of his Salzburg salary.[*]

---

[*] It is practically impossible to estimate what money in mid-eighteenth century Vienna would be worth today. It has been calculated that 20 gulden, or florins, might be worth around £500. Given that there were 4.5 gulden in a ducat, 100 ducats might be worth around £11,250, meaning the sum Leopold banked would be around £13,500 in today's currency.

Left

Portraits of Wolfgang
and Nannerl Mozart
in court dress, aged
six and twelve, 1763,
ascribed to Pietro
Antonio Lorenzoni.

We have reason today to be very grateful to the empress for the gifts that she gave to Wolfgang and Nannerl – a set each of full-dress court clothes. These might have been hand-me-downs from royal children, but Wolfgang and Nannerl wore them the following year, back home in Salzburg, for two oil paintings, the first portraits we have of the Mozart children.

The young Wolfgang looks thoroughly regal in lilac jacket and matching brocaded waistcoat, with plentiful gold braid, gold buttons and tassels, white lace collar and cuffs and white stockings. He is holding a black hat and wearing a sword. His left hand is tucked imperiously into his waistcoat, his right rather arrogantly on his hip, one finger extended. He wears a wig, and he gazes unflinchingly at the painter. Were it not for his diminutive size, he could be a decade older than he was.

Nannerl, in a plum-coloured taffeta dress appliquéd with sheer white lace, has an equally self-assured gaze, her right arm bent at the elbow, hand turned with fingers splayed, as if she has been interrupted while playing at the keyboard.

And that, perhaps, is the most interesting feature of the portraits. Both have keyboards. That, now, is the Mozart children's raison d'être. They are musicians.

Leopold Mozart had every reason to be thoroughly pleased with the way things had gone in Vienna. But, as we have seen, he was something of a worrier, a born pessimist perhaps. And the truth was he did have cause, if not for pessimism, then at least for worry.

Leopold held a senior position as musician at the court in Salzburg. The most senior musician at court, the kapellmeister, had died the previous June. It was taken for granted that his deputy would succeed him, which would leave a vacancy for the number-two position.

Leopold Mozart was a leading candidate for deputy kapellmeister, but just when he should have been back in Salzburg pressing his case, manoeuvring along with other candidates, ensuring his name was at the forefront, he was away in Vienna.

Leopold put pen to paper. Using Hagenauer as a conduit, knowing full well his words would reach the court, he stated that if by staying in Vienna he was in any way losing favour with the prince-archbishop, he would leave 'on the instant' by mail coach for Salzburg.

He went further, and his choice of words is interesting. 'I am now in circumstances that allow me to earn my living in Vienna,' he wrote. 'I still prefer Salzburg though, but I must not be held back. If I am, I cannot say what others might persuade me to do.'

It is a veiled threat to resign from the Salzburg court and move, with his family, to Vienna permanently. His children, and in particular Wolfgang, he now knew, would be able to bring money in through their musical talents, and enough for the family to live on.

Leopold must have wondered if he had gone too far. Was he pushing his luck? What if the prince-archbishop called his bluff? It was not entirely a bluff. But here he was relying on his children's continued talent. The old worry resurfaced. What if they failed to improve? What if the aristocracy tired of them, and their earning power dwindled? What if something totally unforeseen were to happen?

And that last worry is exactly what occurred. By the time of the Mozarts' second appearance at Schönbrunn, on 21 October, young Wolfgang was seriously unwell. It had been threatening for some time. His mother was convinced the boat journey on the Danube, which had been unseasonably cold, wet and windy for September, had damaged his health.

So prodigious was Wolfgang's talent that, even suffering from a worsening cold and sore throat, he had been able to play as well as ever in the salons of the nobility. But people – high-ranking aristocratic people – were beginning to talk. Was Leopold pushing his son too hard?

Even the empress was heard to say Leopold was sacrificing his son's health in the pursuit of ducats. It was not looking good for Leopold. Or Wolfgang.

After that return visit to Schönbrunn, Wolfgang came down with a rash and lesions, with pain in his back and hips, which were diagnosed as 'a kind of scarlet fever'. His condition was made more difficult by his adult teeth beginning to come through. (He was just six years and nine months.)

The doctor confined him to his bed, and there he stayed for two weeks, after which time he showed considerable improvement. But word of scarlet fever had spread, and Leopold suddenly found invitations cancelled and others not forthcoming.

Leopold has done himself no favours with posterity by writing to Hagenauer that 'this adventure [Wolfgang's illness] has cost me 50 ducats'. He compounded this by spending an impressive 23 ducats on a private coach. He justified it by claiming they would have returned with fewer ribs had he not done so. He is probably right, in that Wolfgang's health would have suffered even more had he travelled in a more basic form of transport.

He suffered enough as it was. By the time the family arrived home in Salzburg, Wolfgang was so seriously unwell that smallpox was suspected. He had a fever, which prevented him from sleeping, and complained he felt nothing in his lower legs and was unable to move his feet.

He was confined once again to bed, and it was a week before things began to improve. With all the caveats of attempting a diagnosis two and a half centuries after the event, it seems the earlier illness was a streptococcal infection, followed some weeks later by rheumatic fever. Though his young age allowed for a swifter recovery, these were serious ailments for a child as young as Wolfgang.

While Wolfgang's mother worried over his health, Leopold looked beyond that to the effect a serious illness would have on the family finances. He had already seen how in Vienna Wolfgang's poor health had led to an immediate loss of income. If that were to recur, the rosy future he had once seen for the family would swiftly dissipate.

He had his own position to consider too, and it was precarious. Leopold had seriously tried the prince-archbishop's patience by extending his absence for a second time, to fit more recitals in on the journey home.

"Even the empress was heard to say Leopold was sacrificing his son's health in the pursuit of ducats."

In what looks to us like an absurd misjudgement, once back in Salzburg he had defended himself to Archbishop Schrattenbach by saying he had been forced to take the return journey slowly because the extreme cold made it necessary to protect the children's health. He compounded this by saying he had been suffering from dreadful toothache, which so disfigured his face that people who knew him had not recognised him.

If we are not fooled today, neither was the archbishop. But just when things were beginning to look really grim, they started to improve. Although Michael Haydn (the younger brother of Joseph) was brought to Salzburg as court composer and konzertmeister, thus diluting the power of the deputy kapellmeister, Leopold Mozart got the promotion he wanted.

Wolfgang's health improved too, and it was soon evident that his extraordinary young genius had not suffered.

Leopold looked to the future, and with his innate pessimism the future was at worst precarious, but at best ... who could tell? It was time to be bold. Bold and courageous.

Wolfgang had conquered Vienna. Now it was time for him to conquer Europe.

3

THE GRAND TOUR

On 9 June 1763, the Mozart family – mother, father, and two children – left Vienna for an extensive tour of Europe. Leopold had planned an ambitious itinerary. In the event it would be far more ambitious than he had intended, visiting more places and taking much longer than originally planned.

In all, the tour lasted for three and a half years, covered several thousand miles, stopped in eighty-eight towns and cities (several more than once), and the children performed for audiences totalling many thousands.

Leopold was easily able to persuade the benign Archbishop Schrattenbach to give him paid leave of absence, the costs again being partly born by Hagenauer and other wealthy burgers of Salzburg. The musically aware elector had witnessed the Mozart children's skills for himself, and knew any kudos they received would reflect well on Salzburg and its ruler.

That is indeed what happened, but to a degree far beyond anything Schrattenbach, or Salzburg, or indeed Leopold Mozart, might have expected. By the time of the family's return home, the name Mozart was known throughout Europe.

Those who had attended one of their recitals were heard to speak of the experience decades afterwards. In fact Germany's foremost playwright and poet Johann Wolfgang von Goethe, shortly before he died, vividly recalled seeing 'the little man with his wig and his sword'[10] performing in Frankfurt nearly seventy years earlier.

It certainly did not begin auspiciously. The family of four, plus a valet who also dressed wigs, had made less than a day's travel when one of the back wheels on the carriage broke. A temporary replacement was supplied at a coaching inn, but it was not quite the right size.

They had to continue, so Leopold and the valet walked alongside the carriage for two hours to lessen the weight, and they arrived just after midnight in the town of Wasserburg in Bavaria, in search of a cartwright and an inn where they could stay.

It ended up costing Leopold two new wheels, an extra night in the inn, which included a bed for the coachman too, and feeding the team of four horses and replacing them with a new team.

Leopold complained of the extra expense and time lost in a letter to Hagenauer back in Salzburg, but saying also that he put the second day to good use (knowing word would be relayed to Schrattenbach).

While the coach was being repaired, Leopold took Wolfgang to the church in Wasserburg. The organ there had pedals, and the small boy with short legs had not played on an organ with pedals before.

Leopold showed Wolfgang how to play with a pedal board, and then wrote in astonishment: 'Pushing away the stool, he experimented while standing.* Remaining upright, he played as he worked the pedal, and gave the impression of having practised in this manner for several months.' Adding, again – we can assume – in the firm expectation that word would reach the archbishop, 'This is a new sign of God's grace.'

The carriage repaired, they travelled on to Munich, arriving on 12 June. This was a return visit to the Bavarian capital, and here they collected more admiring members of the aristocracy, including the elector himself.

Leopold, always ready to report as much on what went wrong as on any successes, complained in a letter that the custom in Munich was to keep musicians waiting, sometimes for a long time, thus forcing them to run up extra costs for accommodation, meals and so on. To compound matters, he said, at the end it was unlikely any profit would be made. Whatever was received would cover expenses and no more.

He was preparing to move on, having found a brief gap in the elector's schedule of hunting by day and attending French comedies at night to show off his son's virtuosity, when the elector let it be known he wanted to hear the daughter play as well. That meant prolonging the stay.

In the event Nannerl performed admirably, and Leopold was pleasantly surprised to receive generous payment.

---

* Leopold used the Latin phrase, *stante pede*.

They finally got away from Munich after a stay of almost ten days, and headed for Augsburg. Leopold was not looking forward to this part of the trip. He had never been fond of his home town. After all, he had left it at the first opportunity to attend university in Salzburg.

There was also the embarrassment – and guilt, I am certain – of the rift with his mother. So deep was the break, as I have already noted, that his mother did not even come to hear her grandchildren perform.

'I was detained in Augsburg for a long time and profited little or nothing' and 'Everything [in the Zu den drei Mohren inn] was uncommonly expensive' were some of his comments, and as if to justify the surprising lack of interest in his children's recitals, he blamed the fact that 'those who came to the concerts were almost all Lutherans'.

His sourness was at least to some extent unjustified, as the local newspaper eulogised his 'two wonderful children', and wrote of 'the extraordinary gifts a magnanimous God has bestowed in so abundant a measure upon these two dear little ones'.

Ever mindful of money and unnecessary expense, Leopold did invest in one rather surprising acquisition in Augsburg – a keyboard small enough to be carried on their travels. You have to wonder whether maybe the two children ganged up on their father, pointing out that they were unable to practise on their constant travels, since hotel rooms did not boast pianos.[*]

As swiftly as he could, Leopold moved the family on to Ulm, around seventy-five miles west of Munich, another town Leopold had no liking for. 'Loathsome, old-fashioned, tastelessly built,' he wrote back to Salzburg. The quaint crooked streets and half-timbered houses dating from the Middle Ages held no appeal for him. He preferred classical order, balance, symmetry, though one does get the impression that, at that stage of the family's travels, nothing would have satisfied him.

In fact matters were about to get a whole lot worse. Leopold's plan was to head next to Stuttgart, seat of Duke Karl Eugen, known to be a great patron of the arts, and generous with his financial rewards for artists. In Leopold's pocket was a glowing letter of recommendation from a senior canon in Salzburg.

But, en route, while at a coaching station changing horses, Leopold learned that the duke had left for his country palace north of Stuttgart, and intended travelling on from there to his hunting lodge.

Undeterred, but no doubt cursing under his breath, Leopold ordered his coachman to change course, in the hope of catching the duke at his palace. He and the family arrived before the duke had moved on, and Leopold lost no time in making contact with the duke's Italian kapellmeister.

He brandished his letter of recommendation, but the Italian shrugged. Duke Eugen's every minute was taken up with moving, with an entourage of almost two thousand, to his hunting lodge. Even an audience was out of the question, let alone a musical recital.

Leopold appealed to the duke's master of hounds, in a somewhat desperate attempt to persuade him to delay everything. This not only failed; it backfired. The official, knowing the duke was worried that he did not have enough horses for his huge entourage, commandeered Leopold's.

The Mozarts were stranded. Now Leopold really let his venom fly. It was all the dastardly Italian's fault, he wrote home, adding that the wretched man hated Germans and was interested only in Italian musicians.

---

[*] Pianists, along with organists, lament to this day that they are unable to take their instrument with them, and so practice time on the road is severely limited.

Leopold finally secured fresh horses and on 12 July the Mozarts managed to get away and continue their travels. They journeyed on through southern Germany and up through the Rhineland, stopping in Heidelberg, Mainz, Frankfurt and Koblenz.

Leopold kept up a steady stream of letters back to Hagenauer in Salzburg. He chronicles his children's successes, their health – despite a storm more ferocious than any Leopold had ever experienced, the children slept soundly – and copious details about money, how much was earned, how much was spent on food and lodging, whether exchange rates were favourable or otherwise. Interestingly, there is barely a word in his letters about his wife. Certainly Leopold's main concern was to appraise Hagenauer of expenditure and other practical details, but the families were more than business associates; they were friends too. The omission is curious.

They had now been away for over a month, with not very much to show for their efforts. There had been performances, much praise, money had come in, but little more than enough to cover expenses. Leopold was constantly having to justify drawing money on Hagenauer's chain of business accounts.

There was a certain amount of time to relax. In the medieval university town of Heidelberg they became tourists, visiting the fortress set on a height to guard the town. Leopold bemoaned the damage done to it in the recent wars against the French.

They no doubt enjoyed seeing the giant beer cask, famed throughout the region, which held nearly 220,000 litres of the much loved liquid. And maybe father and son purchased fancy waistcoats the town was famous for. Leopold certainly mentions the two of them visiting the factory where they were made.

Frankfurt, commercial and cultural capital of the area, was nothing short of a triumph – something Leopold presumably felt was much needed. He publicly announced that on 18 August a concert would take place that would appeal 'to all those who take pleasure in extraordinary things … with incredible skill a girl of twelve and a boy of seven will play concertos, trios [with Leopold], and sonatas'.

Which is what they did, with such success that the concert was repeated four times. At the fifth concert (possibly at the earlier ones too), Wolfgang invited members of the audience to play single notes or chords on any instrument they wished, even on bells, glasses and clock chimes. He would name the notes.

As a clincher, his *pièce de résistance*, he would play the keyboard with the keys covered by a cloth – not just play, but improvise 'in all keys, even the most difficult'.

"*Frankfurt, commercial and cultural capital of the area, was nothing short of a triumph.*"

The audience was suitably stunned, and it was this concert Goethe recalled attending at the age of fourteen all those decades later.

There was one small fly in the ointment. Hagenauer was beginning to become just a little concerned about the amount of money it was all costing. His letter to Leopold has not survived, but Leopold's reply has, and in it he laments the high cost of hotels, laundry, food and tips. He makes the point that the money accruing to them through the children's efforts is keeping pace with expenditure, and appeals to Hagenauer's – and the archbishop's – vanity when he writes, 'We must travel nobly or worthily in order to preserve our health and the reputation of my court.'

And travel nobly he continued to do. He now most certainly had the appetite for continued journeying and more performances to show off his children. He had three goals in his sights, of increasing importance: Brussels, Paris and, most prestigious of all, London.

Crossing the border from Germany into the Austrian Netherlands* could be said to be the first time the Mozarts had travelled abroad. Technically they were still within the Holy Roman Empire, in its most westerly outpost, but to Leopold, at least, they were firmly in alien territory. The locals had no command of the German language, so Leopold found himself at a disadvantage when it came to haggling over price. He complained that publicans and innkeepers immediately inflated the bill when they realised he was a foreigner.

He was in a bad mood even before arriving in the capital. The iron hoops on the carriage wheels had burst, meaning extra stops for repairs, and more expense.

Once in Brussels, he complained that he was unable to negotiate a preferential rate at the exorbitant Hôtel d'Angleterre. His mood was darkened still further when the local ruler, Prince Karl Alexander von Lothringen, let it be known he would like to hear the Mozart children play 'within a few days', but those days soon became weeks, with no further word from the palace.

In a classic fit of Leopold pique, after five weeks of waiting he wrote to Hagenauer that 'the Prince spends his time hunting, eating, and drinking, and in the end it appears he has no money'. He did concede, though, that the recitals the children had given in the meantime to various members of the local nobility had been well rewarded, though he had not received as much in cash as he had hoped.

---

* Equivalent to present-day Belgium and Luxembourg.

'Little Wolfgang has been given two magnificent swords … My little girl has received Dutch lace from the archbishop, and other courtiers have given cloaks, coats, and so forth. With snuffboxes, needle cases, and such things, we should soon be able to set up a shop.' Leopold was clearly hoping to raise a smile back in Salzburg, but the underlying disappointment and frustration in his words come clearly through.

As on various other stops, the Mozarts did some sightseeing on their idle days. Coming from landlocked Salzburg, they delighted in seeing ocean-going ships sailing right through the centre of the city, gliding through the paved banks of the canal that led to Antwerp and the open sea.

Leopold took in a bit of culture. He admired works by the great Flemish artists, such as van Eyck, Rubens and Van Dyck, while *A Last Supper* by Dirk Bouts he confessed had rooted him to the spot. He wandered in and out of Flemish churches, with their stark altars of black and white marble.

He remarked on how almost everyone had heavy wooden shoes, and the women wore hooded cloaks. A meal in an inn was meat and turnips ladled from a cauldron suspended above a hearth. In an inn outside the city he laughed when a herd of pigs invaded the dining room and waddled and grunted beneath the tables. He imagined himself in one of the medieval paintings he had seen.

Finally, the waiting was over. On 7 November, after almost six weeks, a 'big concert' was held in the presence of Prince Karl. It was, as always, a huge success. Leopold was delighted to report back to his paymasters in Salzburg that he had received 'a rich booty of fat thalers and louis d'or'.

Eight days later he packed his family into the now rather battered coach and set out for Paris. The journey took four days, with three overnight stops. Leopold reverted to his habitual complaining. The rates for hiring horses were astonishingly high; the ubiquitous cobbles wreaked havoc on the carriage's suspension, particularly since the coachmen whipped the horses to a gallop, and men and horses were changed every two hours (Leopold had paid extra for express travel, to save on more overnight stops). As for the men he saw climb aboard to take the reins, it is worth quoting him in full. It is a delightful mix of humour, sarcasm and, one suspects since this is Leopold, frustration.

> *Sometimes I took them for a pair of pedlars, sometimes for a pair of rogues from a farce, sometimes for a pair of Italian donkey drivers, sometimes for a pair of vagabond hairdressers, or dismissed jobless lackeys, or even valets, sometimes for a pair of discharged sergeant majors.*

He added, just in case Hagenauer and company had not got the point, that they travelled at such speed and in such chaos that he felt like 'a soldier in the Army of Empire pursued by two divisions of Prussians'.

The Mozarts arrived in the outskirts of Paris on the afternoon of 18 November. Lying before them was a great European capital without ramparts and fortified gates – a sight for central European eyes to marvel at.

The family was now truly abroad and the city they were about to take up residence in was a place of contrasts. Leopold lost no time in relaying his impressions to Salzburg. The streets were malodorous with no effective drainage, yet along them travelled coaches that amazed him with their beauty, many of them japanned, he said, like harpsichords.

He found 'very few beautiful churches'. Apparently not even Notre-Dame impressed him. To make up for it, there was a 'large number of beautiful hôtels or palaces on whose interior decoration no expense has been spared, each of them containing extraordinary things, all in all everything a person can ever imagine as necessary to the comfort of his body and delight of his senses'.

As for the comfort of the body, he was so impressed by an English import that he described it in detail to Hagenauer – or at least in as much detail as sensibilities would allow. It was the flushing toilet:

> On both sides are handles that can be turned after the business has been done. One handle causes water to spurt downwards, the other sends the water – which can even be warm – spurting upwards. I do not know how to explain it to you more fully in polite and respectable language. You must imagine the rest or ask me in good time.

He added that the toilet cabinets were beautifully tiled in the Dutch manner, and that on highly decorated pedestals were exquisitely painted porcelain chamber pots. Nearby were glasses of perfumed water and pots filled with aromatic plants.

And the exquisite line: 'Usually one finds a handsome sofa nearby – for a sudden fainting spell, I believe.'

Paris was also – and this was of somewhat more importance to the Mozarts than even a flushing toilet – the musical capital of mainland Europe. It had a grand opera house, and a smaller rival one that was giving rise to a new form of entertainment, *opéra comique*, something at which Wolfgang in years to come would excel.

Many wealthy aristocrats were patrons of the arts, and the city had a flourishing music-publishing industry. It is therefore surprising that there were few public concerts; the Mozarts' best hope lay in performing at the palaces of the nobility, and the ultimate prize, at the Versailles court of Louis XV.

They were offered accommodation at the palace of Count van Eyck, the Bavarian minister in the city. This arrangement pleased Leopold, allowing him to cancel the expensive rooms he had reserved.

He was even more pleased to find that their room was large and comfortable, containing a double-keyboard harpsichord. He was also intrigued to discover that in a secluded corner of the mansion the Count ran a gambling casino, protected against French law by being technically in Bavarian territory.

All was set fair for the Mozart children to conquer Paris. But fate intervened. One of King Louis's grandchildren had contracted smallpox and died suddenly. The court wore black and all entertainments were suspended.

As they were used to doing, the Mozarts made good use of the time. The family had by now travelled far and wide, and word about them had travelled even further and faster. There was never any shortage of invitations to play in the palaces of the aristocracy wherever they went, and Paris was no exception.

One man in particular eased their way in Paris, and he has thereby earned a small place in musical history. His name was Friedrich Melchior Grimm, a Bavarian who had become secretary to Louis Philippe, Duc d'Orléans.

With access to high places he arranged concerts and soirées for the Mozarts, even to the extent of selling tickets and arranging for wax to light the hall. In short, he managed their musical activities. He also coached Leopold in court etiquette and what particular turns of phrase were popular at court, in preparation for the anticipated invitation to travel to Versailles.

Leopold was naturally delighted to be in the hands of a fellow Bavarian, with whom he would have so much in common, not least the language.

And how did Herr Grimm earn his place in musical history? Young Wolfgang had been using his time well, particularly since he now had a harpsichord at his disposal. He had composed two sets of sonatas for harpsichord and violin. It was Grimm who advised him on which members of French royalty and aristocracy he should dedicate them to, and it is more than likely that the dedications, in flowery French, were written by him.

Of perhaps greater service to the boy genius – and musical history – Grimm wrote in his fortnightly newsletter, the *Correspondance Littéraire, Philosophique et Critique* that at one concert a woman had asked Wolfgang if he would accompany her as she sang an Italian song she knew by heart.

Wolfgang did not know the song, wrote Grimm, and so his accompaniment had a few mistakes in the bass. At the end of the song, Wolfgang asked the woman to sing it again. This time, he not only played the entire melody with his right hand, but with his left added the correct bass. Twice more he asked the woman to sing, and each time he varied the accompaniment. 'He would have gone on twenty times had we not stepped in,' Grimm wrote. With deliberate hyperbole he described 'such an extraordinary phenomenon that one

has difficulty believing what one sees with one's eyes and hears with one's ears … Now I understand why St Paul fell into a trance after his strange vision.'[11]

As far as I am aware, this is the first description we have of what Wolfgang was actually capable of achieving at the keyboard, as opposed to general descriptions such as being able to play with his hands covered.

The period of court mourning over, the Mozarts duly travelled to Versailles, where Wolfgang and Nannerl performed before the king and queen, to predictable acclaim. Leopold was pleased to report a payment of 1,200 livres.

He also wrote with paternal pride that his son 'bewitched almost everyone'. It is not difficult to see why. At the age of just eight, and small for his age, dressed in a black suit and three-cornered hat, he drew attention like a magnet.

The king's daughters allowed him to kiss their hands, and returned his kisses. The queen, Polish-born and fluent in German, conversed easily with him. Members of the royal family were seen to hurry along corridors in the hope of catching a glimpse of him. The English and Russian ambassadors sought him out.

Only one personage seemed to be less than entirely welcoming. Also living in apartments in Versailles was the most notorious woman in France, Jeanne Antoinette Poisson, otherwise known as Madame de Pompadour, mistress of the king.

Although widely unpopular in France for the influence she had on the king, Madame de Pompadour was a generous patron of the arts, and something of a musician herself. She was competent on the harpsichord. It was therefore deemed appropriate for Leopold Mozart to take his young son to meet her.

Wolfgang, as expected, thrilled La Pompadour with his playing. When he finished, she bent to help him down from the piano stool. He, expecting a warm embrace, flung his arms round her neck and reached forward to kiss her. Shocked and somewhat horrified, she pulled her head back to avoid the kiss. Pleasantries were exchanged, and the Mozarts departed.

Wolfgang, genuinely shocked and disappointed at the rebuff, reminded his father of what had happened at court in Vienna. 'Who does she think she is, not wanting to kiss me? Why, the Empress herself kissed me!' In reporting this to Salzburg, Leopold added his own critique of the royal mistress: 'Handsome and well proportioned, but extremely haughty.'

It was time to leave Paris, but once more fate intervened. Wolfgang fell ill, and quite seriously. He had a high fever, severe inflammation of the throat, and brought up phlegm in such quantities that he appeared to be in danger of choking. Nannerl too fell ill, but not so severely.

Leopold put it down to poor hygiene. The family, used to fresh-water fish from the lakes of Germany, stared with disgust at the fish on Paris stalls. They boiled all their food and water. But still they had all been afflicted with diarrhoea.

The children recovered after rest and recuperation, and on 10 April 1764 they left Paris on the next leg of their tour. Ahead of them, the biggest prize of all: London.

4

PRODIGIES OF NATURE

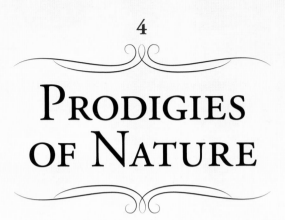

*I*f Paris was a thriving bustling city and the musical capital of Europe, London put it completely in the shade. The English capital was, quite simply, the largest and richest city in the world. Great Britain had recently emerged victorious from the Seven Years War, its navy supreme, and acquired new territory overseas, largely at the expense of France.

A new emerging middle class saw opportunities for making money. London became the thriving hub, as people from around the country, and from abroad, flocked to the city in the hope of making their fortune.

In the all-important world of music too, Paris could not compete with London. There were more music publishers in London than in Paris, and London was the first city in Europe to have purpose-built concert halls. There was a flourishing concert life in London, both in public and private.

When Leopold had planned the tour, it had not been his intention to travel as far as London, but having been received with such acclaim in Paris – by the king and queen, no less – it would have been unthinkable to turn round now and head back home.

As always word had travelled ahead of him. The French court had written to its ambassador in London. At Versailles Wolfgang had played for the Duke of Bedford, a senior British aristocrat who was in Paris to negotiate peace terms with the French after the war. He too encouraged Leopold to take his family to London, and sent word to the court there.

The Mozarts, it seemed, wherever they went, moved in the highest social circles, thanks to the remarkable talents of the two children, Wolfgang in particular.

Leopold has left a compelling account of the journey, particularly the Channel crossing. I shall relate the details in full, as a timely reminder that superb musician though Leopold might be, his daughter a brilliant one, and his son a genius unlike any before, still they were not immune from the problems that might beset any other traveller.

In the first place, they had too much luggage. The family had to pare down to the essentials. This was not easy, since it was impossible to gauge how long they might remain in London. It might be days, or it might be weeks. In the event they left a lot of their belongings in the care of their Parisian banker. That would mean, whether they wanted it or not, the return trip would have to take them back through Paris.

Secondly, their carriage, which had undergone repairs more than once, would have to be left behind at Calais. That meant more expense on the other side of the Channel.

As before, though, Leopold – much as he might complain about costs – was reluctant to stint on travel. He understood that his children had to be kept as comfortable as possible if they were to perform to their best, all the more so after their most recent bout of ill health.

And so he hired a second servant for the crossing, a man with experience of what was involved. He was an Italian by the name of Porta, and he was to prove a wise investment.

Porta advised Leopold to hire a boat that would take extra passengers, so as to cut down on expense. He settled on a boat that would take fourteen, at a cost of five louis d'or. Four extra passengers meant a saving of two louis d'or.

The Mozarts had never seen the sea before. One can only begin to imagine the children's excitement, and perhaps the trepidation of their parents. Nannerl wrote in her diary of the wonder of watching the tide ebb and flow against the shingle.

The actual crossing was thoroughly uncomfortable. There were too many people on board for a start, so that privacy was almost impossible. Every member of the Mozart family was seasick. Leopold, with self-mocking humour, wrote that the Mozart family made a sizeable liquid contribution to the Channel – at least saving money on emetics.

On arrival outside Dover harbour, Porta helped them in the tricky manoeuvre of transferring, along with their luggage, to a smaller boat to take them ashore. Once on the quayside they were instantly surrounded by thirty or forty porters jostling to carry their luggage, touching their forelocks or caps, in a cacophony of 'your most obedient servant'.

Porta, with a smattering of English, managed to see most of them off, but one look at the exhausted travellers told the men they would be going nowhere that night, and before they knew it their bags were being carried off to the nearest hotel – or at least the one from which the porters could be sure of a commission.

Leopold probably gave in gracefully. The Mozarts were in no fit state to continue their journey. But it allowed him his customary moan. 'Whoever has too much money need only undertake a journey from Paris to London,' he wrote, 'and his purse will certainly be lightened.'

Leopold has left us no details of the journey from Dover to London, but we know the family arrived in the capital on 23 April 1764, almost two weeks after leaving Paris. It had been a long and gruelling journey, particularly coming so soon after the children's illnesses, Wolfgang's having been especially draining. It must certainly have made it easier for Leopold to have their mother to look after them – although again not a word in his letters about her – but he must have wondered if Wolfgang would be physically up to what lay ahead.

The family stayed for their first night in London at the White Bear hotel in Piccadilly, which was a main gathering place for travellers arriving from Continental Europe. Probably with Porta's help, they swiftly found lodgings – three small rooms – above a barber's shop in Cecil Court, just off St Martin's Lane.

Things moved swiftly, possibly too swiftly for Leopold's liking after such an arduous journey. The high-level recommendations from Paris had found their mark. Added to this Leopold had, once again, impressive letters of commendation. Probably the clinching factor was the fact that the Mozarts were German, and on the throne was a Hanoverian, albeit the first to be born in London and have English as a first language. George's wife, Queen Charlotte, was German born and a native German speaker.

A mere four days after arriving in London, probably not yet fully recovered from their travels, the Mozarts were summoned to Buckingham House to perform before King George III and Queen Charlotte.

Unlike some high-born personages, rulers even, for whom the Mozart children had played, here they could be sure of an appreciative reception. Music had played an important role at the Hanoverian court since the accession of George I. George Frideric Handel, who had died only five years earlier, and whose achievements were well known to Leopold Mozart, had been closely associated with the London court.

George III himself delighted in his own personal band, enjoying having to guess which piece they were playing; usually it was by Handel. The king played violin and flute to a high level, and was competent at the harpsichord.

"The Mozarts, wherever they went, moved in the highest social circles, thanks to the remarkable talents of the two children."

Queen Charlotte played the harpsichord 'quite well, for a queen', as Joseph Haydn was later to observe rather drily.

Leopold has left us no detail of exactly how the children performed at Buckingham House. We can assume Nannerl played with her usual skill, and that Wolfgang carried out his familiar tricks of guessing notes accurately, playing difficult music by sight, and his *tour de force* of playing on a covered keyboard.

We do know that the Mozarts were received in the most welcoming manner by the royal couple. 'Their unpretentious manner and friendly ways made one forget that we were with the King and Queen of England,' Leopold wrote home. 'At all courts we have been courteously received, but here our welcome surpassed all others.'

He added that fully a week later he and the family were walking in St James's Park, dressed in different, more casual, clothes. 'The King and Queen rode by, recognised us, greeted us, and what is more the King opened the window, saluting us cheerfully, especially our Master Wolfgang, nodding his head and waving his hand.'

It is a beguiling image, the king of England smiling, nodding, and waving to an eight-year-old boy.

Proof of how well the Mozart children had performed came when they were summoned to return to Buckingham House three weeks later. This time princes joined the king and queen to marvel at the extraordinary musical talent on display.

Leopold, always ready to see the downside, lamented that he was paid only 24 guineas for the first appearance, but that at least it had been paid immediately. His mood was improved by the unexpected second invitation, and the payment of a further 24 guineas.

From here things seemed to go rather unexpectedly downhill. Leopold made bookings for Wolfgang to perform, but there was little interest. Unaware of the habits of the English aristocracy, Leopold did not know that come May anyone with means and leisure on their hands left London for the country.

So fulsome had been his announcements, and so thin the interest, he was forced to announce postponements and then cancellations due to Wolfgang's ill health. It was almost certainly not true.

He was alerted to the fact that the concert-going aristocracy would need to be back in town by 4 June, the king's birthday. In the meantime, as they had in other towns and cities, the Mozarts became tourists.

Leopold wrote home amusingly about Londoners and their city. In the first place the family went shopping for clothes. Why? Because they had bought new outfits in Paris and thus resembled a French family. They soon

Left
180 Ebury Street
(now Mozart Terrace),
the Mozart family's
London residence during
1764. Mozart composed
his first symphony in
the house.

realised this was a mistake. Street urchins followed them, teasing and mocking them, and shouting, 'Bugger the French!'

Leopold wrote that it was best to keep quiet and act as if they didn't hear anything. Even better, he took the family shopping for a more English look. This his wife and daughter achieved – a rare mention here of Anna Maria in a letter – by wearing a hat wherever they went. 'No woman crosses the street without a hat on her head', Leopold wrote.

London, to Leopold's observant – and critical – eye, was 'nothing but a masquerade', and it could be a surprising one at that. The royal palaces, for instance, were much less ostentatious than similar buildings in Paris and

Vienna. They were unobtrusive, almost anonymous, and 'rather middle-class, certainly not royal'.

The same was true of the aristocratic ladies. It is difficult, he wrote, 'to distinguish a tailor's or a shoemaker's wife from a Mylady. Except that the first two are much of the time better turned out than the last.' He added that if a 'Mylady' had no reason to 'display herself', then she did not do so.

Certainly London had its aristocracy, not to mention royalty, but for me Leopold's description came as a complete surprise. Were these high-born dukes and duchesses really that much less ostentatious than their Continental counterparts? And if so, might that be one of the underlying reasons the revolutions and upheavals to sweep across Europe never took root on the English side of the Channel?

Not that London was without its political protests, and Leopold witnessed them. He watched astounded as thousands of marchers, 'honest people who earn their bread by the sweat of their brow', were allowed to demonstrate for better working conditions, something that would have been utterly unthinkable in Vienna.

Leopold became quite enamoured of London and the English. He might have bemoaned the state of the roads, riddled with potholes – 'Better to walk than run, because if you run you risk falling and breaking a couple of ribs' – but he read (or claimed to have read) two volumes on the history of London. He also said he picked up the English language really quickly, and it is true that he continued to study it when he returned home to Salzburg.

As for the sights, he was as impressed as anybody. 'When one stands on London Bridge and contemplates the host of ships always lying in the Thames, the amazing multitude of masts makes one seem to behold a thick forest ahead.'

Leopold would not be Leopold, though, without words of criticism. Breakfast of tea with milk and buttered toast was the sort of thing the lowliest soldiers in the imperial army would eat. It was not fit food for the Mozarts, though he rather liked the custom of keeping a kettle on the boil to serve visitors tea with bread and butter later in the day.

It was impossible, too, to escape street hawkers, determined to relieve you of your money. 'One holds out a pot of flowers, another toothpicks made of quill, another copper engravings, another sulphur matches, another sewing thread, another ribbons of various colours.'

Worst of all, beggars would sing in the street, and they would be the commonest songs doing the rounds, 'which one hears with disgust hour after hour'. Not ideal for a true musician's sensibilities.

Leopold confessed both he and Anna Maria (another rare inclusion) were utterly spellbound by the largest pleasure park in London, Vauxhall

"Every Body will be astonished to hear a Child of such tender Age playing the Harpsichord in such a Perfection."

Leopold Mozart promoting his son.

Gardens[*] – like the Elysian Fields, with night transformed into day by no fewer than a thousand lamps, floodlit pyramids and arches, pavilions, and a fine concert hall. People had to pay no more than a shilling for entrance, and this son of a class-conscious empire again marvelled at how noblemen and commoners mixed happily.

There was, naturally, a hitch and it was, naturally, financial. You may resolve firmly not to waste money, Leopold wrote, but it is a futile hope. You walk and walk, you become tired, you sit down, you allow yourself a bottle of wine, perhaps with some biscuits, and that's four or five shillings gone. Still hungry, you see a few roasted chickens being carried past, you beckon, they come over. 'Thus are guineas lured from one's purse.'

Once again it is a captivating image, the Mozart family enjoying themselves in Vauxhall Gardens, eating, drinking, perhaps listening to music, looking just like any other family.

<hr>

With the nobility back in town, it was time to earn some money. Wolfgang and Nannerl made their public London debut on 5 June 1764. Leopold had not undersold the concert:

> *Miss Mozart of eleven and Master Mozart of seven Years of Age, Prodigies of Nature, taking the opportunity of representing to the Public the greatest Prodigy that Europe or that Human Nature has to boast of. Every Body will be astonished to hear a Child of such tender Age playing the Harpsichord in such a Perfection – it surmounts all Fantastic and Imagination* [sic]*, and it is hard to express which is more astonishing, his Execution upon the Harpsichord playing at Sight, or his own Composition.*

Knowing what we know today, it is hard to argue with Leopold or accuse him of exaggeration. Except in one respect. Nannerl was twelve years of age, Wolfgang eight.[†]

The concert, in the Great Room in Spring Garden near St James's Park, was a triumph. Leopold related, probably with slight overstatement, that 'not only all the ambassadors, but the principal families in England, attended'.

---

[*] A century later it gave the word *vokzal*, meaning 'central railway station', to the Russian language, when a music pavilion was built next to the railway station in Pavlovsk and named the Vauxhall Pavilion.

[†] Little over a decade later, Johann van Beethoven – quite possibly taking his cue from Leopold Mozart – was to practise a similar deception at his son Ludwig's first public recital in Cologne, advertising his age as six when he was in fact seven.

The applause, he reported, was tumultuous, and he was delighted to confess himself shocked that after the costs of renting the hall, two harpsichords, other musicians, music stands and candles, were deducted, he took in 100 guineas within three hours.

More concerts followed, more success, more money coming in. London had taken the Mozarts to its heart. But here is where Leopold made something of a miscalculation. He showed he had not understood the English character quite as well as he believed he had.

In short he oversold his children. He put them on daily view to anyone who might care to come and witness their talents. He advertised that the family would be at home 'Every Day in the Week from Twelve to Two o'clock' for the children to be put to the test.

Leopold was acquiring a reputation for having his children perform on any occasion that might bring a financial return. This was considered to be in somewhat poor taste and, together with a corresponding lack of exclusivity, led to a falling off of private engagements.

There was one more invitation, the third, to perform before the royal couple at Buckingham House, but it was to be the last, despite the Mozart family remaining in London for a further nine months.

Leopold was perplexed. He might have been poking fun at the eccentricity of English currency when he said, 'Once I leave England I shall never see guineas again. So we must make the most of our opportunity.' But the lack of income clearly worried him.

A few months later, with the situation not improving, he reported that attendance at a concert by the children at the Little Theatre in the Haymarket was 'not as strong as I hoped', and wondered 'why we are not being treated more generously'.

If public displays were slowing down, that at least afforded young Wolfgang the time to indulge his rapidly growing passion for composition. During the entire stay in London, a period of almost sixteen months, he composed his first symphonies, several keyboard pieces, as well as a set of six violin (or flute) sonatas K. 10–15, which he dedicated to the queen. There were vocal pieces too.

It is beyond doubt that Leopold oversaw many of these, but he professed himself impressed beyond words at his son's talent for composition.

There was one encounter for Wolfgang that was to lead to his name being associated with one of the greatest family names in music, even at this tender age. Resident in London for the past several years had been Johann Christian Bach, youngest son of the great Johann Sebastian. A complete Anglophile, he was known as John Bach, as well as 'The London Bach', and would spend the rest of his life in London.

Left

'God is our Refuge',
K. 20, a motet written
by Mozart in July of
1765 during the family's
stay in London.

Probably on the recommendation of the royal couple, to whom Bach was well known and highly respected, a meeting was arranged between him and young Wolfgang. Leopold, surprisingly, barely refers to this in his letters, but Nannerl – writing many years later – gives us an entrancing description of the encounter between a well-established musician close to thirty years of age, and the boy of eight.

Bach, she writes, took Wolfgang

between his knees, the former played a few bars, and then the other continued, and in this way they played a whole sonata, and anyone not watching would have thought it was played by one person alone.[12]

Another of those present confirmed that Bach sat Wolfgang on his lap and they played together. He wrote that they led each other into 'very abstruse harmonies and extraneous modulations' in which, he stated categorically, 'the child beat the man'.[13]

There is no doubt that Bach spread the word of the boy's remarkable talent, and Wolfgang himself remembered J. C. Bach for the rest of his life with affection.

The Mozarts finally left London on 24 July 1765. The prolonged stay in the British capital – more than fifteen months – might not have been the unalloyed success Leopold was hoping for, and he confessed himself disappointed. But he left having amassed a considerable amount of money; several times he had sent earnings back to Salzburg.

There is also no doubting the fact that his young son – and to a lesser extent his daughter – had conquered London. Wolfgang had played before royalty, the aristocracy, and the general populace. He had been feted at every turn. His name was now spoken of with awe in the most sophisticated and important capital in Europe.

More importantly for the history of music, Wolfgang had begun to compose. These were not childish jottings; they were already showing some of the genius that was to emerge in the coming years.

Could it be possible for a child of such a tender age to emerge from all this unscathed? Leopold clearly thought so, but he was wrong.

HE IS SKIN AND BONE

We have to be grateful to Leopold Mozart for so completely chronicling the family's travels in copious letters home. Without them we would know precious little of this extraordinary voyage that spread the Mozart name across Europe.

It is as if Leopold's thoughts minute by minute are being put down on paper, including the most mundane – which are themselves totally fascinating. It is so easy to picture him standing, frustrated, scratching his head, one hand on his hip, probably blaming his wife, when he writes on leaving London, 'Just to look at our baggage makes the perspiration run down my face. We cannot leave everything here, yet we cannot take everything with us.' What modern traveller, looking at too much luggage, has not felt that exact sentiment?

Just for once, one aspect of the journey did not cause problems. The graphic description of the seasickness the Mozarts had suffered crossing the Channel persuaded Hagenauer and his wife to invoke divine intervention for the return journey, by praying to the Madonna of Maria Plain at the church dedicated to her just outside Salzburg.

It worked. The weather was glorious, the sky blue, the wind favourable. The family disembarked at Calais with sharpened appetites for lunch.

It had been Leopold's plan to return to Paris, pick up the belongings they had left there, and head for home. It did not work out quite that way, thanks initially to a very persistent Dutchman.

Shortly before the Mozarts had left London, the Dutch ambassador called on them to try to persuade Leopold to take the family to The Hague, so that Wolfgang could perform before Princess Caroline of Nassau-Weilburg, sister of William V of Orange. It seems Leopold had politely declined, because just a few days later, on 24 July, the envoy called again, to find the Mozarts had left that very day. Undeterred, he pursued them to Canterbury.

It's not surprising Leopold had declined. He had already written to Hagenauer stating he had no intention of taking the family to The Hague, 'of that I can assure you'. The Dutch he had come across so far, mostly innkeepers, he had found 'a bit uncouth'. In any case the family had been away from home for long enough. It was time they returned to Salzburg.

But the envoy's persistence paid off, no doubt to his relief. The Princess had heard from her relatives in the English royal family how remarkable Wolfgang was, and insisted on seeing him for herself. The ambassador was able to offer Leopold a financial inducement he simply could not refuse. And so it was back on the road again, north to The Hague, not south-east towards Salzburg and home.

It was now that the rigours of the journey finally caught up with the Mozarts. There had been bouts of illness in London, but now they were truly laid low. First Wolfgang, and then his father, came down with severe colds, forcing them to remain in Lille for a full month.

Leopold was still not fully recovered when they packed up and moved on again. With stops on the way, during which Wolfgang performed on the organ, the family arrived by canal boat in the Hague on 10 or 11 September.

Within a day Wolfgang was performing for the Princess, but Nannerl stayed behind at their lodgings. She was feeling unwell, with symptoms of a chest cold. It appeared not to be too serious, and Leopold went ahead and scheduled a 'Grand Concert' for the evening of 30 September. Both Nannerl and Wolfgang were to perform keyboard concertos with full orchestra, and the orchestra was to perform two of Wolfgang's symphonies.

But Nannerl suddenly took a turn for the worse, and on the evening of the 26th she started to shiver and had to lie down. Soon she was gripped by a high fever. Her throat was inflamed and Leopold summoned a doctor, recommended by the diplomatic corps, who bled her. Over the ensuing days more doctors came to inspect Nannerl and offer advice.

Nannerl became more emaciated by the day. Leopold and his wife were advised that nothing else could be done for her, and that they should prepare for the worst. Leopold summoned a priest and Nannerl was given the last rites. Leopold and Anna Maria kept a constant vigil at her bedside, taking it in turns so the other could get some sleep.

Later he wrote, 'Though my poor daughter did not breathe her last, I have seen her near the agonies of death.' We must forgive Leopold a certain

"*It was now that the rigours of the journey finally caught up with the Mozarts*"

callousness, even humour, in his description of worrying events, since he was writing after Nannerl had recovered, but he left those back in Salzburg in no doubt as to how close Nannerl had come to death.

> *Had anyone heard the several evenings of conversation among the three of us – my wife, myself, and my daughter – during which we persuaded her of the vanity of this world and of the blessedly happy death of children, he would not have listened with dry eyes.*

Nannerl was delirious, and Leopold describes her rambling in English, French and German. He and his wife, he confessed, could not help laughing, in spite of their distress. And he rounded off the drama with what is almost an aside, 'Meanwhile, in the next room, little Wolfgang entertained himself with his music.'

Nannerl was still very unwell, clearly hovering between life and death, when Leopold – his mind, it seems, as much on financial loss as his daughter's precarious state – decided to apportion blame:

> *Now God has upset my calculations. If God spares her, I cannot expose her capriciously to the obvious danger of losing her life through an inopportune journey. You can easily understand that I have derived no advantage from this accident, but the greatest loss.*

Against all odds Nannerl turned the corner. She was well on the road to recovery, Leopold wrote, when the royal physician arrived, dispatched by the Princess herself, just in time to claim credit and receive gratitude. His most effective advice, according to a cynical Leopold, was to prescribe 'good calves soup with well-boiled rice'.

The crisis was over. Nannerl soon felt well enough to get out of bed and attempt to walk. But then crisis number two struck, and it was a crisis that carried a much greater threat to the Mozart family enterprise and its earning power. Wolfgang began to develop the same symptoms as his sister. And now we begin to get a true indication of the effects of the punishing schedule Leopold had inflicted on his young son.

Some week earlier, doctors who had come to see Nannerl also apparently encountered Wolfgang, and reported their concerns that he did not look healthy. In fact, so unhealthy did he appear, according to the British Minister to The Hague, that they agreed he would 'not be long lived'.

They were not entirely wrong. For eight days Wolfgang was nearly comatose, and for four weeks his life hung in the balance. So vivid is Leopold's description of his son's illness that we cannot accuse him of exaggeration. It is quite understandable that he thought his son, who he knew was a musical prodigy unlike any the world had seen – 'this prodigy

of nature' he had called him – was going to die, just a month before his tenth birthday.

Wolfgang's lips turned hard and black, and peeled away three times. His tongue seemed to have turned to wood. He lost all power of speech. For eight days he was unable to utter a single word. On 12 December Leopold wrote, 'He is not only absolutely unrecognisable, but has nothing left except his tender skin and tiny bones, and for the laᶜt five days he has been carried daily from his bed to a chair.' There is a hint that Wolfgang had endured the worst in those last few words. Had he not been showing signs of some recovery, he surely would not have been moved from bed to chair.

As the days progressed the small boy was helped from the chair and encouraged to take a few faltering steps. Leopold and Anna Maria began to lead him gently across the room 'so that little by little he may learn to move his feet again, and also to stand upright unaided'.

For several months past the Mozart family had been struck down by illness. Only Anna Maria appears to have escaped it, although, given Leopold's reluctance – deliberately or otherwise – to give any news about her in his letters, it is quite possible she was unwell too. He does say that for almost three months she did not dare leave the children's rooms, as they were so seriously ill.

With all the caveats about retrospective diagnosis two and a half centuries later, it seems both Nannerl and Wolfgang had succumbed to typhoid. The rigours of travel, poor hygiene, food and drink that was quite possibly contaminated – all point to typhoid, which drains the body of all energy.

A high fever, rashes, sickness, diarrhoea, and the body totally drained, figuratively and literally. In a strange room in a strange town, with no effective treatment, it is no wonder the children were so very ill.

Given what we know of Wolfgang's health during his short life, it is tempting to see this illness as the beginning of it all, and that he never fully recovered his strength. It certainly seems he suffered more acutely than Nannerl. His symptoms sound appalling. Maybe it is not so surprising his sister was to outlive him by so many years.

With both children now recovered, there was work to be done, financial losses to be recouped. Leopold had no time for sentimentality. He couched it in slightly less strident tones in his letters. To head straight home now, a lengthy journey in midwinter with the children so recently ill, would be folly, he wrote.

But there is no doubt he was feeling the loss of income from both children being laid up for so long. Both of them were in front of an audience again on 22 January 1766 in The Hague. Less than a month later the family were in Amsterdam, where they stayed for five weeks.

Leopold was back to his old tricks, as impresario and as an eighteenth-century public relations man. He advertised the children's upcoming performances, subtracting a year from his son's age, and stating that the two of them would play 'not only concertos together on different harpsichords, but also on the same one with four hands, and finally the boy will play on the organ his own caprices, fugues, and other pieces of the most profound music'.

Early in March they were back in The Hague, with Wolfgang composing at least nine new pieces for performance in royal circles. Then it was back to Amsterdam, on to Rotterdam and Antwerp, with yet more performances.

We have an interesting insight into Leopold's character during the stay in Amsterdam. He was, it seems, a deeply religious man, a devout Roman Catholic. He had continually asked Hagenauer back in Salzburg to offer prayers for the children during their illness, and he no doubt ascribed their 'miraculous' (his word) recovery at least in part to divine intervention. This is reinforced by the fact that time and again Leopold attributes his children's otherworldly musical talents – particularly those of Wolfgang – to a divine gift, a gift straight from God.

We have practical evidence of his deep religious conviction. In Amsterdam, he writes that he met an old friend from Salzburg who he was appalled and saddened to find had embraced Calvinism. He says he spent much time and energy trying to draw him back into the Catholic fold. We have no reason to doubt this is true.

Back on the road the family passed through Mechelen (today Malines) in the Austrian Netherlands (now Belgium), where they called on the archbishop. This is the town from which a musician and singer by the name of Ludwig van Beethoven had left for Bonn thirty-four years earlier. His grandson, named for him, was to change the course of music, and be a lifelong admirer of the composer whose life this book chronicles.

Brussels, Valenciennes, Cambrai and finally Paris, with the opportunity to rest – possibly. The family remained in the French capital for two months, and we have very little detail about the stay. However, one witness wrote a vivid account of the children's talents, stating that Nannerl was brilliant on the harpsichord, and the only person who could outplay her was her young brother, who had already composed symphonies, and whose profound grasp of harmony was 'beyond comprehension'.

It is more than likely that there were more performances. Paris was an expensive city, and Leopold would no doubt have wanted to see some return for their stay there.

They left Paris on the evening of 9 July. More cities, more performances. Lyons, then into Switzerland to Geneva, on to Lausanne, Berne, Zurich. Into Germany, to Donaueschingen and Munich. It is exhausting just to contemplate the Mozarts' schedule. It is also almost unnatural. Even if they had not been recovering from serious illness, we would say that Leopold was driving them hard, very hard indeed, and to some extent it is to cover his own increasing sense of unease.

He had now been away from Salzburg, and from the court – the source of his income – for more than three years, and the strain was beginning to show in his letters home to Hagenauer. He was worried on two counts, professional and personal.

Accommodation in Salzburg was weighing heavily on his mind. He would be returning home to very different circumstances from those he had left more than three years ago.

His two children were now recognised throughout Europe as musical prodigies. Of the two, clearly, Wolfgang was the more talented, but Nannerl's skills as a musician were not to be underestimated, and they provided her with one great advantage. She was highly eligible as a wife. Her skills would surely be appreciated by a suitor, and might well bring money in if she chose later to teach.

Nannerl was now fifteen, and that was a marriageable age. In Salzburg she would require some privacy at home. Clearly she could not continue to share her mother's bed, as she had done before and again on tour.

Wolfgang Mozart entertaining the court of Louis François, Prince of Conti in the Four-Mirror Salon of the Palais du Temple, 1766.

The same applied to Wolfgang, only more so. Leopold was a good enough musician himself to know that Wolfgang was talented beyond what was conceivable, even for someone supremely gifted. As a religious man he knew he was dealing here with something outside earthly comprehension.

On a practical level, Leopold understood that Wolfgang's future lay in his extraordinary ability to compose music. Performers, virtuosos, were not in short supply in Vienna, capital city of music, but to compose was to put a musician into an entirely different class.

Compositions were what would ensure immortality, more than skill at the keyboard, and if there were already composers in Vienna, they were far fewer in number than performers, and certainly none possessed the extraordinary talent that Wolfgang did, leaving aside the fact that they were many years older.

Wolfgang was young, very young. He would need nurturing, and he would need guidance, from a fellow musician who understood him completely. There was only one person totally and undeniably qualified to provide that, and that person was, of course, Leopold, his father.

Like his sister, Wolfgang had shared his father's bed on tour, and when he composed he had to find a small corner in a cramped room. The apartment in Salzburg might be slightly more comfortable, but would it do for this new set of circumstances?

'Where will Wolfgang set up?' Leopold wrote to Hagenauer. 'Where will I find a special place for him to study and work, and he will certainly have plenty of work to do.' Leopold is now referring to Wolfgang as 'our little composer'.[*]

As well as worrying about his domestic circumstances, Leopold was concerned about his position at court. He was deputy kapellmeister. But being away for so long made him in effect an absentee. Who could tell what jealousies he might find on his return, what cabals might have been formed to oppose him?

He poured out his worries in letters to Hagenauer:

The nearer I approach Salzburg, the more childish the gossip reaching my ears. I wish to be spared such things. For several years, thank God, things were peaceful and I was free of such annoyances, and I want to remain far away from them. In particular, very odd things are being said about our reception at court. I assure you that I find all this very strange, and it is affecting me in ways I did not expect. After experiencing such great honours, I cannot forgive or forget such rudeness.

---

[*] In the event, it was to be six more years before the family moved to a larger apartment.

The last sentence is particularly to the point. Here is a man who, from humble origins and of middling status in Salzburg, thanks to his children's talents, had met and chatted with the Emperor and Empress of the Holy Roman Empire, the Queen of France, Their Majesties the King and Queen of England, not to mention an almost incalculable list of aristocrats and nobility, archbishops and bishops.

Leopold is hardly to be blamed if he was beginning to think that maybe he had moved beyond the court in Salzburg. He and his family were destined for higher things. There is evidence in his letters that he is already beginning to think of the next move, and it has nothing to do with his home city.

There was a nagging worry, and it was something over which he could have no control. In Munich Wolfgang had succumbed to illness again. He had a fever and pains in his leg. We can probably say with some certainty he had rheumatic fever. In one so young that is a serious cause for concern.

A side trip to Regensburg to perform was called off, but Leopold had Wolfgang at the keyboard again when the opportunity to play at court arose. Given Wolfgang's precarious health, and the chill November temperatures, this was probably not wise.

There was something else. In the three and a half years that the Mozarts had been away, Wolfgang had not grown by a single inch. Before they had left, it had been noted that Wolfgang's hands were so small that they could scarcely span a fifth on the keyboard, let alone an octave. Back then, this had simply led to extraordinary praise for the way he negotiated the keyboard. 'Amazing, considering his little fingers could scarcely reach a fifth on the harpsichord,' observed one. 'At proper speed and with wonderful accuracy he skimmed the octave his short little fingers could not span,' said another.[14]

But when, on the family's return to Salzburg, Wolfgang's fingers could span no more notes than when he had left, there were concerned mutterings. Still some would not let this cloud their admiration. 'That he can still not bridge the octave makes his skill all the more exceptional and admirable,' was one opinion.

Leopold himself, as musician and father, must have noticed. Why else would he write, 'How my children have grown!' It was as if he was flying in the face of reality.

It fed into Leopold's growing conviction that he should waste no time in exploiting Wolfgang's talent. He had always been a worrier and now he was once more in a state of high anxiety. What if God were suddenly to rob his son of the extraordinary gift he had given him?

One acquaintance, who knew the family well, picked up Leopold's concern. As he put it, they should all celebrate the child's 'wit, spirit, grace, and

"That he can still not bridge the octave makes his skill all the more exceptional and admirable."

sweetness' to provide reassurance 'against the fear one has that so premature a fruit might fall before it matures'.[15]

No sooner had they returned home to Salzburg, ten days short of three and a half years since they had left, than Leopold's thoughts turned again to travel. Who could say how much time his son might have?

Wolfgang had been a little less than seven and a half when they had left. He was now ten years and ten months. In the intervening period he had conquered Europe. Well, almost. There was one great prize still to be won: Italy. It would take considerable planning, but as the weeks and months passed Leopold set his sights firmly on it.

6

WOLFGANGGANGGANGERL

Vienna might have been the musical capital of Europe, but music in the Habsburg capital, or indeed Salzburg, was still largely an aristocratic affair. The same, broadly speaking, was true in other European countries. It tended to exist primarily in the capital city, radiating from royalty – whether major ruling houses or petty regional princes – down through the aristocracy, but not much further than that.

Italy, on the other hand, was where people of all classes lived and breathed music. From wealthy aristocrats to street vendors, popular tunes of the day were being whistled and sung. One musical form more than any other belonged to Italy: opera. Almost every city worth its name could boast an opera house, and audiences packed in with little regard to social status.

Wolfgang, while on tour and despite thoroughly unconducive conditions, not to mention illness, had composed whenever he could. Small pieces, sonatas, symphonies, a cantata, as well as an oratorio, other choral pieces and songs. Increasingly he was enjoying writing for voices, and Leopold, to his credit, encouraged him – particularly when commissions began to come in. No money-making opportunity was to be ignored.

The family had been back in Salzburg for just a matter of months, and Wolfgang was barely past his eleventh birthday, when he began work on his first opera. There is no doubt Leopold assisted him, in this and other compositions, as one would expect from a father who was also an accomplished musician. It was a short work, a miniature opera, entitled *Apollo et Hyacinthus*.

Leopold had ceased being surprised at what his son could achieve, even with a little paternal help. He must, though, have allowed himself a small smile of satisfaction as it became increasingly clear that there was no musical form his young son could not turn his hand to. Who could tell what riches his earning powers might one day command?

The path ahead, though, was not entirely smooth, and Leopold must in part be blamed for this. He was, by nature, a boastful man. He can most certainly be forgiven for taking genuine pride in Wolfgang's remarkable talents, and Nannerl's, but he was just a little too strident in his boastfulness for some tastes.

The family had returned from the extended tour of Europe laden down with gifts from admirers. Leopold lost no time in putting them on show and inviting friends and colleagues to come to the small apartment in the Getreidegasse and be impressed.

One friend of the family described the apartment as looking like 'a church treasury'. He listed nine gold watches, twelve gold snuffboxes, more gold rings with precious stones than he could count, earrings, necklaces, knives with gold blades, bottle-holders, pens and writing pads, toothpick boxes, and a snuffbox filled with coins. He estimated the gifts to be worth as much as twelve thousand florins.[*]

As if this ostentatiousness were not enough, Leopold offered some items for sale at what were considered to be shockingly high prices, but he also – it was rumoured – slipped in some items he had himself bought with the intention of reselling them.

In both London and Geneva, he had attempted to set himself up as an importer of pocket watches to Salzburg. Although this had come to nothing, he bought several timepieces, which he added to the pile of gifts from 'great monarchs and princes', inflating their prices accordingly.

Of more potential damage, there were disquieting rumours that he was actually exaggerating Wolfgang's musical powers. The boy might have been brilliant on the keyboard, nobody would dispute that – no less a figure than Michael Haydn said he lacked the confidence to enter into competition on the clavier with this boy – but no child so young could possibly compose works of the complexity and sophistication his father was claiming for him.

The truth was, said the more strident voices, Leopold was composing the pieces himself and passing them off as his son's. And those voices reached right to the top.

---

[*] Using the same calculation as in Chapter 2, this would be roughly equivalent to £300,000 in today's money – a fortune.

Above

Colour engraving of the
house on Getreidegasse,
Salzburg, c. 1830.

The 'Prince of Salzburg', no less – the same archbishop whose patience
had been tested by Leopold's continual prolongation of the family's tour
abroad – decided to take matters into his own hands and put Wolfgang to
the test.

He took the decision to lock Wolfgang in a room for a week, during
which he was not allowed to see anyone, gave him words for an oratorio,
and ordered him to set the words to music.

We have only one source for this drastic action, but it is a fairly impeccable
one. An English lawyer and magistrate who had met the Mozarts in London,
and had in fact put Wolfgang's musical abilities to the test there, confessing
himself amazed, related it in a report to the Royal Society of London.

Wolfgang passed the test with flying colours. There is some doubt as to
exactly which piece emerged, but it is generally believed to be the oratorio
Die Schuldigkeit des ersten Gebots, for which he composed the first part, com-
prising eighteen arias and recitatives, as well as a sinfonia and trio. If that is
excessive even for the genius of this boy, then it might have been the less substantial *Grabmusik*, K. 42. The eleven-year-old's compositional powers were
never called into question again. Leopold was off the hook as far as that was
concerned, but it did not improve his standing one bit.

Deputy kapellmeister he might be, with the respect the position naturally brought, but to say his was a popular appointment would be well wide of the mark. In fact he began to speak now of having enemies in Salzburg, and there might well have been some truth in this.

Increasingly, senior Salzburgers, musical as well as aristocratic patrons, approached Wolfgang directly, commissioning him to write pieces or inviting him to perform at civic or religious events. Leopold began to sense he was losing control of his son.

Leopold had a natural arrogance, which perhaps he had always had trouble curbing. Now that he had travelled further and wider than any of his musical colleagues in Salzburg, met kings, queens, princes, princesses, this arrogance found a natural outlet. One can imagine him regaling his colleagues with tale after tale, anecdote after anecdote, of places and personages they could only dream about.

He might well have exaggerated for effect. The same man who had described the treasure trove of gifts reported the 'strong rumour' that the Mozart family would soon be on their travels again, visiting 'the whole of Scandinavia, the whole of Russia, and perhaps even travel to China'. Add to that the fact that all knew his son had a talent none of them could approach, and it is easy to see why a mutual animosity, even jealousy, developed.

Leopold had never liked Salzburg. It was nothing compared to his home town of Augsburg, even if he was none too complimentary about that place either. The fact of the matter is that Leopold was fed up with being a provincial. For goodness' sake, he had lived in Paris, London and The Hague. He had been to Versailles.

It seems Leopold made a conscious decision not to attempt to further his career in Salzburg. He was just one step away from the top musical job in the city: kapellmeister. But he must have suspected he had burned his boats as far as this was concerned. He had spent too much time away; he was blatantly neglecting court duties to concentrate on his children; and he had alienated powerful figures.

He needed to get out of Salzburg, away from his petty rivals, and regain control of his son. It now seemed Wolfgang and his sister between them could provide the ticket by being taken on tour again. Leopold was still contemplating a trip to Italy, in fact he had already begun making plans, when the perfect opportunity arose to travel once again to the capital of empire.

A wedding was in the offing, and it was a royal one. The emperor's sister was to be married to the King of Naples. It would be a glittering occasion, attracting all the noble families of Austria, Hungary and Bohemia, many of them patrons of the arts. A perfect moment for the extraordinary Mozart children to be heard once again in Vienna.

There seems to have been no block to Leopold leaving his duties behind; some in court circles in Salzburg might well have been pleased to see the back of him, with his constant bragging. The Mozarts left in the family carriage on 11 September 1767. Nannerl was sixteen, Wolfgang eleven and three quarters.

Leopold relished his renewed freedom – away from intrigues at court, and once again in sole control of his son – and was clearly in jovial mood. At their first stop, the monastery town of Melk in the beautiful Wachau valley on the banks of the Danube, they were given a tour of the monastery, and then – as Leopold wrote to Hagenauer – he had 'Wolganggangergl' (as he referred to him in a letter) play at the organ without telling the monks who he was, then hurried out to their carriage leaving everyone bemused, bewildered, impressed, desperate to know who the boy was.

Vienna was a city in celebration, emerging from mourning the sudden death of Emperor Franz in his carriage returning from the opera. Leopold reported that there were performances of opera and plays every night, as well as balls, illuminations and fireworks.

However, strict etiquette demanded that the Mozarts could not visit aristocrats to perform in salons until they had first appeared at court, and no summons from the court was forthcoming. Things were very different from the way they were when the Mozarts were last in Vienna just four years earlier.

The emperor's premature death had changed everything. His widow, Empress Maria Theresa, went into heavy mourning. She cut off her hair, stopped wearing jewels and cosmetics, and wore only black. She no longer held musical gatherings in her apartments, stopped going to the opera and theatre, and to all intents and purposes became a recluse at Schönbrunn.

She took her son, Joseph, as co-regent, and he immediately set about undoing much that his father had put in place, first and foremost cutting down on expenditure. This compounded Maria Theresa's distress, ushering in a period of tension and conflict between mother and son, two strong characters neither inclined to give way.

An invitation to a musical family from Salzburg to come and perform at the palace, even if the family had visited before and was known to them, was a long way down the royal list of priorities. The empress might have been reluctant to receive them because it would revive memories of the last time they were there, and the pleasure it brought to her husband. Besides, there was a wedding to arrange.

Leopold put a brave face on it in letters to Hagenauer back in Salzburg. He needed to draw more money in Vienna to cover accommodation

"Leopold relished his new freedom – away from the intrigues at court and once again in sole control of his son."

costs – four or even five hundred florins – but he told Hagenauer not to worry, the whole amount could be recouped in a single day under the right circumstances.[*]

But the situation was about to get a whole lot worse, and there was nothing Leopold could have done to prevent it. The empress insisted that her daughter, before she leave for Naples with her new husband, should descend with her mother into the imperial crypt and bid her father a final farewell.

This they did together, kneeling at the late emperor's coffin for a full three hours. But near to Emperor Franz's coffin lay the coffin of the new emperor's second wife. She had died of smallpox, and the coffin was still unsealed.

In a letter dated 7 October 1767, Leopold wrote to Hagenauer that on the previous Saturday – four days earlier – the Princess-Bride reported feeling unwell. By Tuesday the smallpox rash had appeared.

Eight days later Leopold reported in flowery language, 'The Princess-Bride has become a bride of the Heavenly Bridegroom.' He confessed himself angry that the empress had insisted her daughter should descend into the crypt. It was small wonder, given the 'terrible odour' from the unsealed coffin, that she fell ill. All Vienna believed she had contracted smallpox from the unsealed coffin in the imperial crypt.

The royal household was thrown into complete confusion by the young princess's sudden death. All the celebrations had proved premature. A gorgeous retinue of thirty-four coaches, specially decorated for the occasion, was disbanded. Official mourning was once again declared – so soon after mourning for the late emperor – and theatres closed for six weeks.

Ever mindful of the costs involved, Leopold wrote that all the towns the newlyweds were to have passed through on their way down to Naples had to cancel festivities on which they had already spent vast amounts of money. With the wry humour of a musician, he noted that three famous singers who were to have serenaded the couple in Florence had all memorised their parts to no avail.

Within a matter of days the disease spread across the city and Vienna was in the grip of a smallpox epidemic. The Viennese now talked of little else but smallpox, wrote Leopold. The disease spared no one, regardless of class. Another of the royal princesses fell ill.

Archduchess Maria Elizabeth was, by general agreement, the most beautiful of the empress's daughters. On receiving the diagnosis, so it was said, she called for a mirror to bid farewell to her face before the pock

---

[*] Evidence that Hagenauer and possibly business colleagues were again subsidising the trip.

marks left their indelible scars. She survived the disease, but with her beauty gone for ever she entered a convent, ultimately becoming abbess in Innsbruck.

The goldsmith in whose house the Mozarts were lodging deliberately hid from them the fact that one of his children had caught the disease. He was forced to own up to the fact when his two other children also came down with it. 'You can imagine how I felt,' Leopold wrote. What should have been a triumphant return to the imperial capital had turned into a catalogue of disasters.

The disease, and the fact that it had struck the royal family so hard, released Leopold from any obligation to remain in Vienna. His priority was to get as far away from any smallpox-affected area as possible, so as soon as he could he left with the family for Moravia, well north of Vienna, where he had contacts. All he could do was pray that his own children did not come down with the dreaded disease.

They did. Both of them. Wolfgang first, and worst.

In the town of Olmütz, the already crowded hotel Zum schwarzen Adler ('At the Black Eagle') could offer only an uncomfortably damp room. A heater was brought in, but it belched smoke and made the family's eyes smart.

It was not long before Wolfgang's cheeks began to glow red and hot. His forehead burned, his hands were as cold as ice. He could not sleep.

The hotel managed to find a more comfortable room, and Wolfgang was carried to it, wrapped in furs. His fever continued to worsen, and he was soon delirious. Leopold suspected immediately that this was smallpox. If it was, then his worst fears would be confirmed.

As it happened, Leopold had an impressive contact in Olmütz – one of the reasons he had journeyed there – a certain Count Podstatsky, nephew of a former archbishop of Salzburg, now dean of the cathedral. Leopold lost no time in contacting him.

The count's response was exemplary. He dispatched his personal doctor to the hotel to examine Wolfgang, and – with no heed to the possible spread of infection – had rooms made up in the deanery for the Mozarts.

The doctor confirmed the worst. Wolfgang was once again wrapped in furs, and this time leather as well, and transported, shivering, to the deanery. His eyes were badly affected. They became painful and he preferred to keep them closed. For nine days it was as if he was blind.

Small red spots appeared on his face, and soon after the smallpox broke out fully. After nine days the fever abated, the spots began to disappear, leaving behind the telltale scars; Nannerl wrote later that his face was heavily scarred from the disease. There are, as far as I can ascertain, fourteen portraits of Mozart done from life, thirteen of them after the smallpox. None shows any sign of the scars. Portrait artists were well used to covering blemishes.[*]

As perhaps only a child can, Wolfgang recovered rapidly as soon as the fever abated. The bishop's chaplain called on him and taught him card tricks, and – unlikely though it might sound – when he had regained enough strength he took fencing lessons from a local fencing instructor.

Leopold was grateful beyond words to Count Podstatsky – though not literally. He had some time since resolved to write a biography of his remarkable son, and he promised that when he came to write it the count's good deeds would 'redound in no small way to his honour'.[†]

For the immediate future, though, Leopold's worries were not over. Nannerl came down with the disease. He could at least be grateful that the attack was mild, she recovered quickly, and her face was left unmarked, thus not impeding her marriage prospects.

Once Wolfgang was fully recovered, he returned to what he loved best, bringing to fruition a new symphony, the Symphony in F (к. 43), its slow movement an orchestral arrangement of a duet from *Apollo et Hyacinthus*. It was Wolfgang's first four-movement symphony.

Both children recovered, it was time for the Mozarts to head south, back to Vienna, to try their luck once more at court. This time they had more success.

It was a difficult journey back, the coach frequently delayed by deep and drifting snow, and maybe the family were grateful for a few days' rest, before receiving a summons to Schönbrunn on 19 July 1768, nine days after they arrived.

It is more than likely the empress had heard of the children's illness, and wanted to offer sympathy and support. In the intervening months she herself had come down with smallpox. Leopold wrote to Hagenauer that he could scarcely believe his eyes to see the empress clutching his wife's hands and stroking her cheeks, the two women speaking intimately not as ruler and subject, but as mothers. One suspects he might even have felt a small pang of envy.

The new emperor proved a slightly tougher nut to crack, at least initially. He seems to have shown little interest in hearing Wolfgang play. The boy was now twelve years of age, on the brink of his teenage years. Young he might be, but with every passing year his precocious talent would seem just that bit less remarkable.

> "Young he might be, but with every passing year Mozart's precocious talent would seem just that bit less remarkable."

---

[*] This is also true of portraits of Beethoven who, like Mozart, contracted smallpox as a child.

[†] In fact the biography was never written.

And then something quite extraordinary happened. Leopold reported to Hagenauer that the emperor – out of the blue – asked Wolfgang if he would like to compose an opera and direct it. Twice he asked him, said Leopold. That was most certainly too good an opportunity to let pass.

To Leopold this would be the passport to Italy, home of opera. In fact soon afterwards he began collecting letters of introduction to influential people in the world of Italian music. The future looked secure.

Wolfgang was excited beyond words. This was something he really wanted to do. For Leopold it represented the logical next step for his son, and of all forms of musical entertainment it was the one most likely to bring in good money. And with the request, in effect an order, coming from the emperor himself, what could possibly go wrong?

A lot, as Leopold was to find out. To compound matters, it was entirely his fault.

Leopold upset just about everyone it was imperative not to upset. His arrogance completely got the better of him.

The first to get a taste of this was the venerable Christoph Willibald Gluck, revered composer of opera, much loved by the Viennese opera-going public. His *Don Juan* and *Orfeo ed Euridice* had been enormously popular, and only weeks earlier his *Alceste* had been a huge hit.

Leopold, it seems, calmly informed him that on nights when he was not leading his opera from the harpsichord, a twelve-year-old boy would be directing his. Gluck was appalled. In his mid-fifties, he considered it thoroughly demeaning that he would in effect be sharing the prestigious Burgtheater with a boy. Leopold left him in no doubt this was sanctioned from the very top.

He then antagonised the director of the Burgtheater, who would have to bear the costs of the production. Wolfgang was raring to go, but Leopold complained the librettist was not supplying the text quickly enough.

The opera was to be called *La finta semplice* ('The feigned simpleton'), and Wolfgang intended it to be a full-length opera of two and a half to three hours.

He began work in late January. At the end of March Leopold reported that it was going well, and that it should be ready for performance before the emperor in June. Things went badly wrong, though. The first rehearsal in late spring was a disaster, with the singers claiming the work was unsingable, and members of the orchestra complaining they did not want to be directed by a boy.

Musical circles in Vienna were intrigued by the goings-on. Rumour spread that the music was in fact written by the boy's father, and was 'not worth a fig'. Calamity ensued when the theatre director cancelled the production outright, refusing to pay any fee as the work was 'untheatrical'.

At this point Leopold's arrogance got the better of him. He blamed anyone and everyone. He wrote home about 'all sorts of concocted intrigues and malicious persecutions'. Gluck, he said, persuaded all other composers to join him in opposing the project. The singers and orchestra, according to Leopold, were persuaded to say the opera was unsingable and unplayable, even though he knew perfectly well they actually admired it greatly.

Leopold was in high dudgeon and he took the moral high ground. 'Had I known all that I know now,' he wrote to Hagenauer, 'Wolfgang would never have written a note, but would have been home long ago.'

In fact Leopold was facing a dilemma. If he left now and took the family home to Salzburg, he would have to carry the burden of total failure. If he stayed, it might be to no avail and increase his costs considerably.

It was at this point that he overreached himself. What he did next showed an appalling ignorance of etiquette, of just how little he understood about rank and hierarchy. In fact he unwittingly proved himself to be the complete outsider, the provincial adrift in the capital city of empire. He wrote directly to the emperor himself, blaming the director and management of the court theatres, people whose appointment was ultimately sanctioned by the emperor himself. He declared himself entitled to compensation for the cancellation of the opera and reimbursement of his costs.

Verbally he complained to senior figures that the cancellation of the opera was proof of Vienna's contempt for provincial Salzburg and its archbishop. Not words likely to earn him any friends.

All this from a Salzburger who, it was well known in musical circles, was on protracted unpaid leave, and in danger of dismissal from the court on his return.

The emperor accepted Leopold's complaints and promised they would be thoroughly investigated. And that was the last Leopold heard about it. He had thoroughly burned his boats in the one place that really mattered to an aspiring musician.

His arrogance had upset his son's plans not only in the short term but in the longer term as well. Some years later the empress opposed giving Wolfgang a permanent position at the Habsburg court because that would have meant putting up with his family, 'people of no use to us'.

Wolfgang consoled himself by writing several small works, as well as a Mass, and an operetta entitled *Bastien und Bastienne*.

The Mozarts returned to Salzburg after a difficult year away. It really was now time for Leopold to put his grander plan into action. Enough of Salzburg, enough of Vienna and the Habsburgs. Italy was there, waiting to be conquered.

7

CHEVALIER DE MOZART

By the end of the year, Leopold and Wolfgang were on their way to Italy. It was no thanks to Leopold. A cheeky demand he had made to the archbishop for the salary that had been withheld from him while he was away in Vienna was rejected out of hand.

Archbishop Schrattenbach, who had nurtured other local musical talent, made it clear he would subsidise the trip purely on account of young Wolfgang's extraordinary musical gifts, and he expected the boy to return to his native city polished by Italian culture and ready to contribute to Salzburg's musical life.

Leopold wanted to set out as soon as possible, but he was made to wait, as if the court was reluctant to give way on everything. It was almost at the end of the year, on 13 December 1769, that the carriage rolled out of Salzburg.

There were only two people in it. This moment was a turning point in the lives of the Mozart family. Leopold, paterfamilias, decided that he and his son Wolfgang would travel alone.

The lower costs of just two people travelling played a part in his decision, but there was more to it than that. Leopold could see how much more impressive Wolfgang was than his elder sister. She was good at the keyboard, but he was very much better. And so far she had shown little inclination to compose. As for Wolfgang, he could barely compose fast enough.

There was also the matter of age. Nannerl was now eighteen, an adult. She might be very accomplished at the keyboard, but she was no longer the child wonder she had been on earlier tours. Remaining at home, she could

be expected to take in a few students, thus bringing some money in. She was also of marriageable age. Leopold had every reason to hope that during his absence she might make a good match.

Wolfgang was six weeks short of his fourteenth birthday. He too was no longer a wunderkind. He was still short of stature (which his father admitted was something of a concern), with sparkling eyes and a beguiling face that slipped into a smile at the slightest opportunity. His skill at the keyboard, not to mention tricks such as playing on a covered keyboard, stunned and baffled professional musicians twenty and more years older than him. Leopold was in no doubt of the effect he would have on Italian audiences.

There was the added bonus that much of the music Wolfgang would play was also composed by him. These were not childish jottings, but works of such maturity and complexity that doubts always arose as to whether he could possibly have composed them. Leopold had by now learned how to dispel these suspicions and, given his tender age, Wolfgang was more than happy to obey instructions and oblige his father.

To this end father and son took with them a stack of manuscripts, from chamber pieces, choral works, to symphonies and piano pieces – all the work of Wolfgang. And Leopold had done his homework. He had made use of the delay in departure to contact noble houses in northern Italy that belonged to Habsburg aristocracy, as northern Italy was part of the Habsburg empire and was ruled from Vienna. Leopold knew even before they left that they would be received, royally in some cases, in major cities across the north of Italy.

Perhaps even he could not have foreseen the full extent of what he and his son were embarking on. In the event they would stay on tour for fifteen months. Wolfgang would perform in almost forty cities and towns, travelling all the way down to Naples in the south. As well as numerous private recitals, he would give at least twenty-five public performances – and he would still find time to compose around twenty new pieces of music.

Verona, Mantua, Milan, Bologna, Florence, Rome, Naples – and these are only the principal towns and cities. The teenage boy would be feted in some of the most musical, musically sophisticated, and indeed musically critical, cities in the whole of Europe.

We have copious information on the tour, since Leopold continued to be an indisputably prodigious letter writer. All the more so, since he was now separated from his wife. And since it was his wife he was writing to, rather than a friend, there is more intimacy in the letters than there was on previous tours.

At the bottom of almost all Leopold's letters, Wolfgang added a postscript to his sister or less often to his mother. Often he would enclose a separate letter to Nannerl. It is the first opportunity we have to hear Wolfgang's own words, allowing us for the first time to form a true picture of the young genius's personality.

Verona and Mantua were almost like warm-up destinations ahead of the biggest prize in northern Italy, Milan. In both cities Wolfgang performed, to much praise and adulation. Now Leopold had his sights firmly set on Milan. It was imperative Wolfgang was well received there.

Milan was the centre of Austrian government in northern Italy. Senior members of the Habsburg aristocracy had homes there. There was constant communication between Vienna and Milan at a senior level. It is beyond doubt that word of Wolfgang's achievements throughout Europe had reached Milan. We can also assume Leopold would have had letters of recommendation in his pocket bearing many an aristocratic seal.

The two, father and son, arrived in Milan at noon on 23 January 1770. On the journey their feet were enveloped in muffs lined with wolf fur against the bitter cold. They lodged in the Augustinian monastery of San Marco, which was warm and comfortable, much to Wolfgang's relief.

The journey across the Alps into northern Italy and then west across Veneto and Lombardy to Milan had taken its toll. Wolfgang's face had become red and leathery in the icy temperatures 'as if he had been on a military expedition', Leopold wrote. Worse, much worse, his hands showed signs of frostbite.

The nobleman who was Leopold's main contact in Milan, Count Karl Joseph von Firmian, was unwell, which at least allowed Wolfgang some time to recuperate. A kindly Brother Alphonso provided him with four mattresses to curl up on, to which he added a warming pan every night. Wolfgang was soon able to shake off the rigours of the journey.

Count Firmian, a nephew of a former archbishop of Salzburg and now governor-general of Lombardy, is one of those characters whose place in history is assured by his ability to recognise youthful genius and nurture it. A highly cultured man, he spoke several languages and had a library of forty thousand books. He was to be a constant advocate of Wolfgang, directly or indirectly, in Italy, and would be responsible for the commission of several future operas. He was the perfect contact.[*]

As soon as Count Firmian was recovered, he summoned the Mozarts and laid plans for Wolfgang to demonstrate his powers to the aristocracy and cognoscenti of Milan. A first concert was held at the count's palace on

---

[*] Similarly, nearly two decades later in Bonn, Count Waldstein was to nurture the youthful genius of Ludwig van Beethoven.

18 February, at which the guests of honour were the Duke of Modena and his daughter, who was about to marry into the Habsburg royal family.

Count Firmian was so impressed with Wolfgang that he arranged for him to give a public concert just five days later. He also decided to subsidise it so it would be free to the public, which was rare in itself. It is easy to imagine Leopold being less than pleased, and this might be why, in a letter home, he said no more than that the concert went off 'just as all our concerts have done everywhere'.

The main event of the stay came two and a half weeks later, again at the count's palace. It was a special gala evening for a select audience of a hundred and fifty guests. The crème de la crème of Milanese society was there.

It was, predictably, a triumph. Count Firmian immediately commissioned Wolfgang to write an opera for the following season at Milan's prestigious and renowned opera house, the Teatro Regio Ducal.[*]

Leopold's eyes must have watered when he saw the contract, which was for 100 cigliati.[†] Count Firmian had worked out a sensible timetable. A libretto would be forwarded to the Mozarts as they headed south from Milan. Wolfgang could begin work, and then return to Milan in early November with enough time to work with the singers.

A sweetener, should Leopold have required it, was a gift from the count to Wolfgang of a snuffbox set in gold containing 20 cigliati. Leopold might well have been irritated by Count Firmian's decision to allow Wolfgang to perform free of charge, but it had most certainly paid dividends.

Father and son left Milan on 15 March, knowing they would be back towards the end of the year, and with a very nice contract burning a hole in Leopold's pocket.

Let us look at this boy by the name of Wolfgang Mozart who had just passed his fourteenth birthday. Wolfgang, Wolferl to his family and friends, a boisterous, energetic, hyper (as we might say today) live wire, with boundless energy, albeit prone to sudden and severe illness, was entering adolescence. And what fascinates adolescent boys? Girls, of course. Just because Wolfgang is an unsurpassed musical genius does not mean he is not subject to the same thoughts and desires as any other adolescent boy.

In a letter to his sister from Milan, Wolfgang writes of a prima ballerina he has seen at the ballet: 'They say she is not at all bad looking, but I haven't seen her up close.' And of one of the singers at the opera: 'The second Dona

"Just because Wolfgang is an unsurpassed musical genius does not mean he is not subject to the same thoughts and desires as any adolescent boy."

---

[*] The building would be destroyed by fire in 1776. Rebuilt, it would open with the new name, which it bears to this day: La Scala.

[†] The equivalent of 100 ducats, in the region of £11,250 today.

is not bad looking on stage, young, but nothing spessial.'[16] To say that this is a foretaste of what is to come is an understatement of gigantic proportions.

The same applies – much, much more so – to another area of fascination for Wolfgang, again something he shares with other adolescent boys, and that is bodily functions. There is a dancer at the ballet who jumps very well, but 'he can't write like me: [I write as easily as] pigs piss'.

More than anything it is bodily functions from the rear end that hold, and will continue to hold, an endless fascination for him. We will come across this time and again, indeed throughout his life, even later – to the bewilderment and embarrassment of learned and academic musicologists from that day to this – gelling with his musical activities.

In this same letter, he writes of a male dancer who 'let out a fart each time he jumped'. And in another to Nannerl, writing of the dance festival he and his father attended in Milan, he adds a postscript sending 'a Thousand Compliments to you from Don Cacarella espessially from the rear'. 'Don Cacarella' being Wolfgang's pet name for diarrhoea, and the rear, naturally, being his bottom.

So the stay in Milan, which lasted seven weeks, represents the first truly significant musical success for Wolfgang, in that he has been awarded a valuable contract to compose a full opera. It also gives us our first invaluable insight into the joyful character of this teenage boy.

South to Lodi, where Wolfgang composed his first string quartet, and on to Parma and Bologna. In Bologna he met the greatest of all the castrati, Farinelli, now in retirement. He was introduced to leading musicians in whatever town they stopped in, performances were given, and to Leopold's delight payments were made in appreciation.

The first major stop was in Florence, where there were more performances and more money earned. Wolfgang's musical powers were still being put to the test, as if surely there had to be some weakness in his armour. Certainly no offence was taken at this, Leopold seemingly happy to allow his son to be challenged, and Wolfgang more than happy to oblige.

We know this from Leopold's account of a meeting with a certain Eugenio Marquess of Ligniville, a director of music known as a scholarly contrapuntalist. He challenged Wolfgang to write counterpoint to several difficult themes, 'which', wrote Leopold, '[Wolfgang] threw off and worked out as others might eat a piece of bread'.

It is perhaps easy for us today, just as it was for those who encountered him, to concentrate and marvel so completely at Wolfgang's musical genius that we forget what sort of life he was actually leading.

No evidence exists that Wolfgang ever attended school; he was on the road throughout his childhood and into his teens, forever on display, and always meeting, playing and conversing with men and musicians decades older than him. It was a lonely life for a growing boy. Where were the friends of his own age, the pranks that they would certainly have got up to?

No wonder, then, that when at last he met a boy of his own age, and a superbly gifted musician to boot, he was over the moon and a friendship quickly formed.

The boy was the English violin prodigy Thomas Linley, who had come from his home in Bath to Florence to study with Pietro Nardini. He was alone, no member of his family accompanying him. Thomas was just three months younger than Wolfgang, and like him was unusually small for his age. Hardly surprising the two boys immediately got on.

"The instant
friendship
Wolfgang formed
with Thomas
emphasises what
a strange life
they both were
leading"

Musically it was a perfect match. Thomas was already being described as the most supremely gifted violinist England had ever produced. They were soon performing together at aristocratic venues in Florence, sometimes both on violin, at other times Wolfgang accompanying Thomas on the piano.

Their closeness was so evident that Leopold wrote that even when performing before nobility they were 'constantly embracing one another'. You can see why. Even if each struggled with the other's language, at last Wolfgang had someone his own age to laugh and giggle with, chatting and joking in broken English and German about the obvious topics that would interest adolescent boys, and certainly they would have performed musical tricks too, delighting in the other's skills and sharing in the adulation they received.

Sadly Wolfgang does not write about Thomas in letters home. We have only Leopold's account, and all that interested him was musical prowess. When it came time for Leopold and Wolfgang to leave Florence, Leopold allows himself a small measure of empathy: 'Little Thomaso accompanied us home and wept the bitterest tears because we were leaving the next day.'

Thomas, on his return to England, went on to a glittering early career, both as performer and composer, earning himself the sobriquet 'The English Mozart'. He no doubt talked of his new-found friend widely and whenever he could. Maybe he met people who had encountered Wolfgang as a child in London.

The story does not have a happy ending. Thomas and Wolfgang never met again. In July 1778 Thomas went with his sisters to Lincolnshire to stay as guests of the Duke of Ancaster. On 5 August Thomas went boating on the lake, a storm blew up, the boat overturned, and Thomas drowned. He was just twenty-two years of age, at the height of fame, with a glittering musical career ahead of him.

To compound the tragedy, his three sisters all died of consumption over the next fifteen years, and his brother drowned in 1795. Their father died in the same year, it was said of a broken heart.

Young Thomas barely earns more than a line or two in Mozart biographies, and then it is only to relate how the two boys made music together. But it is worth pausing for a moment to contemplate the relationship that developed between these two teenage boys, and the similarities they shared. Both had siblings, and had been taken away from them. Now at last they were able to speak 'boyish' language together, laugh, play pranks, talk about girls, their desires and hopes.

It is not fanciful to imagine that it was a total relief for both of them to spend time together *not* making music. The instant friendship Wolfgang formed with Thomas emphasises what a strange life they both were leading. They might have been doing what they loved best, what came most instinctively to them, but it is not an exaggeration to say neither had had a childhood.

⌐⌐

The journey south was difficult. It took five days in rain and wind, the roads were rough, and they stopped at 'disgusting, filthy inns where there was nothing to eat', reported Leopold.

As they approached the Eternal City, Leopold allowed his imagination a little rein. In a thunderous storm, lightning lit up the sky. He and his son, he wrote, felt like great men being welcomed by a firing of salutes.

Leopold had timed their arrival to coincide with Holy Week and Easter, when musical activities would be at their height and the noble families of Rome would be certain to be in their palaces. He had not taken into account the fact that the city would be full. The only accommodation they could find was in a small and uncomfortable boarding house. Wolfgang complained in a letter to his sister that he was having to share a bed with his father, so naturally he was getting no sleep.

The day after their arrival, Maundy Thursday, they pushed their way through the crowds to watch Pope Clement XIV washing the feet of the poor, and they took in the sights of the Vatican City.

Leopold marvelled at the symmetry and order of the architecture, its richness and gigantic scale. Wolfgang, with self-deprecating humour, described how his lack of height proved a real embarrassment. Taking his turn to kiss the feet of a statue of St Peter dating from the thirteenth century, he had to be lifted up so he could reach – 'so small I, the same old numbskull'.

The Mozarts stayed in Rome for a month. They met senior cardinals, and were pleased to find news of Wolfgang's musical prowess had already reached the highest circles. The Pope himself knew of Wolfgang, though no summons to meet him was immediately forthcoming.

No public concerts were given, but Wolfgang performed in the palaces of royalty and aristocrats, as well as ambassadors. As both father and son had come to expect, plaudits were universal and more often than not accompanied by financial reward and gifts.

From this stay in Rome comes one of the best-known legends of the teenage Mozart, and our knowledge of it stems from a letter Leopold wrote home to his wife Anna Maria.

After a tour of St. Peter's, Leopold took his son to the Sistine Chapel to hear the Tenebrae service. Traditionally this concluded with a singing of the *Miserere* by the seventeenth-century Italian composer Gregorio Allegri. This was a work the Vatican reserved to itself. It was so greatly prized, Leopold wrote, that 'the singers in the chapel are forbidden on pain of excommunication to take away a single voice part, copy it, or give it to anyone'.

In short, the Vatican forbade Allegri's *Miserere* to be performed, or in any way heard, outside the Sistine Chapel. It was able to do this by the simple expedient of forbidding any copies of the music to be taken outside. Without copies it would be impossible for any choir to perform it, given that it was a substantial work lasting well over ten minutes.

They reckoned without Wolfgang Mozart. As Leopold relates, after they heard it sung they returned to their lodgings and Wolfgang wrote down, from memory, as much of the music as he could remember. He needed to check on a few passages, so on Good Friday they went again to the Sistine Chapel when it was to be sung again, and Wolfgang was able to complete it.

Leopold wrote to his wife that he had told all and sundry of Wolfgang's achievement. She, panicked, wrote back fearing Wolfgang would be punished. Her husband reassured her. He knew for a fact that the Pope had been told, he said, and no thunderbolts had been hurled. In fact, Leopold told her, it had greatly increased admiration for their son.

As the warm weather of early summer arrived, Leopold headed south with Wolfgang to Naples, where he knew there were prize pickings. In fact their stay in Naples was something of a disappointment. The local nobility showed little interest; there never was a summons from the King and Queen of Naples, and the situation was saved only by the interest of foreign ambassadors, particularly from Britain.

The British ambassador William Hamilton and his wife Catherine had met Wolfgang in London. They lost no time in inviting the Mozarts to their residence. Catherine was in fact an accomplished pianist, though she admitted to 'trembling' in front of Wolfgang. [*]

With the heat of summer worsening his mood, Leopold decided to move north again. Although he admired the huge variety of fruit, vegetables and flowers in Naples, he found the inhabitants almost as rude as those in London, and he deplored the filth, the beggars, 'the godlessness … and the disgraceful way in which children are brought up'.

After Naples, it was back to Rome, where a singular and extraordinary honour awaited. But before that, it was as if the sheer relentlessness of what they were doing caught up with them, both of them.

---

[*] Catherine would die ten years later, after which Hamilton would marry his mistress, Emma, whose name would become forever linked with that of Horatio Nelson.

Leopold was keen to get back to Rome as quickly as possible – too quickly. We cannot be entirely sure why he was in such a hurry: perhaps frustration at time wasted in Naples, more than five fairly unproductive weeks, the heat and noise and bustle of this southern Italian city, coupled with a desire to get back to the capital to see what glory, and remuneration, awaited them there.

It was an overly impatient Leopold who ordered a post-coach, a much smaller two-wheeled coach with a half-open top, which was drawn by a single horse with a postilion riding alongside. This *sedia* could cover the distance to Rome in a little over twenty-four hours without overnight stops, instead of the usual four and a half days.

When a stop was necessary Leopold, using a combination of German and badly accented Italian, ensured swift service and good horses by telling innkeepers and officials he was steward to the ambassador of the Holy Roman Empire. Innkeepers doffed their caps; customs officials employed by the Vatican bowed in respect and waved the travellers on.

The final stage of the journey was over makeshift roads of deep sand and soil, which made progress slow. Leopold ordered the postilion to whip the horse, which he did with such force that the horse reared, stumbled and fell, pulling the carriage down with it.

Leopold instinctively held out an arm to prevent Wolfgang from falling out, but gashed his right shin against the iron bar supporting the mudguard. It was a deep gash, down to the bone and 'the width of a finger', and it was to cause Leopold considerable pain over the ensuing months.

Father and son were exhausted by the time they arrived in Rome. As soon as they got to their room, Wolfgang collapsed in a chair and fell so deeply asleep he snored. Leopold had to lift him up, undress his son and put him underneath the covers. Wolfgang did not wake.

Three days later, on 29 June, Leopold, his leg badly swollen and bandaged, took a recovered Wolfgang to St Peter's to attend services for the Feast of Peter and Paul. A week after this they were invited to call on Cardinal Pallavicini, who informed them that the pope himself was to award Wolfgang a papal knighthood, making him a Knight of the Golden Spur. This carried insignia of cross-studded sash, sword and spurs. A papal patent described Wolfgang as 'a musician who excelled since earliest youth in the sweetest sounding of the harpsichord'.[17]

Three days after this, Leopold and Wolfgang had a formal audience with Pope Clement, who informed him he was now entitled to style himself 'Chevalier de Mozart'.

To a fourteen-year-old boy, especially one with Wolfgang's quirky sense of humour, this was more amusing than impressive, and in a letter to his

"The pope himself was to award Wolfgang a papal knighthood, making him a Knight of the Golden Spur."

Mozart wearing the insignia of a Knight of the Golden Spur; the portrait is a copy of the original, now lost.

sister he indulges in the kind of lavatory humour he is to use more and more. In a combination of French and Italian, as if maybe that is slightly more acceptable than his native German, he writes:

> Mademoiselle, I have the honour of being your very humble servant, and brother,
> Chevalier de Mozart
> Rome, July 7, 1770, Addio, be well and shit in your bed with a resounding noise.

Once again, this is a mere nothing compared to what lies ahead.

8

Ass-Bumping in Venice

Leopold, a natural worrier, had plenty to worry about. His letters home are a catalogue of problems. His injured leg was not healing as it should; in fact it had become worse. The wound opened and his leg and foot swelled. Soon his ankle was the thickness of his calf. To compound his misery, he was in pain in his other foot, probably with an attack of gout.

Constantly on his mind was the danger of contracting malaria, which was prevalent in Italy and came with the hot summer months. For Wolfgang to become ill again would be a disaster. Leopold had a valuable contract in his pocket for an opera that Wolfgang needed to compose by the beginning of the new season in Milan. Already he only had months left to complete it.

A long and difficult journey north lay ahead. Leopold contrived to make it even more difficult, rather as he had done with the shorter journey from Naples to Rome. He decided they would travel by night, to lessen the risk of catching malaria on the road in the heat of day.

They left Rome at six in the evening on 10 July. They travelled right through the night, until five the next morning, when they stopped. By then they were bitterly cold, Leopold writes, even with their furs over their coats. They warmed themselves up with drinks of hot chocolate.

They left again at five in the afternoon. Their destination was Bologna, 240 miles north of Rome as the crow flies, via Florence. But Leopold decided against making it that simple.

Instead they headed across Italy to the Adriatic coast, destination Loreto, where Leopold wished to make devotions at the shrine of the Virgin in the Santa Casa, the house in which the Holy Family had lived in Palestine. The house had been miraculously flown by four angels to Loreto, where for centuries it had been a place of pilgrimage.

From there they took the coastal road up to Rimini – a foolhardy and potentially disastrous decision. Leopold reported that the whole coast was swarming with mounted soldiers and police, deployed to protect travellers, and pilgrims, from Barbary pirates who were attacking and robbing them.

It really is no wonder that when father and son finally arrived in Bologna on 20 July, even if they had escaped the pirates, they were utterly exhausted. They checked into the San Marco inn, and it was never going to be a short stay.

Leopold's leg was now causing him serious problems. He could not walk properly or stand for any length of time, and was in great pain. For the next two weeks he remained in his room, either in bed or with his leg resting on a chair.

For Wolfgang, too, life was not entirely straightforward. He was now fourteen and a half years of age. In the previous weeks his voice had broken, and in Naples his father had noted he had put on a spurt of height – although 'still a little man' – which had meant his clothes needed altering.

Puberty can be tiring for a teenager, even when living a calm life in luxurious surroundings. But Wolfgang, in Italy in high summer, on the road constantly, his eating and sleeping patterns disrupted, performing at the keyboard to order, was being pushed beyond natural limits.

No wonder he wrote to his sister that 'Italy is a drowsy country. I am always sleepy.' It is a mark of his genius, though, that despite being exhausted he was able to tell her he had composed four Italian symphonies, five or six arias, and one motet.

Music was very much on his father's mind too. Wolfgang's voice, it seems, had broken into a shaky scale of barely five notes: 'He has neither a deep voice nor a high one, not even five pure notes; he is very cross about this as he can no longer sing his own compositions, which he would sometimes like to do.'

Despite Leopold's inbuilt pessimism, and therefore the probability of some exaggeration, it is still a beguiling image: the young musical genius struggling to sing his own songs, crying out in frustration at being unable to hit the very notes he had himself written.

Leopold had informed the Milan opera house of their whereabouts, and exactly a week after their arrival in Bologna the libretto and cast list arrived. Wolfgang began work immediately on his new opera, *Mitridate, rè di Ponto*.

Is it too fanciful to imagine Wolfgang, while naturally sympathetic towards his father, being perhaps just a little grateful that, laid up on a chair with his injured leg, Leopold was unable to interfere in his son's creative process quite as much as he was used to doing?

In fact Wolfgang did little work on the opera for the next few weeks. Circumstances were about to change dramatically for father and son. They received an invitation to stay at the country estate outside Bologna of Field-Marshal Count Pallavicini, a distant relative of the cardinal they had come to know in Rome, where they arrived on 10 August.

What a contrast to life on the road! They were given palatial rooms and were waited on by footmen and valets. Their beds were made up with 'sheets of linen finer than many a nobleman's shirt'. They had toiletry pieces made of silver, and a servant sleeping in the anteroom was on hand to attend to their every need, including dressing Wolfgang's hair.

They dined with the Pallavicinis at their sumptuous table in the terrace room. They ate the finest figs, melons and peaches, and delighted at their first encounter with watermelon, which, as Italians say from that day to this, fulfils three functions: you eat it, drink it and wash your face with it.

Leopold spent his days reclining in an easy chair. Wherever he went in the house, servants followed with a comfortable chair and footstool, and his aristocratic hosts forbade him to rise to his feet when they approached. Mass was held privately in the house so Leopold did not need to make the journey to church.

When his leg began to improve, Leopold along with Wolfgang took carriage rides through the lovely countryside. Wolfgang took to riding a donkey, to exercise his muscles a little. When he was well enough, Leopold went with Wolfgang to a sacred concert in the church of San Giovanni in Monte.

There they bumped into the English composer and music historian Charles Burney, who had heard the young Wolfgang in London a few years previously. He was touring Europe to gather material for his history of music, and he wrote that 'there is no musical excellence I do not expect from his extraordinary quickness and talents'. [18]

It was an idyllic existence, something they both needed very much, and they were in no hurry to move on. It had been Leopold's plan to leave at the end of the month and pay another visit to Florence, a city he especially loved. Wolfgang was excited at this prospect, since it would mean a chance to rekindle his friendship with young Thomas Linley.

In the event, though, Leopold's leg was taking a long time to heal, longer than expected. It is impossible for us to judge just how bad it was, but no doubt his kindly hosts encouraged him to stay longer to allow it to heal properly, and he probably would not have taken too much persuading.

"Puberty can be tiring for a teenager, but Wolfgang was being pushed beyond natural limits."

With any fear of outstaying their welcome put to rest, Leopold and Wolfgang remained at the Pallavicinis' estate until the end of September. They finally returned to Bologna, where they spent more than a month leisurely gathering all their things together. They had by now accumulated an array of trunks and boxes, filled with books and music. So much did they have that Leopold started shipping some of it over the Alps to Salzburg to make their return journey easier.

There were more musical honours to be had in Bologna, and Leopold lost no time in putting his son forward for membership of the august Accademia Filarmonica, despite membership being open only to those of more than twenty years of age and with conservatory training. Leopold calmly reminded the distinguished examiners that his fourteen-year-old son was a papal knight. They would certainly have already heard of Wolfgang's extraordinary talents, and agreed to examine him.

Leopold was locked in the library, while Wolfgang was sequestered in another room on the other side of the hall. He was given a plainsong Gregorian chant, which he was required to set in the 'strict style', adding three contrapuntal voices above the bass.

Candidates usually took three hours over this fiendishly difficult exercise. Leopold reported that Wolfgang took just half an hour, probably not much of an exaggeration since the academy itself said it took him less than an hour.

After perusing Wolfgang's efforts, each member of the examining panel raised a white disc. Wolfgang was congratulated, letters patent were prepared, and this fourteen-year-old boy had another honour to his name.

North-west to Parma, in a direct line to Milan, and Leopold had more reason to complain. What should have been a brief stopover was prolonged by torrential rain, so heavy that the city risked being flooded. Leopold's leg might by now have largely healed, but the damp air exacerbated his chronic rheumatism.

Finally arriving in Milan on 18 October, they took up assigned lodgings close to the theatre, consisting of a large room with three windows and a balcony and an equally spacious bedroom, with a huge nine-foot bed and two windows.

Still Leopold was not happy. There might have been a good number of windows, but there was no fireplace. 'We may freeze to death, but we will certainly not smell, since there is plenty of air,' he wrote home to Salzburg.

Wolfgang got down to work, serious work. Two days after arriving in Milan he wrote to his mother that his fingers hurt terribly from writing so many recitatives. Two weeks later in a letter to his sister, he said he had complained to Papa that he was getting sleepy, and Papa said, 'Then stop writing.'

PRINCEPS   CAETERIQUE

ACADEMICI   PHYLHARMONICI.

Omnibus, et singulis praesentes Literas lecturis, felicitatem.

Uamvis ipfa Virtus fibi, fuifque Sectatoribus gloriofum comparet Nomen, attamen pro majori ejufdem majeftate publicam in notitiam decuit propagari. Hinc eft, quòd hujufce noftrae **PHYLHARMONCAE ACADEMIAE** exiftimationi, & incremento confulere, fingulorumque Academicorum Scientiam, & profectum patefacere intendentes, Teftamur *Domin Wolfgango Amadeus Mozart e Salisburgo* fub die 9 Menfis *Octobris* — Anni *1770* inter Academiae noftrae *Magistros Compositores* adfcriptum fuiffe. Tanti igitur Coacademici virtutem, & merita perenni benevolentiae monumento profequentes, hafce Patentes, Literas fubfcriptas, noftrique Confeffus Sigillo impreffo obfignatas dedimus.

Bononiae ex noftra Refidentia die *10* · Menfis *Octobris* Anni *1770*

                       Princeps. *Petronius Lanzi*

                                 a Secretis.

Regiftr. in Libro Camplono G — *pag. 147.*

                                   Camplonerius. Cajetanus Croci

With humour, but with signs of exhaustion showing through, he signs off the short note to his sister:

> *I am, as always, Your*
>
> > *brother wolfgang Mozart*
> > *whose fingers are*
> > *Tiherd Tiherd Tiredh*
> > *tired from writing.*[*]

Six weeks later rehearsals began, and the opening night, on 26 December 1770, with Wolfgang himself at the keyboard – wearing a new scarlet coat with gold trim and light-blue lining – was a triumph.

Cries of *Viva il maestrino!* ('Long live the little maestro!') rang out. Wolfgang directed the first three performances from the keyboard, then handed over to his deputy, while he and his father watched further performances from different parts of the auditorium.

Above

Mozart's letter of admission to the Accademia Filarmonica of Bologna.

---

[*] *dessen finger von schreiben / Müdhe Müdhe Müedhes / müde sind.*

Traditionally the first opera of the new season drew small audiences, but not *Mitridate*. It played to full houses every night, as Wolfgang wrote to his mother, and ran for twenty-two performances. 'Many are saying that as long as they have lived in Milano they have never seen a first opera so full,' he wrote.[*]

Leopold, ever the pessimist, refused to allow himself unalloyed joy. 'My son's opera has been received most favourably,' he wrote to a colleague he had met in Bologna, 'in spite of the great opposition of his enemies and detractors, who before hearing a single note had spread the rumour that it was a barbarous German composition.'

Wolfgang was the toast of Milan. The city of Verona joined in, appointing him Honorary Kapellmeister of the Accademia Filarmonica, and he was feted on a more personal level too. On the night of 3 January Madame d'Asti von Asteburg, a family friend, cooked him liver dumplings and sauerkraut, his favourite dish. Other guests ate capon and pheasant.

It was soon time to bid farewell to Milan and begin the journey home to Salzburg. First, though, a detour south-west to Turin, a city Leopold was keen to visit at the start of its new opera season.

It was as though there was no Italian city that Leopold was prepared to miss, if there was the slightest chance of making musical contacts. They remained in Turin for two weeks, then back to Milan to pack everything up and begin the journey home to Salzburg. First stop, Venice, and the chance to hear more performances, show off his son's skills, and make more contacts.

It should have been an easy couple of days, but once again appalling weather delayed them – 'astonishing' winds – and it took them a full week to reach Venice. They arrived on Monday, 11 February, in the city known since its golden age as La Serenissima, the most exotic city in Europe, suffused with romance and intrigue, where masks were worn to conceal identities, and who knew what else?

One can imagine the excitement of a boy just turned fifteen, past puberty, boarding a boat to make the short crossing to the city of canals. Who could tell what adventure might lie ahead?

That was exactly what worried Leopold. Venice was the pleasure seeker's capital of Italy, if not Europe, a reputation acquired nearly five centuries

---

[*] It is possible the Milanese allowed themselves to be influenced unduly by Mozart's tender age. He himself subsequently dropped the work. There is no mention of it in any of his letters after March 1771. It fell out of the repertoire, and was revived only as recently as 1971 in Salzburg.

earlier when masks were first worn at balls and parties to celebrate a famous military victory of the Serene Republic. It had grown steadily since, allowing people of all classes and ranks to mingle freely – and anonymously. Passions were ignited, fantasies played out.

Courtesans were more numerous in Venice than in any other Italian city. Far from being frowned on, they led fashion, and many were known for their musical accomplishments. Young men from across Europe, when they came to Venice, knew what they could expect.

'As for women,' wrote the French philosopher Jean-Jacques Rousseau only a few years before the Mozarts arrived there, 'it is not in a city like Venice that a man abstains from them.'[19] Leopold used more direct language. '[Venice is] the most dangerous place in all Italy.'

His fears were compounded by the fact that he and Wolfgang were arriving in the final days of the annual Carnival, a mighty letting-off of steam before the rigours of Lent. There was another factor too. They were staying in the house of a friend of their Salzburg landlord Hagenauer,* but their main contact was with a business associate of Hagenauer by the name of Johannes Wider.

Wider, a Salzburg merchant, was particularly popular since he had an attractive wife and six beautiful daughters. This was enough to cause Leopold serious concern.

It is easy to raise a wry smile thinking of a father who is a touch worried that his teenage son – a young man, by eighteenth-century standards – might get himself into a spot of trouble, or find himself led astray. What parent has ever been immune from such thoughts?

But to Leopold this was no laughing matter. Wolfgang had responsibilities. He was already the family's most effective breadwinner. Momentum was building across Europe, and must not be allowed to flag. If he was to continue to compose then he needed to remain serious, and focused. Any whiff of scandal, however slight, could put paid to his reputation.

There was, too, the undoubted fact that Leopold was a deeply religious man. This was not a father who was prepared to allow his son any leeway in his social activities. Underlying this, I am convinced, is the realisation – for the first time – on the part of Leopold that Wolfgang might feel the urge to

"One can imagine the excitement of a boy just turned fifteen, boarding a boat to the city of canals."

---

*The house, owned by the Ceseletti family, was by the Ponte dei Barcaroli, in the centre of the city and on the water. It still stands, with a plaque on the wall commemorating the stay in 1771 of 'the boy from Salzburg in whom musical genius fused with the grace of the eighteenth century in the purest poetry' (*Nel quale la grazia del genio musicale e il garbo settecentesco su fusero in una purissima poesia*).

distance himself, however slightly, from his father's influence; to break away, in however small a way, from his control. That, to Leopold, was unthinkable.

As it happens, we know frustratingly little about the social side of the stay in Venice. The little we do know, though, is utterly fascinating. We have only a short letter from Wolfgang to his sister as evidence, but he most certainly had fun with the Wider females.

He refers to the six daughters as 'pearls', and recounts how they, and their mother, attempted to initiate him as a true Venetian. This is the process known as the 'treatment'. Bavarians who are familiar with it have a more expressive name: 'Ass-bumping' (*Arschprellen*).

It involves wrestling the initiate to the floor, then raising him aloft by the arms and legs, swinging him back and forth, then bumping his bottom against the floor. In his letter Wolfgang described this as the way you become a true Venetian.

Then he adds, tantalisingly, 'They wanted to do it to me too, and all 7 women got together and attacked me, but they couldn't get me down to the floor, addio.'

Once again, for a seemingly insignificant event that rarely merits more than a line or two, or none, in Mozart biographies, it is worth pausing for a moment to take a closer look. If it is my aim in this book to reveal the man, then this qualifies for more than a mere passing reference, and surely allows for a certain amount of speculation.

First, picture the scene. You can almost hear the squeals of delight from the girls as, encouraged by their mother, they grab Wolfgang by the arms and legs and try to force him down to the floor. I imagine Wolfgang – knowing, as we do, that infectious personality – convulsed in laughter, embarrassed no doubt, but most certainly enjoying the close physical contact with attractive members of the opposite sex.

Where was Leopold? I suspect he absented himself in disgust. His son does not tell us. Will he have given the boy a ticking off afterwards? Most certainly, probably accompanied by a stern lecture. Frivolity was not something Leopold understood.

For my part, the thought of the greatest musical genius who ever lived being bumped on the floor by six beautiful girls, encouraged by their mother, is an unforgettable image. But wait. Did he not say they couldn't get him down to the floor? He wrote that as a postscript to a letter his father had written, so he would say that, wouldn't he?

Musically the stay in Venice was not an unalloyed success. Leopold wrote home that he and his son were invited to lunch with the great noble families of the city, who sent their private gondolas to collect them, and then personally accompanied them home afterwards.

Above
Carnival time in
eighteenth-century
Venice: 'the most
dangerous place in
all Italy.'

It seems Wolfgang gave at most four private recitals in aristocratic salons, and he might have performed in establishments that cared for orphaned girls, for which Venice was renowned, and in which music played a major role.[*]

But Leopold, as always, was not happy, and it showed. A priest who met them wrote to a colleague that he did not believe Leopold liked Venice, and the probable reason was that, as had happened elsewhere, he expected musical invitations to come to him, not that he would have to go out to find them.

The colleague who received that letter responded in kind, and it is worth quoting him at some length, because it gives a true sense of how, although Leopold managed to upset just about everyone, this did not detract from the lovely character, and extraordinary musical talent, of his son – loved and admired by everyone:

> *The young Mozart is certainly wonderful for his age, and indeed I love him infinitely. The father, as I see the man, is equally discontent everywhere. He made the same complaints here as he did elsewhere. He idolises his son a little too much, and thus does all he can to spoil him. But I have so good an opinion of the boy's natural good sense that I*

---

[*]Vivaldi had been appointed *maestro di violino* in one of these 'ospedali' in 1703.

hope he will not, in spite of the father's flattery, be spoilt, but will grow instead into a fine man.[20]

Leopold was determined to reach home by Easter, and he and Wolfgang left Venice on 12 March, after a stay of a month. More towns and more recitals – Padua, Vicenza, Verona – and then, at last, across the Alps into Austria.

This was not the route Leopold wanted to take – 'I have already seen the Tyrol, and there is no pleasure in taking the same route twice, as if we were dogs' – but his mood was considerably lightened by news that reached him in Verona, before they set out for the mountains.

A personal message arrived from Empress Maria Theresa, no less, commissioning Wolfgang to compose a second opera for the Teatro Regio Ducal in Milan. The opera was to honour the marriage between one of her sons and an Italian princess. The wedding was due to take place the following October in Milan.

The empress knew exactly what she wanted. Wolfgang was to set a work by the Milanese court poet entitled *Ascanio in Alba*; a story of the wise goddess of love, Venus, bringing together an adoring couple who first must be tested to ensure their love is real. In case anyone was in any doubt, the empress herself was, of course, the wise goddess; she determines the young couple's love is real, and everyone lives happily ever after.

There was even more reason now to arrive home as swiftly as possible. Wolfgang would need to get to work immediately. They crossed the Alps via the Brenner Pass again, this time heading north. A violent gale, bitter cold and snow delayed them for a day in Innsbruck, but on Maundy Thursday, 28 March 1771, they arrived home in Salzburg.

Leopold and Wolfgang had been away for more than fifteen months. Much had happened. Wolfgang had made the transition from boyhood to youth. He had firmly cemented his reputation as a composer of the first rank in the country in Europe where it mattered most. Leopold might have found much to grumble about on the trip, but he was arriving home with yet another valuable commission in his pocket, and it had come, as it were, out of nowhere.

He knew, too, it meant within a matter of months that he and Wolfgang would leave home once again and head south to Milan. There was now no going back. Leopold might still have been employed at the court in Salzburg, but he – and they – knew he had a more important musical task on his hands: to guide his uniquely talented son to ever more musical heights, and bring glory to his home city.

Nothing could now impede this. The future seemed set. But father and son were soon to encounter an intractable obstacle.

9

BRAVISSIMO MAESTRO!

*L*ife back home in Salzburg was anything but comfortable. Leopold knew even before he and Wolfgang arrived home that things could not continue as they were. The apartment they rented from Hagenauer was small and cramped, and he and his wife were no longer a couple with small children.

'Wolfgang is not seven any more,' Leopold wrote to his wife from Venice. In fact Wolfgang was fifteen, Nannerl nearly twenty. There was a simple solution: move to a larger apartment. But why go through that when there was the prospect of more travel? Wolfgang's new opera was due to be performed in Milan in a matter of months. With rehearsals and general preparations they would be on the road again very soon.

With few creature comforts at home and the court largely hostile – if not openly so, certainly under the surface – Leopold must rather have been looking forward to the next trip. Wherever he and his son went, they were treated like nobility and they mixed with the highest in the land. What a contrast to dull provincial Salzburg!

This must surely have been Leopold's thinking, and I am convinced – given what we know of future years – that it rubbed off on his son. Who can blame a teenage boy for enjoying the constant praise and flattery, from royal personages down? In time Wolfgang would come to despise his home city, and those who lived there. Like father, like son.

Salzburg was preparing itself for celebrations – discreet celebrations, nothing too showy, in keeping with the pious modesty of the man in whose honour they would be held. The following January, on the 10th to be precise, less than two months before his seventy-second birthday, Siegmund Schrattenbach, Prince-Archbishop of Salzburg, would celebrate fifty years in the service of the Church.

The Archbishop was a man much loved by his people. He was of the old school. Deeply religious, he would attend up to five church services daily. He marked every feast day in the calendar, and it was said – not in an unkind way — that if you wanted to become one of his privy councillors, simply let him see you saying the rosary at an open window.

He was happy to attend weddings, loved children, and was generous with gifts to his subjects of all ages. And he loved music. Many a young musician in Salzburg found himself en route to study in musical cities such as Venice, with a court appointment awaiting him on his return.

It was Schrattenbach who had allowed Leopold extended leave of absence, on full salary, for his first trip with Wolfgang to Vienna, for the extensive European tour that had taken the two of them to London and Paris, and for most of the second visit to Vienna. I suspect it was only under pressure from jealous rivals that he docked Leopold's pay on that last trip for prolonging his absence without authorisation.

And it was Schrattenbach who had appointed Wolfgang konzertmeister at the age of thirteen, albeit without salary, and authorised payment of two years' salary in advance to Leopold for the first visit to Italy.

Leopold could look forward to many more years of patronage and support from the very top, to allow his son's career to advance. If Wolfgang had already shown himself without equal in the world of music, Leopold knew everything he had achieved so far would pale before the accomplishments that lay ahead.

But Schrattenbach would not see either of the two anniversaries that were approaching, and under his successor things would never be the same again for the Mozarts.

After less than five months father and son left Salzburg once again, en route for Venice and further musical glory. This time the journey took only eight days – the Brenner Pass now more familiar than daunting – and they arrived in Milan in blistering summer heat.

It had not rained in Milan for a whole month, and when it tried, just a few drops fell before the sun blazed out again. 'It was so dusty and hot on our trip, that if we hadn't been so clever we would have choked and died of thirst for sure,' Wolfgang wrote home to his sister three days after arriving. 'I am panting it is so hot! I am tearing open my waistcoat right this minute!' He was not suffering as much as some. 'The princess [Maria Beatrice of Modena] had the runs the other day – or a shit-fit,' was his graphic description.

But despite the lack of creature comforts, Wolfgang was in his element. He and his father took the same lodgings they had taken previously, and the building was a cacophony of sound. Above and below them lived violinists, constantly scraping away. In the room next door a singing teacher gave lessons, and across the hall lived an oboist. 'It's all such fun for Composing! gives you lots of ideas,' he wrote, in a marvellous insight not just into his joyous character, but into how he lived and breathed music.

The libretto for *Ascanio* arrived in Milan a week after the Mozarts, and Wolfgang worked feverishly on it. 'My fingers are so sore from writing.' It was completed – a three-hour opera with overture, choruses, recitatives, a 'rather long' allegro, an andante, as well as ballets to be danced at the end of each act – in under seven weeks, remarkable by any standards.

The premiere took place, as scheduled, on 17 October 1771 at the Teatro Regio Ducal, two days after the wedding ceremonies for which it had been commissioned. It was a triumph.

'Our heads are spinning,' Leopold wrote home to his wife and daughter. In the days following, they were stopped in the street to be congratulated. After a few performances, the newly wedded royal couple came to see it. At the final curtain, they leaned over their box, clapping and shouting 'Bravissimo maestro!' to the diminutive character seated at the harpsichord below.

The groom, young Archduke Ferdinand, was apparently so impressed he went to his mother the empress and asked her advice on whether he might offer young Wolfgang a position at the court of Milan. Empress Maria Theresa's response has gone down in history.

> *You are requesting that I take the young Salzburger into your service. I do not know, nor do I believe, that you would need a composer or useless people. If that would give you pleasure, I don't want to keep you from it. I am saying what I am saying to prevent you from being burdened with useless people and giving titles to them.*[21]

Useless people! She says it twice so she must have meant it. She goes further. She refers to people such as the Mozarts going 'around the world like beggars'.

Beloved of her people, the empress, who did so much to retain the Habsburgs and their empire as the dominant force in mainland Europe, who indeed had met young Wolfgang and marvelled at his skills, suffered a lapse of judgement that will always blight her name when her artistic

"Leopold knew everything Wolfgang had achieved so far would pale before the accomplishments that lay ahead."

Right

Ferdinand, Archduke of Austria and Duke of Breisgau and Ortenau.

sensibilities are assessed. The archduke must have taken his mother's advice. No offer of a position at court was forthcoming.

This second trip to Italy lasted just four months, and was intense from start to finish. Wolfgang's postscripts to his sister, added to his father's letters, are short and lacking in any really interesting observations – in contrast to his outpourings from the previous trip.

What comes through is sheer fatigue, which clearly causes him an uncharacteristic lack of motivation. 'I cannot write allot. first: I don't know what. second: my fingers are so sore from writing …' 'I have no desire to go to Salzburg any more. I am afraid I might go crazy …' 'I know nothing new, except that next Tuesday will be another rehearsal …' 'I am well, god be praised and thancked! but always sleepy …'

In fact he was not all that well. He had a heavy cold, and his father's rheumatism was so bad that he would not leave their lodgings. His final postscript, on 30 November 1771, is his shortest of the trip. He is clearly utterly exhausted, and he sounds thoroughly depressed too.

He denies being unwell, but without conviction, and in just a single sentence describes a harrowing event he has witnessed. He suggests he saw something similar back in Lyons on his earlier trip. There is no reference to this anywhere else in any letters written either by him or by his father. Is it a product of his general tiredness and depression? Or did it happen, and he is pretending he was there? We cannot know. But it is a bizarre thing to write – in a single sentence, with no embellishment. Whatever the truth, it is testament to a fifteen-year-old boy who has worked himself not just to the limit, but beyond it.

> *So that you won't thinck I am sick, I'll write these two lines. farewell to you all. a handkiss for mama. and greetings to all good friends. I saw 4 fellows hanged on the piazza del Duomo. They hang them here just as in Lyon.*

The fact that as well as composing an opera, Wolfgang also composed a concerto and two symphonies during the stay in Milan, far from evidence that he overworked himself, to me suggests that composing is what he turned to when he needed to relax, when he had time on his hands, even if for a brief hour or two.

It was a thoroughly weary father and son who left Milan on 5 December 1771. They were, naturally, flushed with the success of *Ascanio*, but success was what they had become used to. Leopold was truly disappointed that no offer of employment at court had come to Wolfgang. Twice he had delayed departure in the hope that Archduke Ferdinand would extend an invitation to work for him. But no offer came.

The journey back took ten days, and we have no information about it. I suspect they were simply both too tired to be bothered with writing, particularly since they knew they would be home in a short time.

Leopold and Wolfgang arrived home in Salzburg on 15 December. One day later the kindly and pious Archbishop Schrattenbach died.

The death was sudden and unexpected, and it threw Salzburg into turmoil. The forthcoming celebrations, naturally, were called off. It was a time for score-settling, for factions and rivalry to break out.

Schrattenbach was not of this world, said some. His piety and deep faith had led him to lose his grasp on politics and governance. He was too much archbishop and not enough prince. Under his rule expenditure was unchecked, and he had left behind a city deep in debt.

Yes, debt, said his supporters, but in a thoroughly good cause. Why else was he so beloved of his people? His beneficence towards them ensured their loyalty and their love. They had lost a man who would speak up for the poorest among them. Was that not exactly what an archbishop should strive to achieve?

The succession was obvious, and should have been a straightforward matter for the churchmen who made up the elective council, in whose power the appointment lay. There was a highly qualified, and enormously popular, local candidate, by the name of Count Waldburg-Zeil, who was dean at Salzburg Cathedral.

Well known, and much respected by the local populace, he was overwhelmingly the choice of the people of Salzburg. But unusually the court in Vienna decided to stick its nose into Salzburg's affairs. Vienna, imperial capital of the Habsburg empire, wanted one of its own in Salzburg.

Vienna's choice – in an open and blatant piece of nepotism – was the son of the imperial vice-chancellor, no less. He was the thirty-nine-year-old Count Hieronymus Franz de Paula Joseph Colloredo.

Although he had been born in Vienna, Count Colloredo[*] was no stranger to Salzburg. He was appointed canon there at the tender age of fifteen, and had spent every second winter there. The Salzburgers knew him well – and disliked him intensely. Aloof and haughty from his teenage years, he cared deeply about rank, and expected the utmost respect from his subordinates. Only with those of the highest rank did he feel at ease.

Weeks of wrangling followed the death of Archbishop Schrattenbach, as the rulers of Vienna attempted to impose their will on Salzburg, and the local people made clear to the elective council who they wanted to rule over them. It took no fewer than forty-nine ballots before a name with a majority of votes emerged.

On 14 March 1772 a crowd of Salzburgers gathered underneath the balcony of the palace, and were stunned into shock and silence when the name of Archbishop Colloredo was announced as the next prince-archbishop of Salzburg.

They had not recovered as Colloredo and his attendants processed to the cathedral for the Te Deum to celebrate his accession. They looked on in total silence.

Colloredo was known to the Mozarts as well. He had most certainly heard Wolfgang perform during his winter stays in Salzburg; it is possible he met them too in Schönbrunn Palace in Vienna and on their visit to Rome, where he was studying.

---

[*]The Italian name comes from the site of the family castle in the Friuli area of north-east Italy.

Relations between the newly appointed archbishop and the Mozarts began well enough. Indeed it would be some years before they soured irretrievably, and Colloredo would become the 'villain of the piece', an unenviable role he maintains to this day.

One of Colloredo's earliest actions, in fact, was to take Wolfgang into paid employment at court. On 9 July 1772, at the age of sixteen, Wolfgang was formally appointed konzertmeister at a salary of 150 gulden a year – a third of his father's salary.

His duties required him to lead the court orchestra from the violin, something he had regularly done on an informal basis for some time. Wolfgang was soon composing pieces, and adapting others, to mark Colloredo's accession.

The archbishop was also prepared to allow father and son to make yet another trip to Milan – their third – for the performance of an opera Wolfgang had been commissioned to write for the Teatro Regio Ducal.

There was a possible fly in the ointment, and it was once again Wolfgang's precarious health. Nannerl recalled – half a century later – that on her brother's return from the second Milan trip, he suffered a very serious illness, which gave him 'extremely yellow' skin.

We cannot say for sure whether Wolfgang had contracted jaundice, or exactly when this happened. What we most certainly *can* say is that, once again, Wolfgang was overworking.

As well as the opera for Milan, which would become *Lucio Silla*, Wolfgang had been commissioned to write *another* opera immediately after that for Venice. He was also working on several orchestral pieces. The work took its toll, but it was as if he needed to do it. In the event – possibly because his father realised the workload was too much even for this sixteen-year-old – the Venice commission was dropped.

Father and son left Salzburg once again on 24 October 1772, taking the familiar route via the Brenner Pass south to Milan. Wolfgang had clearly not recovered fully from his illness. He penned his first postscript to his sister from the beautiful little wine-growing village of Bozen[*] on the other side of the pass, four days after leaving Salzburg. He is not in a good mood:

> *We are now in Botzen. already? only! I'm thirsty, I'm sleepy, I'm lazy, but*
> *I am well … Botzen is a shit hole …*
>> *Before I come back to this Botzen place,*
>> *I'd rather smack myself in the face.*

Things were most certainly to improve in Milan. Wolfgang once again worked feverishly to complete his opera, and it was given its premiere on schedule on 26 December 1772.

It was not an auspicious beginning. Archduke Ferdinand (the same royal personage whose marriage Wolfgang's earlier opera had celebrated) arrived three hours late for the premiere, offering apologies for spending too long writing New Year's greetings. 'He writes very slowly,' Leopold reported sarcastically.

The opera, full length and with two ballets, lasted an enormous six hours in performance. Due to the late start on opening night, it did not finish until two in the morning. But it was, predictably, a triumph.

Almost as if it was now his due, Wolfgang was feted throughout the city, and *Lucio Silla* was given no fewer than twenty-six performances, displacing the opera that was due to succeed it.

Within just three weeks of the premiere, and clearly flushed with the success of the opera, Wolfgang dashed off – in a matter of days – a vocal

---

[*] Now Bolzano.

piece for one of the singers who had performed in the opera, the renowned Italian male soprano, the castrato Venanzio Rauzzini.

And not just any vocal piece, but without question one of the greatest – in my opinion *the* greatest – of all Wolfgang's youthful works. It is a three-movement piece, and is almost a concerto for the voice. Although based on a sacred text, in places it is mischievous; it has offbeat themes and harmonic surprises, and its treatment of the single word 'Alleluia' must be unique in all music.

It is, I believe, unlike anything else Mozart was to write. It is suffused with joyfulness, and to this day it remains one of his most popular pieces. It is the *Exsultate, jubilate* (к.165).

This motet was given its first performance by Rauzzini in Milan's church of the Theatines. We can be sure Wolfgang knew he had written something very special, though it is not obvious from the deliberately jumbled way he wrote to Nannerl about it: 'I for the primo a homo motet to make had tomorrow that at the Theatines performed will be. Well be to you I ask. Farewell. addio.' It makes sense if you put the words in the right order. But that's Wolfgang the teenage tease. Why make it straightforward when you can raise a smile?

The stay in Milan lasted for a little under five months, and could actually have been considerably less, but Leopold was determined to get his son paid employment at Archduke Ferdinand's court. He kept delaying departure in the expectation of a job offer.

The excuses he offered to the court back home in Salzburg border on the farcical. He wrote to his wife that he was suffering from searing attacks of rheumatism, so severe that he could not leave his room. The thought of crossing the Alps in bitter temperatures and thick snow before he had fully recovered made the condition even worse.

It was all lies. He began to write in secret code, interchanging consonants with vowels – not difficult to decipher. On 30 January 1773 he wrote to his wife: 'What I have written about my illness is all untrue. I was in bed for a few days, but I am now back in good health and am going to the opera today.'

To compound the absurdity of it, he advised Anna Maria to cut this portion of the letter off so no one else would see it. She clearly did not, and so Leopold's folly is fully exposed. Maybe she showed it to close friends, no doubt with a disbelieving shake of the head. Leopold must have known the censors would have seen the letter in any case, and would have had no trouble decoding it.

When it was reported to Colloredo, the new broom, he might at first have been amused at Leopold's deception, but then surely his attitude will have hardened and he would certainly have resolved not to make the same

"Nannerl recalled that on her brother's return from the second Milan trip, he suffered a very serious illness."

mistake as his late predecessor, who had been so lenient with the Mozarts. The future history of mutual antagonism between the court and the Mozarts had its beginnings here.

Leopold finally gave up hope of any offer of employment for Wolfgang, and they left Milan on 4 March, arriving in Salzburg nine days later.

It brought to a close their third – and final – visit to Italy. They crossed the Brenner Pass for the last time. Neither expected this to be their last visit to the land of music, but Milan never asked Wolfgang for another opera, nor did a commission come from any other Italian centre. Neither father nor son was ever to cross into Italy again.

For Leopold, although he wrote, 'I find it difficult to leave Italy', it was in effect mission accomplished. He had established his son's reputation as a serious composer who could be relied on to fulfil operatic commissions for the most prestigious opera houses, and who had beyond doubt shown himself – even at such a young age – capable of carrying out the duties of kapellmeister at a major European court.

That remained Leopold's principal aim. If full-time employment could be secured for his son at a royal court, the family's income would be guaranteed for the future. He was also a good enough musician to know his son's name would be known and extolled across Europe, and who can blame him if the thought of basking in reflected glory appealed to him?

Wolfgang, too, was sorry to leave Italy. He had enjoyed its warmth, colour and the cacophony of different sounds he had heard and absorbed. He would remain nostalgic for Italy for the rest of his life.

Fresh from the successes of Italy, Leopold might well have been expecting something of a hero's return. Indeed, the thought of trying his luck once more in the imperial capital of Vienna must have already been crossing his mind. Given the rapturous reception in Milan from the archduke, surely his mother the empress herself might now be persuaded to offer Wolfgang employment.

In fact, in both Salzburg and Vienna, the Mozarts were in for a rude shock.

10

GNAGFLOW TRAZOM

*T*he city of **Salzburg** might always have been smaller, less grand, less important, more provincial than Vienna, but from before Mozart's time to the present day, it has never been burdened with a sense of inferiority.

There was, and is, an insularity about Salzburgers, born of pride in belonging to a beautiful city with a rich cultural heritage. A traveller, writing just a few years after Leopold and Wolfgang arrived home from Italy, describes a city sitting in the midst of 'a vast amphitheatre, the background occupied by high rocks lifting up their heads to heaven … wooded mountains to the back and beautiful and cultivated hills to the side … the town commanded by the castle standing on a high rock'.

He continues:

> *[Salzburg] itself is very handsome – the houses are high, and built all of stone. The roofs of the houses are in the Italian style, and you may walk out upon them. The cathedral is the handsomest building I have seen since I left Paris … and is an imitation of St Peter's at Rome … This town contains many more excellent buildings and statues, which remind you that the borders of Italy are not far distant.*[22]

In other words, Salzburg is closer in style and sophistication to Rome than it is to Vienna. Salzburgers much preferred to look south than east, but best of all they liked to look no further than their own city walls. Outsiders could

View of modern
Salzburg across the
Salzach river.

Above

live in Salzburg for as long as they wished, identify themselves with the city as closely as they liked, but they would forever remain outsiders.

Leopold Mozart was an outsider. Augsburg, the city of his birth, was a hundred and fifty miles from Salzburg – beyond Munich. It might as well have been a thousand miles. Leopold would never fit in, however hard he tried.

The truth was he had never tried particularly hard. He might not have been overly fond of his home city, but it was a Free Imperial City, responsible for its own governance. It had a wealthy aristocracy, and this attracted artists seeking patrons.

In these respects Augsburg was the equal of Salzburg, and it is easy to imagine Leopold reminding Salzburgers of this, making no attempt to disguise his markedly different accent.

Then along came his prodigiously talented children, and the beginning of the touring life that took him to Europe's great capitals and into the palaces of monarchs.

Still Leopold could have striven to make himself just a touch more popular in the city he had chosen to make home, but that was not his style. He was openly contemptuous of Salzburg, and notoriously short tempered and patronising towards its inhabitants.

Fellow musicians employed at court were well aware of his antics – that he had been given leave of absence time after time to travel with his son; that

Above

Salzburg Cathedral, built in the seventeenth century. The original baptismal font, in which Mozart was baptised, is still to be found inside.

he had extended trips sometimes with permission, sometimes without; and it is more than probable word had got around about his absurd attempt to feign illness to excuse prolonging the most recent trip.

There was a mutual animosity, and it went to the very top. Leopold had not got off to the best possible start with Archbishop Colloredo. It is not an exaggeration to say Leopold might have found himself generally ostracised had it not been for the extraordinary talent of his son.

Conversely, of course, had it not been for Wolfgang, Leopold himself might have settled more contentedly into the life of a court musician of above average talent, living relatively comfortably on the salary of a deputy kapellmeister.

Wolfgang's genius, though, had changed everything. Leopold could not wait to get out of provincial Salzburg for good. The simple way of achieving this was for his son to secure paid employment at a royal court in one of the great cities of Europe, and the family would take up residence there with him.

The most likely place for this to happen was the capital of the Habsburg empire, where Wolfgang had first performed as a child, stunning the emperor and empress. It was an easy journey from Salzburg, language would be no problem, and Leopold had a large list of contacts, all the way to the very top.

There was another factor that made Vienna the city of choice for Leopold's efforts. The chief kapellmeister, head of all music in the city, was terminally ill and close to death. This, coupled with the fact that Colloredo himself was planning a trip to Vienna anyway, made Leopold's mind up.

He petitioned the archbishop for permission to travel to Vienna with his son, to visit friends and musical colleagues, to make further contacts, and generally to disseminate word of Salzburg's musical prowess. With his grace's own absence, father and son would surely not be missed.

Somewhat surprisingly, Colloredo granted Leopold's request. On 14 July 1773 Leopold and Wolfgang left once more for Vienna – to the chagrin of Anna Maria, who saw no reason why she and Nannerl should not accompany them. No, said Leopold, it would cost extra money, and might start unpalatable rumours in Salzburg.

Those rumours were circulating anyway. It was general gossip in court musical circles that Leopold had his eye on the hofkapellmeister's job for Wolfgang. What a coincidence that he should apply for leave of absence just at the time the prestigious appointment was about to fall vacant. 'Fools are fools, wherever they are!' was Leopold's response.

Everything seemed set fair when the Mozarts received a summons to the palace for an audience with the empress, even if it was nearly three weeks after their arrival. Undoubtedly Wolfgang performed for Maria Theresa, but nothing further was forthcoming.

'Her Majesty the Empress was very gracious to us, but that was all,' Leopold wrote candidly. The truth was probably considerably more prosaic. We can assume that Leopold put in a pitch for his son to get the top job after the sad demise of the current holder, but the empress was giving nothing away. It is probable she told him she would take advice from expert courtiers. We can be sure she offered no encouragement.

Even more worrying, no invitations came in from the nobility. Leopold took to promenading with his son on the Bastei, the huge wall that encircled the inner city, where it was de rigueur to see and be seen. Still no invitations. It was true that many of the aristocratic families had left the city for the summer, but it was nevertheless a disappointment.

It seems Wolfgang did not give a single recital in an aristocratic salon. This was a first, and an unwelcome one at that. Leopold was forced to confront the fact that, at the age of seventeen and a half, Wolfgang was simply not the astonishing child virtuoso any more.

To compound his misery, Leopold noted that the hofkapellmeister had made something of a recovery (he lived on until the new year). If misery summed up Leopold's mood, the same was most certainly not true of Wolfgang, if the postscripts to his father's letters are anything to go by.

He is full of mischief. Word games, languages jumbled, offering (fictional) greetings from the empress, pretending he is his father and using nicknames for himself – Wolfgangerl, Wolferl, Wolfi; and my favourite – he signs one postscript 'gnagflow Trazom'.[*]

Father and son remained in Vienna for a little over two months, returning to Salzburg empty-handed. It must have been galling for Leopold. In court musical circles it will have been no secret that the trip – with dubious motive in the first place – had yielded nothing. And he is sure to have endured harsh words from his wife, who was denied a visit to the imperial capital – some clothing purchases, 'corselets, caps and so on', the latest in fashion, might have mollified her somewhat.

One of the first tasks Leopold undertook on their return was to move the family into a larger apartment. As we have seen, he complained regularly in letters about how small and cramped the apartment in the Getreidegasse was, becoming more and more unsuitable as the children grew older.

Nannerl was now twenty-two years of age, Wolfgang nearly eighteen. It was time they all stopped sharing beds and 'sleeping like soldiers'. Leopold had clearly been putting off a move, in the hope that a court appointment would come for Wolfgang and the family would leave Salzburg altogether. The failure to make any headway on the recent visit to Vienna must finally have persuaded him that this was a forlorn hope.

Late in September 1773 the Mozarts left the apartment in the Getreidegasse, in which Leopold and Anna Maria had lived all their married life, and where all their children had been born, and moved across the river to the Hannibalplatz.

There they rented a large eight-roomed apartment on the first floor of the house known as the Tanzmeisterhaus ('Dancing Master's House').[†] It was large enough to accommodate servants, and Leopold was soon running what amounted to a music business from the house.

Both Leopold and Nannerl took in students, and Leopold bought and sold musical instruments on the premises. Most importantly, it was as if the spaciousness unlocked doors in Wolfgang's brain. His creativity had never been low, but here it soared.

By the end of the year he had written seven symphonies, four divertimentos, six string quartets, a string quintet, a piano concerto, a set of

---

[*] His name backwards.

[†] The building stood until the Second World War, when large parts of it were destroyed in bombing raids. After the war it was sold to an insurance company. The International Mozart Foundation acquired it in 1989, rebuilt it to resemble as closely as possible the building the Mozarts knew, and opened it to the public. Today it is an important repository of manuscripts and letters.

Above

The Tanzmeisterhaus, into which the Mozart family moved in 1773. It is now a museum known as Mozart Wohnhaus (Mozart's Residence).

keyboard variations, sixteen minuets for orchestra, a mass and more. In the following year he composed three more symphonies, a piano sonata, two church sonatas, a set of variations, two concertos, two masses and several other sacred works.

These were not average pieces composed to while away the time. They included the 'Little' Symphony in G minor (к. 183), considered a masterpiece, and the six string quartets (к. 168–73), dedicated to Haydn, are among the finest he would ever write.

To this prodigious output, he was about to add an opera. In the late summer of 1774, a commission arrived from the court of Elector Maximilian III of Bavaria. He wanted a comic opera for the 1775 carnival season in Munich. The libretto had already been written; it was entitled *La finta giardiniera* ('The pretend garden-girl').

Father and son were delighted – for rather different reasons. Wolfgang relished the opportunity to work on something substantial. He had learned a lot from his earlier comic opera, *La finta semplice*, and could hardly wait to write for the stage again.

For Leopold, this was surely the prelude to something much bigger. It was time to resurrect his dream scenario. The opera would be a huge success,

naturally, and Wolfgang would subsequently be offered a permanent position at the court in Munich. Milan and Vienna had failed to deliver; the
same would most certainly not be true of Munich. Why else would the
elector personally authorise the commission?

On 6 December father and son left Salzburg for the Bavarian capital. We
can assume that Colloredo did not take kindly to yet another absence, but
he was powerless to argue against a summons from a personage as exalted
as the elector.

It is worth pausing for a moment to look more closely at Leopold's
behaviour at this juncture, because it gives us an insight not just into his
character, but also helps us to understand why Wolfgang subsequently behaved towards his father in the way he did.

A deep resentment was growing inside Wolfgang. Here was a young
man, almost nineteen years of age, whose life – every aspect of it – was being
controlled by his father. Given his diminutive size, and his predilection for
undoubtedly childish behaviour – pranks, practical jokes, smutty humour
– it is easy for us today to continue to think of him as an overgrown child.

*"Is it unfair
to be critical of
Leopold? After
all, he knew
Wolfgang better
than anybody."*

His father most certainly did. Not only did he make every arrangement for the trip to Munich, he even packed for his son. It was a bitterly cold winter, and Leopold laid out every piece of clothing and footwear that Wolfgang should take.

Is it unfair to be critical of Leopold? After all, he knew Wolfgang better than anybody. He had spent more time with him than anyone else, even his mother. Maybe Wolfgang really was incapable of taking care of himself, even to the extent of selecting the appropriate clothing for a harsh winter.

I doubt it, particularly since Wolfgang was not alone in being treated like this. The same applied to his sister. Munich being an easy day's journey from Salzburg – less than half the distance to Vienna – Leopold agreed to allow Nannerl to come to Munich a month later for the premiere of her brother's new opera.

Once again he took total control. He sent explicit instructions about what clothing she should bring, just as he had done with Wolfgang. More than that, he told her how she should wrap her head and how many layers she should wear on her feet to ward off the cold. He even went so far as to tell her exactly when she should ask for a bundle of hay to be spread on the floor of the coach to help keep her warm.

Was she also completely helpless, a young woman in her early twenties? It seems unlikely. In today's parlance, we would have no hesitation in labelling Leopold a control freak.

Wolfgang got straight down to work in Munich, and had soon produced enough for the singers to start learning their parts. Rehearsals, though, proved difficult and sections of the libretto had to be substantially rewritten.

There was a lot of tension in the air when *La finta giardiniera* premiered on 13 January 1775. Perhaps it showed. The critics were not impressed. 'Flames of genius quiver here and there; but it is not yet that still, calm altar-fire that mounts towards heaven in clouds of incense, a scent beloved of the gods,' was one particularly florid assessment. 'A motley business', 'nearly always difficult', 'in the highest degree tasteless and tedious' were other descriptions.[23]

Wolfgang had a flop on his hands. The opera was performed only twice more and no further commissions were forthcoming. Any offer of a permanent position at court was out of the question.

Leopold's dream had evaporated once again. He blamed it on other factors. The Munich season had 'more entertainments than any other place known to me'. He attempted to put a brave face on it, encouraging his son and daughter to dress up in fancy costumes for the parades and masquerades.

The bitter truth was that the Mozarts had outstayed their welcome in Munich. The opera had failed; no invitations to perform in aristocratic salons came their way; Leopold's forlorn hope of a commission for the following season did not materialise, let alone a job offer for Wolfgang.

It was, we can surmise, a dejected father, son and daughter, who left Munich on 1 March to return to the new apartment in the Hannibalplatz in Salzburg. Neither could know it, but Wolfgang had just completed his final tour with his father.

For the next two and half years Wolfgang remained in Salzburg – the longest unbroken period he had spent in his native city since his infancy. It was a difficult time. Archbishop Colloredo and the court were now openly contemptuous of Leopold Mozart, their deputy kapellmeister, who himself made no secret of his desire to leave the city, or his dislike of Salzburgers.

Wolfgang was accorded more respect, since his musical talents were so astounding. But it was not all sweetness and light for him. Had he not been turned down for employment time after time in other cities – a fact that was well known in musical circles? And had not his latest commission resulted in a thorough flop? Salzburg really had had enough of the boastful father and his undoubtedly talented – but not altogether reliable – son.

Wolfgang's talents, as we have seen, had secured him a position at the court in Salzburg. He retained his position as konzertmeister on a meagre salary of 150 gulden a year.[*] For the foreseeable future the Mozart family would have to live on that, plus Leopold's salary as deputy kapellmeister, and whatever he and his son and daughter could bring in from teaching. It had been made clear to father and son that neither could expect any further advancement at court.

Leopold may have lapsed into a grumpy sullenness, refusing to put himself out for the archbishop, doing only what was formally required of him and no more. The same was most certainly not true of his son.

If Wolfgang was able to be productive while on the road constantly travelling, how much more productive could he be in his own home and in his home city, with no immediate travel plans in the offing?

The following months and years saw a wealth of compositions. In the remaining six months of 1775 alone, he composed no fewer than five violin concertos. Each one is utterly perfect in its own way, and all five are among the best-loved concertos for violin ever written. They remain a staple of every violin virtuoso's repertoire to this day.

---

[*] Less than £4,000 in today's money.

He composed six piano sonatas, as well as the Haffner Serenade (K. 250), an eight-movement piece commissioned by one of the most prominent families in Salzburg.[*] He also wrote several religious pieces and a divertimento.

In 1777 he composed his most important piano concerto to date, No. 9 in E flat major (K. 271). The name it has become known by, 'Jeunehomme', is actually a misnomer, a corruption of the name 'Jenamy', the married name of a French woman for whom he composed it. It was unlike any previous piano concerto, by Wolfgang or anyone else, in both style and scope. I have seen it described as his most important composition to date, in any form.

We have little concrete information on the activities of the Mozarts during this period, for the simple reason that, since they were living under the same roof, no letters were being written.

We do know, though, from future correspondence that Leopold's contempt for Salzburg, the court, as well as the city's inhabitants, was being subconsciously absorbed by his son. Wolfgang, in clear imitation of his father, began to despise the city that, as a child on his travels, he had written fondly of, frequently expressing a desire to return to its familiar surroundings as soon as possible.

The atmosphere inside the Tanzmeisterhaus must have been tense. An increasingly discontent and dissatisfied father and husband, a son quite prepared to parrot his father's misgivings. We can assume the women of the house either went along with their men, or kept their opinions to themselves.

Things were, inevitably, coming to a head, and come to a head they were soon to do. The Mozart family was about to be split apart for ever.

---

[*] Seven years later the family would commission the symphony known as the Haffner Symphony, No. 35 in D major (K. 385).

11

THERE IS
NO VACANCY

Leopold Mozart was about to make a disastrous miscalculation. It was as if he really could not see how unpopular he had already made himself with the all-important Archbishop Colloredo, how he had used up any reservoir of goodwill a long time ago.

His self-confidence can have been founded on only two factors: his own status as deputy kapellmeister, and the inordinate ability of his son – these combined of course with a character which can only politely be described as self-assured.

There can be no excuse for his failure to read the runes. It had already been made clear to him that no further promotion at court would ever be forthcoming, and his son, at the age now of twenty-one, was far from being a child genius. Wolfgang was now just one young professional musician among many, albeit with an ability to compose as well as perform.

What then possessed Leopold to petition Colloredo for yet another leave of absence for himself and his son, in order to seek employment outside Salzburg, we can only guess. Perhaps it was based on the flimsy logic that, three years earlier, Colloredo had advised that Wolfgang should seek employment elsewhere.

But times had changed. The court was busy with visits by important personages, including the emperor, and Colloredo needed his full complement of musicians. To make matters worse, the petition Leopold wrote was arrogant, lecturing the archbishop on the teaching of the Gospels, and ironic, stating that the forthcoming winter and the cold temperatures it would bring would be deleterious to his health. Whose health? Wolfgang's health. Yes, in an extraordinarily ill-judged decision, Leopold decided to write the petition in his son's name. Every word of it is pure Leopold, lacking any element of Wolfgang's humour and banter. Colloredo was not fooled for a minute. It is impossible to imagine how Leopold thought he would be.

Colloredo had the measure of Leopold, and he knew exactly what course of action to take – one that would seem to be positive but that would hit Leopold where it hurt most. Of course father and son should be allowed to travel, he replied on 1 September, to seek their fortune elsewhere, and to that end they were both dismissed from court service.

Any suspicion we might have that Leopold had calculated in some devious way that this was the outcome he wanted, and that he had been successful in engineering it, can quickly be dispelled. A family friend visiting the Mozarts reported that Leopold was so stunned by the archbishop's response that he was physically ill with shock.

It was as if Leopold had finally come to realise the truth: that he, his son and in effect the whole Mozart family were out of favour with the court, and could expect nothing more from it. Literally nothing. No employment, nothing.

Leopold now understood, from one brutal missive from Archbishop Colloredo, that he had brought his family to the brink of ruin. He was, truly, a humbled man. All was lost, and it was his doing.

Well, not quite. Colloredo knew the character of the man he was dealing with. He left a small chink of light. Colloredo never actually stopped Leopold's salary, ordering it should only be stopped 'in the event of his leaving service'. Could reinstatement be a possibility?

Leopold petitioned Colloredo, assuring him he would not travel and pleading with him to be reinstated. Colloredo let Leopold twist in the wind for several weeks, suffering anguish and also public disgrace. He then announced, in language calculated to demean him, that Leopold would be reinstated, provided he conduct himself 'calmly and peacefully' with other court musicians, and that he 'take pains to render good service to the Church as well as to His Grace's Person'. Wolfgang remained dismissed.

Leopold's public humiliation was complete. Colloredo had broken him. Leopold was approaching his fifty-ninth birthday. Friends noted that his notorious self-confidence, his audacity and bluster, had gone. In a matter of months he went from middle age to old age.

Leopold was truly caught on the horns of a dilemma. He knew the only hope for the family's welfare, and reputation, was for Wolfgang to secure paid employment somewhere outside Salzburg. Given that he had lost his job at court, Wolfgang needed to embark on a lengthy trip as soon as possible.

"Leopold now understood that he had brought his family to the brink of ruin"

At the same time, Leopold knew that he could no longer accompany him. If he did, he would certainly lose his job at court. But Wolfgang had never been on any trip, anywhere, without his father. It was Leopold who had planned every aspect of every trip – plotting the routes, choosing the mode of travel, booking coaches, finding inns or monasteries to stay in, making contact with local musicians, organising the music they would play, establishing contact with members of the local nobility to arrange salon recitals, even contacting royalty.

It was a measure of just how controlling Leopold had been, that even at twenty-one years of age, a grown man, Wolfgang had no experience whatsoever of the practical side of travelling. His sole task was to perform, to stun with his talent wherever he played. Leopold had protected him from every other annoying little detail.

And now? If Wolfgang travelled, he would be on his own. How could he possibly handle all these other matters? Leopold knew he was not capable of it. But the only alternative was for Wolfgang not to travel and reapply for his job at the Salzburg court. To give up trying to get a job abroad, give up playing for aristocratic audiences across Europe, earning good fees and furthering his already well-established reputation.

It was unthinkable. He had to travel. Leopold knew that, and fight it as he might, he also knew there was a very simple solution to the problem, and it was staring him in the face.

We cannot know how Anna Maria reacted when he told her, since neither of them wrote about it. We can be certain Leopold lectured her, told her exactly what was expected of her. He will, no doubt, have stressed the domestic issues, such as clothes and food. He will also certainly have given her strict instructions regarding expenditure, expecting her to keep a careful eye on costs, to rent only reasonably priced rooms, and so on.

And from Anna Maria's point of view? We might imagine her relishing the opportunity to get to know her talented son better. Most of his teenage years had been spent away from her, and a distance would surely have grown up between them.

As for Nannerl, just when she was beginning to get to know her brother again after so many prolonged absences, he was about to leave once more. Can we assume she was not overjoyed at being in the house alone with a domineering and demanding father, and no one close to her own age to share things? Probably.

The Mozarts were to split again, though for the first time in this way. New relationships, new dynamics. The family had never been normal; it was about to become even less so.

Anna Maria and Wolfgang set out from Salzburg at six o'clock on the morning of 23 September 1777. It is easy to imagine Leopold issuing last-minute instructions, possibly even shouting after the coach as it drew away.

Leopold was still unwell, suffering from catarrh, and had been up until two in the morning giving orders about what clothes to pack. Shouting hurt his chest, and it is likely he stood there uncomfortably in the early-morning air, perhaps pounding his chest with his fist to release the phlegm.

Suddenly he realised he had forgotten to give his son a fatherly blessing. He ran upstairs, stood at the window, and sent his blessings after both wife and son. But the carriage had already passed out of sight, through the Klausentor gate on the first leg of its journey to Munich. It is a moving image, a sick and elderly man, frantically waving after his wife and son and mumbling blessings.

His prayers would remain unanswered. The family of four had parted for the last time.

Leopold and Nannerl were devastated at the separation. They both took to their beds and slept from emotional exhaustion. Nannerl wrote that she was 'sick to the stomach'.

That was not the case with the travellers. This might have been the first time Wolfgang had ever been on the road without his father, but at the age of twenty-one he relished the freedom.

Wolfgang had now truly come of age. He saw it as his filial duty to look after his mother – 'the secondt Papa' ('der anderte Papa'), as he wrote in his first letter to his father. As far as he could, given that Leopold had meticulously planned every detail of the trip, he took control.

Within just a couple of days of leaving home, letters began to wing their way to and from Salzburg. In the ensuing sixteen months, no fewer than 131 letters would be written, roughly half in each direction.

For any biographer of Mozart, indeed for anyone interested in his remarkable life, it is ironic that we have more information about his younger years than his later ones, simply because letters were flying to and fro with all sorts of useful information, musical of course, but also about the minutiae of travel and being away from home, which gives a wonderful insight into his character.

Hardly had Wolfgang departed than his father began lecturing him. On the dangers of too much alcohol: 'Avoid strong wines, and too much of them,' he admonishes. On his behaviour to courtiers: 'Be inordinately polite.' This, to a twenty-one-year-old!

And now, for the first time, we can get an idea of the personality of Wolfgang's mother, Anna Maria. Until now she has been a shadowy figure, by virtue of her virtual exclusion from letters by Leopold on earlier travels.

Above

Nymphenburg Palace in Munich, where Mozart played as a child.

Given that her voice is so rarely heard, we have to assume Leopold required her subservience, and she acquiesced. Roles were now reversed. Leopold was relying on her to ensure Wolfgang worked hard and tried with all his might to land permanent employment, and to prevent him from being distracted.

Leopold was well aware of the greatest temptation facing his son, and that was interest in the opposite sex. We can be in no doubt that Leopold gave his wife a strong talking-to about how she must not allow their son to be distracted in any way. It was up to her to keep him on the straight and narrow, and keep him focused.

He must have known it was a forlorn hope. Anna Maria was weak willed. Any opinions of her own, if she ever had any, were long since suppressed in the face of a dominant and domineering husband. This was unlikely to change.

He must have known too that she had a slightly strange sense of humour, and now for the first time we are able to see where Wolfgang might have got his own similarly bizarre flights of fancy. Consider this postscript, written with a little Italian and the rest in Salzburg dialect, that Anna Maria appended to the first letter Wolfgang wrote home, two days after arriving in Munich:

> *Farewell, stay well and healthy,*
> *and try to kiss your own behind,*
> *I wish you a very good night,*
> *shit in your bed with all your might.*[*]

---

[*] *Adio ben mio leb gesund / Reck den arsch zum mund / ich winsch ein guete nacht / scheiss ins beth das Kracht.*

These are the words of a fifty-six year old mother of two, one of whom has clearly inherited her predilection for toilet humour, of which we are very soon to hear much, much more.

Munich was, to all intents and purposes, a waste of time. Humiliating too. All the more surprising since Leopold had always assumed this was the most likely place for Wolfgang to find permanent employment.

It was the first place he had taken Wolfgang, as a child of just six (with Nannerl). Twice more Wolfgang had been to Munich and performed for Elector Maximilian III. On the most recent visit, the elector had hummed a tune and Wolfgang had composed a piece based on it.

It is probably not too far-fetched to suppose that Leopold considered it possible the journey he had sent his wife and son on would begin and end in Munich, and he and Nannerl would soon be leaving Salzburg to join them.

Far from it, although it did not at first seem like that. Count Seeau, whom Mozart knew from earlier visits, was optimistic. A good composer was needed at court, he said, and he should seek an immediate audience with the elector.

Before he could manage this, the elector himself intervened. He sent Wolfgang a message, via Count Zeil, Bishop of Chiemsee, that it was too soon to consider employment. Wolfgang should travel to Italy and make his name there first.

This was particularly galling. Had he not already toured the entire country, writing three operas in the process? He decided he needed to meet the elector face to face, put his case to him, man to man. He described in detail in a letter to his father how this then happened. It must have made Leopold's blood boil.

At nine o'clock on 30 September Wolfgang went to the court, where he met a contact who had promised to take him to where he would be sure to meet the elector. At just after ten o'clock, Maximilian was due to pass through a 'narrow little room' on his way to hear Mass before the hunt.

At ten o'clock Wolfgang was taken to the small room, where he positioned himself in the elector's path. Sure enough Maximilian walked into the room on schedule, to be confronted by an eager twenty-one-year-old composer, well known to him, who was looking for full-time employment at court.

It could hardly have been auspicious. Maximilian was likely to be in a hurry, excited with the prospect of a day's hunting ahead. Not ideal conditions for what amounted to a job interview. But it was the best chance Wolfgang was likely to have.

As Wolfgang described it in his letter, the elector walked up to him, and Wolfgang began immediately, 'With your Highness's permission, may I humbly lay myself at your feet and offer you my services?'

Maximilian had obviously been briefed. We can assume he had been warned that he would encounter Wolfgang, and he had either been made aware, or knew anyway, of the troubles the Mozarts had encountered in Salzburg.

> *'Well now, so you are gone from Salzburg for good, are you?'*
> *'Yes, Your Highness, for good.'*
> *'But why? Did you have a quarrel with [Archbishop Colloredo]?'*
> *'Not at all, Your Highness, I only requested permission to travel, but he refused it. So I was forced to take this step; although I had wanted to leave anyway for quite some time. Salzbourg* [sic] *is no place for me. No, absolutely not!'*
> *'My god, what a young Man! but your father is still in Salzbourg?'*

Wolfgang then lays out his credentials, in a way he would be able to do only face to face. It is all or nothing.

'Yes, Your Highness, and he too throws himself most humbly, Etc. I have been to Italy Three Times, have written 3 operas, I am a member of the accademie of Bologna, I had to take a Test at which many maestri had to work and sweat 4 to 5 hours, but I did it in one hour. That may serve as proof that I am able to serve at any court. But my one and only wish is to serve Your Highness, who himself is a great – '

'But my dear child, there is no vacancy. I am sorry, if only there were a vacancy.'

'I can assure Your Highness, I would bring great Honor to Munich.'

'Yes, but it's of no use; there just isn't any vacancy.'

That is the conversation, as Wolfgang described it verbatim in the letter. He leaves the most galling bit to the end. As the elector uttered those final words – *there just isn't any vacancy* – he was already walking away. Wolfgang commended himself to the elector's good graces, in effect addressing his back.

Given that he was relaying the conversation to his father, thereby wanting it to be clear he had done his very best against an implacable elector, it is possible there is an exaggeration or two in there. Maybe the elector wasn't quite so dismissive; maybe he didn't walk away as he spoke those last words. But it is impossible to read the letter without gaining the impression that, to some degree or other, Wolfgang was not just rejected, but humiliated.

One element of the conversation is worth highlighting. It is clear that Maximilian, royalty though he was, had no desire to do anything that might offend Archbishop Colloredo, which would certainly be the case if he gave employment to a musician the Archbishop had sacked (even if Wolfgang denied that was the case). By insulting Salzburg, Wolfgang had done himself no favours. Colloredo really was a powerful man, and his influence reached Munich.

All was not entirely lost. Wolfgang wrote to his father that a scheme had been proposed, whereby ten musical connoisseurs would pay him five gulden each a month to compose and perform new music, amounting to 600 gulden a year, which could probably be augmented with other work to 800. Was that not more than the family was earning in Salzburg?

Leopold was having none of it. Who were these philanthropists, and how could they be relied on to pay five gulden a month? What exactly would they expect in return? How long would Wolfgang have to wait in Munich to see if the scheme was practicable?

'If [the arrangement] cannot be made at once,' Leopold, ever controlling and in charge, wrote, 'then you simply must not lounge about, use up your money and waste your time.'

Leopold had finally come to terms with the incontrovertible fact that Wolfgang was not going to secure a position at the Munich court. He complained that Wolfgang and his mother had already stayed too long there (almost three weeks), and spent too much money for no return. He ordered them to move on to the next destination, the city of his birth, Augsburg.

There is some delightful banter in the last letter Wolfgang wrote from Munich, just before departure. Anna Maria writes that she is busy packing and that she has to do it all by herself, since 'Wolfgang is not able to help me in the slightest.'[24]

Wolfgang – and you can see the mischievous smile on his face as he writes this, teasing his mother at the same time, who no doubt feigned indignation – described how he and his mother were invited out to coffee, but she, instead of coffee, drank two bottles of Tyrolean wine.

Anna Maria, probably snatching the pen out of Wolfgang's hand, writes graphically about the arduous task of packing. 'I am sweating so much the water is running down my face with all this packing. The devil take all this travelling. I feel like shoving my feet into my mouth, that's how tired I am.'

Like mother, like son. The two left Munich at noon on 11 October 1777, and arrived in Augsburg at nine o'clock on the same evening.

The visit to Augsburg, an exception on the tour, was not to seek employment. There was no court there that could offer Wolfgang a job. It was, though, on a direct route to Mannheim, the next scheduled stop, which most certainly did have a court, and a very musical one at that.

Augsburg was nevertheless a cultural city, home to many musicians and opera singers, and Wolfgang made contact with many of them. But he did not take to the place, or its aristocratic inhabitants.

He was taken to a café (*Coffèhaus*), where as he entered he thought he would be blown backward from all 'the stink and smoke of Tobacco', and might as well have been in Turkey. And the aristocrats to whom he was introduced? 'A goodly number of high Nobility, the Duchess Kickass, the Countess Pisshappy, also the Princess Smellshit.'[*]

He gave two public performances, which were well received, but it is a revealing insight into his character that he describes his own playing in mundane terms: 'I took a theme for a walk and returned it assbackwards [*arschling*].'

The main purpose of the stay in Augsburg was to visit family. Leopold's brother Franz Alois, who continued the family tradition of bookbinding, lived there with his wife and daughter.

That daughter, Maria Anna Thekla, has a deserved place in any biography of her cousin Wolfgang. She is always accorded a mention, and I use the word 'mention' advisedly. That is very often all she gets, usually couched

> *"Leopold had finally come to terms with the fact that Wolfgang was not going to secure a position at the Munich court."*

---

[*] *Duchesse arschbömerl', gräfin brunzgern', fürstin riechzumtreck.*

in embarrassed turns of phrase, a reluctance to delve too deeply, a sense of 'How could a musical genius such as Mozart allow himself to behave in such base ways with this young woman?'

Maria Anna was one year and eight months younger than Wolfgang, and they shared a single, and very powerful, characteristic. Both had strong sexual impulses, and swiftly discovered this in each other.

Once discovered, they indulged it. We know this from a series of letters Wolfgang wrote to her after he and his mother had left Augsburg. He wrote twelve in the four-year period between October 1777 and October 1781, nine of which have survived. It is a miracle – nothing short of it – that these nine have survived. There were serious moves in the nineteenth century to have them destroyed, on the basis that they sullied the reputation of this purest of geniuses.

They were not published in full until 1938, even then heavily expurgated. Not until the 1980s were they translated as closely into English as possible, given the eccentricities and idiosyncrasies of Wolfgang's writing.

The letters are about as intimate and sexually charged as it is possible for letters to be. There are indirect sexual allusions, and positively direct ones. There are puns, jokes and declarations of love.

Most striking of all – and what has stunned biographers and Mozart admirers ever since – is the abundance of toilet humour. We have already seen examples of this in Wolfgang's earlier letters home. Now they reach whole new heights (or maybe depths). To call them disgusting, by standards of his day and ours too, would be an understatement.

Sadly none of his cousin's letters have survived, but it is clear from Wolfgang's wording that she responded totally in kind. There is no other way of putting it, other than to use modern vernacular and say the two of them loved 'talking dirty' together.

Can we state that it was with his cousin Wolfgang lost his virginity? We cannot, given that he did not confirm it definitively in any of the letters. In fact, as we shall see from a later letter to his father, he explicitly denies his father's accusation that the two have had sexual relations. But, as I have said before, he would say that, wouldn't he?

I shall lay out the facts as we know them, and then draw a conclusion. If I am truly to present Mozart, the man revealed, then this relationship deserves to be explored closely and in detail. And what an extraordinary insight it gives us into this remarkable young man!

12

Wolfgang Amadé Rosenkranz

Maria Anna Mozart, Wolfgang's first cousin, is known to history as Bäsle, or the Bäsle, from the Swabian word for 'little female cousin', the term by which Wolfgang most often refers to her.

She had just turned nineteen years of age when Wolfgang and his mother arrived in Augsburg. They stayed at the Zum weissen Lamm ('The White Lamb'), which was just a few steps from the Mozarts' house in the Jesuitengasse, behind the cathedral. The two branches of the family were soon united.

There is a pencil drawing of Bäsle, actually a self-portrait, done at the time of her cousin's visit. It shows a pretty, pert, even flirtatious face, with wide eyes and sensuously shaped lips. The upper lip is finely drawn in the perfect shape of a Cupid's bow.

Wolfgang and Bäsle, it is clear from the letters that followed, spent a lot of time in each other's company, and Wolfgang's letters leave us in no doubt as to the sort of activity they indulged in.

Before we come to that, though, there were musical matters to attend to. Even with these, there was fun to be had. Wolfgang went to see the piano-maker Johann Andreas Stein,* and Bäsle and his mother went with him.

---

*Whose daughter Nanette would later marry Johann Andreas Streicher, carry on the piano-making tradition, and become a close friend of Beethoven.

There, to Stein's surprise, Wolfgang performed on an organ with as much accomplishment as he had shown on the piano. Afterwards they went into a room where a certain Pater Emilian, 'a conceited ass and simpleminded clerical wag', as Wolfgang described him, was waiting.

Wolfgang writes to his father that this man tried to flirt with Bäsle, 'but she instead had her fun with him'. The man then got tipsy very quickly. He sang a canon and asked Wolfgang to sing along with him.

Wolfgang excused himself, saying nature had not endowed him with the gift of carrying a tune(!). 'That doesn't matter,' the man said, and started singing. When it was Wolfgang's turn to enter, instead of singing the proper text, he sang, 'P.E., oh you prick, why don't you kiss my ass.'

Wolfgang says he sang it quietly so only Bäsle would hear, and afterwards 'we were laughing for half an hour'. The unfortunate man then said he would like to discuss composition with Wolfgang. 'Well,' wrote Wolfgang, 'I said that would be a very short discussion. *Swallow that, you imbecile!*'

Even allowing for a certain amount of exaggeration, Wolfgang obviously taunted the man to a degree, pricking his pomposity. And you can just see Wolfgang and his cousin doubled up with laughter afterwards.

Five days after leaving Augsburg, Wolfgang wrote a short letter to Bäsle asking about some music that was due to be sent to him. But he begins with the enigmatic line: 'That's so strange! I'm supposed to write something sensible, but nothing sensible comes to my mind.'

I imagine his mother was aware of the shenanigans he and his cousin had got up to in Augsburg, and told him not to write anything silly. A few lines later, even more enigmatically, he writes, 'Don't forget your Promise. I certainly won't forget mine.'

Then: 'Very soon I'll write you a letter all in French, which you can have yourself translated by the Postmaster.' That letter will come shortly, and it would have made the postmaster blush.

Five days later another letter to Bäsle, and we now have a very different Wolfgang. The letter is long, and works properly only in the original German. It is full of internal rhymes, synonyms, echo effects, and extremely down-to-earth language.*

The first paragraph alone gives a flavour of the convoluted humour, with a translation trying as far as possible to render the sexual puns and rhymes into English:

---

* As Robert Spaethling points out in his *Mozart's Letters, Mozart's Life*, it is this particular letter that has led some medical specialists to suggest that Mozart suffered from Tourette's syndrome.

Left
A self-portrait pencil sketch of Maria Anna Mozart (c. 1777), Wolfgang's cousin, known as Bäsle.

Dearest cozz buzz!

I have received reprieved your highly esteemed writing biting, and I have noted doted that my uncle garfuncle, my aunt slant, and you too, are all well mell. We, too, thank god, are in good fettle kettle. Today I got the letter setter from my Papa Haha safely into my paws claws. I hope you too have gotten rotten my note quote that I wrote to you from Mannheim. So much the better, better the much so!

The letter continues in the same vein, with more sexual puns and rhymes. Then, after a promise to send Bäsle his portrait, as she has asked, he writes this extraordinary rhyme:

Oui, by the love of my skin,
I shit on your nose,
so it runs down your chin.

Two paragraphs further down, the sort of scatological language we have encountered before from Wolfgang, but the sentence ends with very intimate words:

I now wish you a good night, shit in your bed with all your might, sleep with peace on your mind, and try to kiss your own behind ... Oh my ass burns like fire! what on earth is the meaning of this! – maybe muck *wants to come out? yes, yes,* muck, *I know you, see you, taste you –*

The letter rambles on, largely nonsensically, with words seeming to pour from his pen meaninglessly and at random. He ends the letter with his crudest piece of humour to date:

Wherever I go it stinks, when I look out the window, the smell goes away, when I turn my head back to the room, the smell comes back – finally My Mama says to me: I bet you let one go? – I don't think so, Mama. yes, yes, I'm quite certain, I put it to the test, stick my finger in my ass, then put it to my nose, and ... Mama was right! Now farewell, I kiss you 10,000 times, and I remain as always your
  old young Sauschwanz
  Wolfgang Amadé Rosenkranz

Sauschwanz means 'pig's tail', but *schwanz* is also German slang for 'penis', so *Sauschwanz* can also mean 'pig's dick'.

Eight days later, Wolfgang again writes to Bäsle from Mannheim. After more nonsensical wordplay, he tells Bäsle how much he is missing her, then comes this:

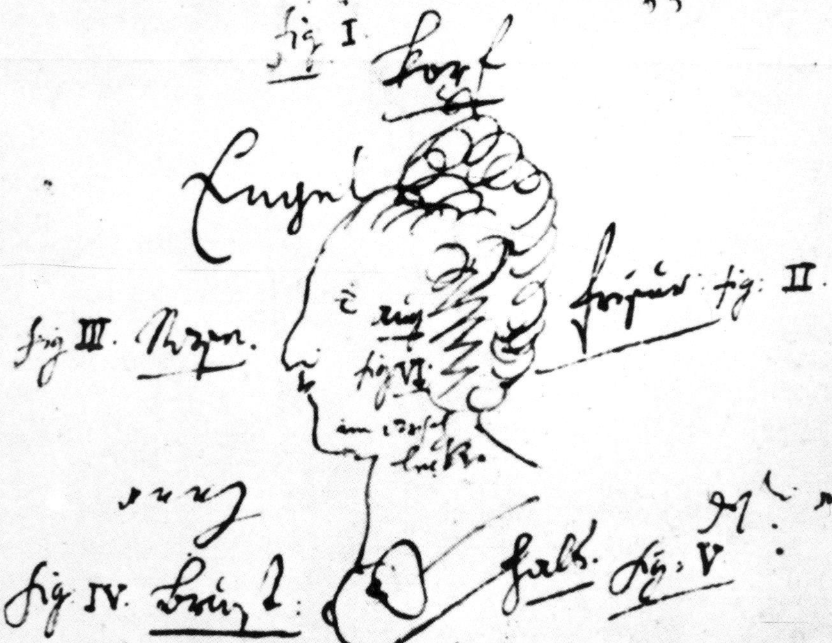

fig. I   Kopf

Augen

fig. III   Nase   Stirn   fig. II

fig. VI

fig. IV   Aug'   Hals   fig. V

Now I have been shitting for nearly 22 years out of the same old hole and yet it's not torn a whit! – although I used it so often to shit – and then chewed off the muck bit by bit.

It seems as if the dirty talk is becoming dirtier and more extreme, yet one cannot fail to admire the lengths Wolfgang has gone to in order to make it rhyme. To deny there is any sexual excitement in this seems to me to be folly, even given the coarse humour we know to exist in the Mozart family, and which was prevalent too in eighteenth-century Bavaria.

It has to be the case that both Wolfgang and Bäsle were mutually excited by such talk. Another similar sentence follows, immediately succeeded by an unexpected declaration of love:

Now I must close because I am not dressed yet, and we'll be eating soon so that afterward we can go and shit again. Do go on loving me, as I love you, then we'll never stop loving each other.

From Mannheim on 3 December there is more of the same, before a sentence in which he seems to be reassuring Bäsle he has remained faithful to her:

My mind is made up: if I have to go, I go. But it all depends. If I have the runs, I must run; and if I can't hold it any longer, I'll shit in my pants … A propos, I have not taken off my pants since I left Augsburg – except at night before going to bed.

And three months later:

If I have already left this place, instead of a letter I'll get muck in my face. muck! – muck! – oh muck! – o sweet word! – muck! – chuck! That's good too! – muck, chuck! – muck! – suck – oh charmante! – muck, suck! – love this stuff! – muck, chuck and suck! – chuck muck and suck muck! – now let's talk about something else …

After this outpouring he moves on to more mundane matters. Wolfgang is obviously having fun, but is he having more than that? Is he referring in these letters to activities he and his cousin have indulged in, or is it fantasy? And if it is fantasy, how much is fantasy?

Of course we cannot be 100 per cent sure either way, but to give an indication of how divided the world of musicological academia is on the subject, I shall give just a couple of examples.

At the end of that last letter from which I quoted, Wolfgang writes:

Whoever doesn't believe me, can kiss my rear end, from now until eternity, or until I regain my sanity, in which case he will have to lick and lick, and I must worry myself quite sick that there won't be sufficient muck and he won't have enough to suck, adieu Bäsle!

The American musicologist and Mozart biographer Maynard Solomon sees this as a reference to oral sex. He concludes, along with the German musicologist and Mozart biographer Wolfgang Hildesheimer, that Wolfgang and Bäsle had a full sexual relationship.

Robert Gutman, American Mozart biographer, disputes this interpretation. His conclusion is that Wolfgang sought release in this safe form of love play, and held back from a complete sexual relationship until he married.[25]

One sentence settles it for me. It comes in the letter of 13 November 1777. This is where Wolfgang switches into French. He concludes the letter with this sentence:

Je vous baise vos mains, votre visage, vos genoux et votre ——, afin, tout ce que vous me permettes [sic] *de baiser.*

This could translate as: 'I kiss your hands, your face, your knees and your ——, in fact everything that you allow me to kiss.' But 'baiser' has a double meaning; as well as meaning 'to kiss', it is also slang for 'to fuck'. If we conflate Mozart's sentence to: '*Je vous baise votre ——*' it is more than a double entendre; it is blatant. I am certain Mozart knew exactly what he was saying when he wrote that.

One other aspect of this extraordinary relationship between the two cousins merits a mention. Bäsle might have been only nineteen years of age, but she clearly already had something of a reputation. Back in Salzburg Leopold had got wind of his son's closeness to his cousin, probably from Anna Maria.

He writes to Wolfgang, warning him not to let himself be carried away by infatuation. It is well known, he writes, that Maria Anna has too intimate a relationship with certain priests. It seems from Wolfgang's reply that Leopold has used the word *Pfaffenschnitzl*, which translates roughly as 'a tasty morsel for a priest'.

Wolfgang angrily denies his father's accusation, saying his 'dear Bäsle' is nothing of the sort, adding, 'Yesterday she dressed up in the French fashion just to please me.' Which might not entirely have put his father's mind at rest.

Leopold might have had a point. It is a fact that seven years later Maria Anna Thekla, the Bäsle, gave birth to an illegitimate child whose father was an Augsburg clergyman.

I believe, looking at all the evidence we have, that the obviously more experienced Bäsle initiated Wolfgang into the joys of sex, they enjoyed a hearty romp together, they will most certainly have indulged in the 'you

"I believe that the obviously more experienced Bäsle initiated Wolfgang into the joys of sex."

show me yours and I'll show you mine' humour of young people, they probably masturbated together. One way or another, however far things were carried, I believe neither of them were virgins when Wolfgang and his mother left Augsburg.

Not everyone will be of the same opinion, not least because the Wolfgang who arrived in Mannheim was an entirely different individual from the one who had left Augsburg. He was about to meet more young women, and his behaviour could not have been more different.

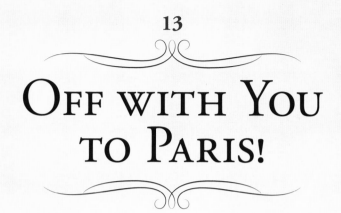

13

OFF WITH YOU TO PARIS!

Wolfgang and his mother arrived in Mannheim, the next stop on their tour, at six o'clock in the evening on 30 October 1777. The journey from Augsburg had taken four days. They were now outside Bavaria, in the highly sophisticated capital of the Electorate of the Palatinate, close to the university town of Heidelberg and the Black Forest.

Sophisticated, and very musical too, Mannheim was ruled by Elector Karl Theodor, a keen patron of the arts. The name-days of both the elector and his wife were celebrated with grand masses, operas, ballets, comic operas and concerts.

Mannheim was famous for its orchestra. The English composer Charles Burney wrote, five years before the Mozarts' arrival there, 'There are more solo players and good composers in this, than perhaps in any other orchestra in Europe; it is an army of generals, equally fit to plan a battle, as to fight it.'

The profusion of musical events attracted skilled players from across Europe, including a famous section of horn players from Bohemia. The orchestra was renowned for its discipline, its precise attacks, attention to dynamics, and uniform bowing.

Leopold Mozart was well aware of the reputation of Mannheim as a centre of musical excellence. 'Its rays,' he declared, 'like the sun's, spread through the whole of Germany, indeed through the whole of Europe.'

If his son had failed to find employment in Munich, then that would surely be remedied in Mannheim. Just wait till they discover how talented Wolfgang is, Leopold must have thought.

In the event, mother and son remained in Mannheim for almost five months. Wolfgang would leave Mannheim empty handed, with nothing to show for his stay there – in terms of musical employment, that is.

In another, more private, area, his life was about to change forever, even though it would be a few years before he, or anybody else, realised it.

Things got off to a bad start in Mannheim, and did not improve. Wolfgang was different. Suddenly he was less of an ingénue. He was more self-assured, with a touch of arrogance that others did not find appealing.

It might be far-fetched to use this as another argument for a sexual relationship having taken place between him and his cousin, but it is not unheard of for a young man to walk that bit taller once he has lost his virginity – become a man in the true sense, so to speak. That, coupled with a definite lacking when it came to social graces, could well explain his demeanour in Mannheim.

His new self-confidence bordered on conceit. In letters to his father, he described the deputy kapellmeister as 'conceited and incompetent', the choir as 'feeble', and the playing of the two court organists as 'wretched'.

He performed for the elector, for which he received a gold watch – *another* gold watch.

I now have five watches, and am seriously considering having another watch pocket on each leg of my trousers so that, when I visit some great lord, I shall wear both watches – that way it will not occur to him to present me with another.

One can't help feeling that his sense of humour is wearing thin. There seems to be a new cynicism in his words.

Wolfgang spent time with other musicians. He lunched and dined with them, he made music with them most evenings, and he attended parties. Given his social antennae were not his sharpest asset, it is more than likely he expressed opinions that were less than well received.

Why else would he write to his father, 'They seem to think that be-cause of my small size and youth I possess no importance or maturity. They will soon learn.' It was an attitude hardly calculated to endear him to his fellow musicians.

It was notable that invitations to perform began to dry up, and once again no offer of employment was forthcoming. This was a source of ever increasing worry to his father back in Salzburg, who urged him repeatedly to try harder, to ingratiate himself more readily. This trip was costing money, and so far it had yielded precious little.

It is extraordinary that Wolfgang seemed so completely insensitive to any concerns he was causing his father. It is almost as if – now that he was free of his father's domineering personality – he was setting out to cause him even more worry, to hurt him more.

If that was his aim, he certainly achieved it with a remarkable letter that he wrote on 14 November. He opens it with a parody of the Catholic confessional prayer, calculated to offend his father's sensibilities. The sins he is confessing to are also clearly designed to upset and worry his father. In fact, the letter bears the hallmarks of a young man getting home late and drunk, and picking up a pen:

> *I, Johannes Chrisostomus Amadeus Wolfgangus Sigismundus Mozart, am guilty of not coming home until 12 o'clock midnight, the day before yesterday and yesterday, and often times before, and that from 10 o'clock until said hour I did some rhyming – nothing too serious but rather light and frothy, actually, nothing but crude stuff, such as Muck, shitting, and ass licking, all of it in thoughts, words … I must also confess that I thoroughly enjoyed it all. I confess all these my sins and transgressions from the bottom of my heart, and, in the hope that I can confess them more often, I am fully committed to perfecting the sinful life that I have begun. I, therefore, beg for holy dispensation if it can be obtained easily; if not, well, it's all the same to me because the play must go on.*

This is a son rebelling against his father, pure and simple.

Tensions were rising, too, between mother and son. It was perhaps inevitable, given that this was the first time they had been in such close contact, and over an extended period of time.

Anna Maria, not possessing musical talent, was naturally excluded from her son's activities. She was actually quite distressed, and it seems Wolfgang either had no idea, or simply did not care.

She was rarely able to write to her husband without Wolfgang finding out, and if she added a postscript to his letters, he made sure he read it. Just once she managed to add a quick word to a letter 'in greatest secrecy and haste while he is at table so that I am not caught'.

Given the subterfuge she had to go to, it makes for even more painful reading. Anna Maria wrote, 'In a word, he prefers being with others to being with me. If I take exception to one or other thing that is not to my taste, that makes him angry.'

"Anna Maria, not possessing musical talent, was naturally excluded from her son's activities."

She describes how Wolfgang seemed to have forgotten she existed. 'I am at home alone, as is the case most of the time.' She said she ate and drank only what they could afford: 'I never drink wine at the inn, except when Wolfgang takes a meal there, and then we share a glass.'

Most portentously of all, she states that she orders a fire only when dressing or undressing. Her health is beginning to suffer. Winter was harsh that year in Mannheim, and at the age of fifty-seven Anna Maria was beginning to decline.

Wolfgang was hurting both his parents, and he seemed oblivious to it. He was about to make matters a thousand times worse.

On 8 December Wolfgang was formally told that there was no appointment for him at court. Leopold, suspecting this would be the case, had already written to his son urging him to leave as soon as possible for Paris. The French capital was the last – and greatest – hope. There, everything would surely come right.

But winter had set in, the roads were icy and Anna Maria's health was not good. Travel was impossible. Wolfgang and his mother had no choice but to wait for spring, kicking their heels with little to do, and eating more and more into their limited funds.

But there was something occupying Wolfgang's mind. He had hinted at it in a convoluted passage in a letter to his father written in the previous November. It is worth quoting, for it is an elaborate, tortuous – and typical – attempt of a young man suffering under his father's controlling influence, attempting to lay the ground for what he knows will unleash a thunderstorm. And because this is Wolfgang, there has to be a scatological reference, used almost as a way of trying to introduce a little levity.

I don't want to talk about things before their time. everything will turn out fine. Maybe I can report to you in my next letter about something that is very good *for you but only* good *for me, or something that is* very bad *in your eyes, but* Acceptable *in mine, perhaps also something* Acceptable *to you, however,* very good, dear*, and* precious *for me! This is all rather like an oracle, isn't it? – well, it sounds mysterious but can be understood … One of those Oracular sayings will have to come to pass – I think it will either be the one in the middle or the last one – it doesn't matter which; because it's one thing whether I eat the muck or Papa shits it – it seems I can never get this thing right! I wanted to say: it's one thing whether Papa shits the muck or I eat it! – now I better quit, I can tell, it's useless for me to try …*

If Leopold was able to guess what was afoot, he gave no hint of it in his letters. Then, three months later, in a letter written on 17 January 1778, Wolfgang broaches the subject, but with a studied insouciance:

The copying of the arias didn't cost me much either, because it was done by a certain Herr Weber, who will accompany me on the trip. I'm not sure whether I have mentioned his daughter to you – she sings superbly and has a beautifully clear voice. The only thing she lacks is some experience in acting, but once she has mastered that she can be a Prima donna in any theatre. She is only sixteen. Her father is a good, honest German who is raising his children properly, and that's the very reason why everyone is after the girl.

Wolfgang is in love, and sure enough the storm is unleashed. Leopold is utterly appalled. He pours the guilt onto Wolfgang's shoulders.

We have done everything to make you happier and through you to bring happiness to ourselves and to set your future at least on a firm footing. But Fate has willed that we should not achieve our purpose … I am now in very deep waters, in debt to the extent of 700 gulden … So it must be clear as noonday to you that the future of your old parents and of your good sister who loves you with all her heart, is entirely in your hands … If you think it over, you will realise that not only have I never spent a farthing on the smallest pleasure for myself but that without God's special mercy I should never have succeeded in spite of all my efforts in keeping out of debt. When you were children I gave up all my time to you in the hope that not only would you be able to provide later on for yourselves, but also that I might enjoy a comfortable old age, be able to give an account to God of the education of my children, be free from all anxiety, devote myself to the welfare of my soul and thus be enabled to meet my death in peace.

What a turnaround! Leopold, the father, is throwing himself at his son's feet. And that son, perhaps for the first time in his twenty-two years, appears unmoved. In fact, he ups the ante. Not only does he have no desire to go to Paris; he wishes instead to go on tour with the Webers – father and two daughters. This is open defiance:

Herr Weber will attempt to organise some concert tours for me and him; we want to go on tour together. That is why I like him so much because, apart from his outside appearance, he is so much like you … I am so fond of this unfortunate family that I wish nothing more than to make them happy; and maybe I can do that. My advice to them is to go to Italy … If

*our plans could be realised, we, that is Monsieur We-
ber, two of his daughters, and I, will have the honour
of visiting my dear Papa and my dear sister on the
way to Italy for 2 weeks.*

If Leopold was angry before, he is now apoplectic.
'MY DEAR SON! I have read your letter with amazement and horror. I am beginning to answer it only
today, the 11th, for the whole night long I was unable
to sleep and am so exhausted that I can only write
quite slowly.' He accuses Wolfgang of being easily led
and letting others sway him as they like.

'As for your proposal to travel about with Herr Weber,' he writes, 'and, be it noted, his two daughters – it
has nearly made me lose my reason! My dearest son!
How can you have allowed yourself to be bewitched
even for an hour by such a horrible idea, which must
have been suggested to you by someone or other!'

He rants on, and then comes the imperious command: *'Off with you to
Paris! and that soon!'* In case Wolfgang is in any doubt: 'You want to spare me
anxiety and in the end you suddenly overturn a whole bucketful of worries
on my head, which almost kill me! … Though half-dead, I have managed
to think out and arrange everything connected with your journey to Paris.'

Leopold is re-exerting paternal control, and Wolfgang, ultimately, is
powerless to disobey. Obedience to his father was ingrained in him so deeply, from his earliest years, that it was inevitable he would revert to type.
He has no choice but to take his leave of the Weber family, and prepare to
depart with his mother for Paris.

So who exactly was the object of Wolfgang's affections? She was Aloysia, the
second of four daughters of Fridolin and Marie Cäcilia Weber, and Wolfgang had fallen head over heels in love with her.

Fridolin Weber* was a bass singer, prompter and copyist at the Mannheim
theatre, and all four of his daughters were singers. At first, it seems, the family
was overwhelmed by Wolfgang's musical talents. When he began to talk of
going on tour with them to Italy, they must have been even more impressed.

---

* Future uncle of the composer Carl Maria von Weber, born 18 November 1786.

'We owe everything to your son,' Wolfgang quoted Weber to his father. 'He has done a great deal for my daughter and has taken an interest in her and she can never be grateful enough to him.' Wolfgang's words, rather than Weber's, but the sentiment is surely correct.

It slowly dawned on Herr Weber, however, that although Wolfgang was always smartly turned out and had impressive musical contacts in the city, he was far from being a man of means. It was obvious to him, also, that it was Wolfgang's father back in Salzburg who was issuing orders. We can assume Wolfgang will have expressed his interest in Aloysia to her father, and that Fridolin was lukewarm.

We know tantalisingly little of how Wolfgang's attraction to Aloysia progressed, other than from his letters, which are always calculated to portray her in a favourable light for his father's benefit. She was certainly an accomplished singer, even if – according to one observer – falling short of Wolfgang's extravagant praise. The sole portrait of her, made a few years after Wolfgang's stay in Mannheim, shows an elegant young woman, with sharply defined nose, full lips and an alluring half-smile. It is easy to see how Wolfgang was attracted to her.

Sadly we know nothing of Aloysia's feelings towards her suitor. Wolfgang gives us no indication in his letters. Possibly we can infer from this that she was less than responsive, otherwise he would have been sure to mention it in making his case to his father.

Future events were to bear this out. For the moment, suffice it to say that the love affair – one-sided from the start – would end in tears. But that was not the end of Mozart's connection with the Weber family. In fact he would indeed find love within the family, and the Weber name would be linked to his from that day to this.

14

MY DEAR DEPARTED MOTHER

olfgang and his mother set out from Mannheim on a sunny morning in March 1778, destination Paris, but the mood inside the carriage was anything but sunny. Neither of them wanted to be there.

Wolfgang had no desire to go to Paris. He wanted to be on tour with the woman he loved, preferably in Italy. Aloysia had knitted him some mittens, her father had given him a copy of Molière's comedies (in German). Was that not proof of her love for him, and her father's affection? Wolfgang no doubt thought so, though they were more likely to be compensation for his unreturned advances.

As for Anna Maria, she was totally out of her depth, away from everything that made her feel safe and secure, and it had been that way since the day she had left Salzburg. She spoke not a word of French and disliked, even feared, big cities. It is likely that she missed her husband's controlling hand: even if there was a deep-seated resentment, she had long since learned that sub-servience was her best ally, and she had grown accustomed to acquiescence.

Three months earlier, in Mannheim, in an attempt to take control of the situation, Wolfgang had proposed that his mother should return to Salzburg, while he went on to Paris alone. He wrote to his father and told him she was in agreement with this plan. 'It only remains for you to give your consent,' he added tellingly, showing who was really in control.

Anna Maria was certainly in favour of the plan. She wrote that she was so cold in Mannheim she could hardly hold the pen to write. 'I myself do not like to let him go,' she added in a postscript to his letter, 'nor do I like to have to travel home alone, it is such an awful distance. I can't bear to think of it. But what can we do? I am too old to undertake such a long journey to Paris and' – no doubt hoping this would be the clincher, given how worried Leopold was about finances – 'besides it would cost too much.' She even points out pitifully that she cannot go out because she had not spent money on an 'umbrella to put up when it snows or rains'.

After several not very helpful suggestions as to how she might keep warm in the cold winter – 'lie in bed, covered up' – Leopold appeared to agree to the plan, suggesting possible routes for her return to Salzburg. It was only the realisation by both parents that if they left Wolfgang alone he would surely travel to Italy with the Webers, rather than go on to Paris, that scuppered the plan.

Wolfgang knew this, and no doubt felt a certain amount of guilt that he had caused his mother to endure an uncomfortable and unwanted journey. That guilt was soon to increase to an almost unbearable level.

The journey to Paris was long and uncomfortable. It took them more than nine days to cover little over three hundred miles, through the relatively featureless countryside of north-east France. We can imagine them sitting miserably in the carriage, being jostled and bumped, barely talking to each other.

Two days before reaching Paris, they were hit by an awful storm. 'The wind and rain almost choked and drowned us,' Anna Maria wrote. 'We both got soaking wet in the carriage and could scarcely breathe.'

It was an inauspicious start, and things did not improve. Leopold, as ever directing matters from Salzburg, had arranged lodgings for them in the house of a secondhand-goods dealer from Augsburg, assuring his wife she would enjoy the German atmosphere and home cooking there.

He could not have been more wrong. The single room was small, cramped and cold. Anna Maria was soon complaining to Leopold that her life in Paris was 'not at all a pleasant one. I sit alone in our room the whole day long as if I were in jail, and as the room is very dark and looks out on a little courtyard, I cannot see the sun all day long and I don't even know what the weather is like.' It was small consolation that 'with difficulty I manage to knit a little by the daylight that struggles in'.

Leopold must have sunk his head in despair when he read that. Here were his wife and son, in the greatest city on the continent of Europe, a leading centre of music, a music-loving public, many music-publishing houses, a busy operatic life and plenty of concerts. Yet both were unhappy.

Wolfgang, with the arrogance that had come over him in Mannheim still very much in evidence, took an instant dislike to Paris, Parisians and all things French.

Everything here is too far to walk – or too muddy; for the dirt in Paris is beyond all description. And to go by cab – there you have the honour of spending about 4 to 5 livres a day, and all in vain. They give you many Compliments, but that's it … If you are not here yourself to experience these things, you cannot possibly imagine how dreadful it is. Paris has changed quite a bit. The French are by far no longer as Polite as they were 15 years ago, their manners now border on rudeness, and they have become terribly conceited.

There was no stopping the bile that poured from his pen:

In truth, the devil invented the [French] language. If only damned French were not so contemptible for music. That is the misery of it. By comparison even German is divine … [I am an] honest German struggling among downright cattle and beasts.

This was not the Wolfgang of previous years, the carefree laughing teenager who loved to joke and tease. He was now a young man of twenty-two, who deeply resented the influence of his father, wished to be free of the burden of looking after his mother, and more than anything wanted to be away from Paris in the company of the woman he loved.

There were matters outside his control, too, that militated against success in Paris. Musical circles were consumed with a feud between two of its most prominent composers, Niccolò Piccinni and Christoph Willibald Gluck, over the direction opera should take.

Why should they spend any time with a practically unknown young musician from Salzburg, who would not have any opinion on the matter anyway? The bald truth was that Wolfgang could not have chosen a worse time to come to Paris.

To give Wolfgang his due, he soon realised he had to make an effort. He quickly made contact with influential names his father had furnished him with. One of these, Baron von Grimm, who had been the Mozarts' chief patron during their earlier stay in Paris, found more comfortable lodgings for him and his mother.

He did the rounds of aristocratic salons, but loathed every minute of it. In a long letter to his father dated 1 May 1778 – the first he had written for nearly a month, an unusually long gap for him – he gives an extraordinary and compelling account of just how painful it was performing for the aristocracy.

Through one of his father's contacts, he had been invited to the residence of the Duchesse de Chabot. He writes that he had to wait for half an hour in a large, ice-cold room that did not even have a fireplace. At last the Duchesse entered and asked him, 'with the greatest politeness', to play.

He demurred. One can imagine the frosty smile becoming even more frozen on her face at his refusal. He explained that his hands were so cold he could not even feel his fingers. He asked if there was a room with a fire where he could warm his hands.

'*O oui, Monsieur, vous avez raison*,' he quoted her as saying. She then proceeded, without another word, to sit at a table 'in the company of gentlemen' and draw for a whole hour, completely ignoring him.

It got worse:

Windows and doors were open. Not only my hands but my whole body and my feet were freezing cold, and my head began to ache. In the room was utter silence. I didn't know what to do for all the cold, headache, and boredom. Several times I thought I should just get up and leave like a shot. At last, to make a long story short, I did play on the miserable, Wretched Pianoforte. And what really galled me was that Mad. and her gentlemen never interrupted their drawing for one moment, they just continued, and I had to play for the chairs, tables, and walls.

It is possible, of course, that there is an element of exaggeration in Wolfgang's account, but to me there is truth ringing out of every word. It is an extraordinary image, the greatest natural genius that music has known, whose name will be revered for all time, sitting there shivering, uncomfortable, ignored, playing for the furniture and walls.

This account summed up Wolfgang's general reception in Paris – by and large, a lack of interest. Evidence of this is that his creative juices seemed to have dried up. Initially he had thrown himself into all kinds of projects. He began writing new parts for a choral work, he embarked on a sinfonia concertante for wind, and he started to plot out a new opera. None of these was brought to fruition.

With the arrival of warmer weather, things seemed to improve a little. Wolfgang had taken on three pupils, and their lessons were bringing in a little money. His mother wrote to Leopold that she was considering renting larger rooms, even possibly buying their own furniture, in the autumn.

She even began to venture out a little. She wrote a long letter to her husband – Wolfgang must by now have become more relaxed about this – in which she told him how utterly Paris had changed since they were last there together. 'It is much bigger and is so spread out that I simply cannot describe it,' she wrote. She walked along the 'broad and shiny' boulevards, and even did some sightseeing.

A rare insight into her character comes in the same letter, asking Leopold to tell their daughter Nannerl that 'the mode here is to wear no earrings, nothing round your neck, no jewelled pins in your hair, in fact no sparkling jewels, either real or imitation'. She makes a special mention of how the women of Paris wear their hair: 'extraordinarily high, not a heart-shaped toupée, but the same height all round, more than a foot … behind is the plait which is worn right down low into the neck with lots of curls on either side'.

At one time, she said, the women wore their hair so high that the roofs of the carriages had to be raised, otherwise no woman would be able to sit upright in them. But presumably fashions swiftly changed, because 'they have now lowered them again'.

With a feminine eye for detail, she informs Nannerl that 'the corselets worn by spinsters are smooth round the waist in front and have no folds', concluding that 'Nannerl will now know enough about fashion here for some time.'

I have quoted her observations about fashion at some length, since it is a rare insight into the character of a woman who for much of the story so far has remained in shadow. At last, now that she has begun writing to her husband, it is possible to form a slightly clearer picture of her.

But if mother and son were beginning to contemplate prolonging their stay in Paris, Leopold, unsurprisingly, was thinking along rather different lines. His son's letters had left him in no doubt about how the stay in Paris was going. Badly, in a word. More expense, for very little return, and an ever receding prospect of paid employment or even lucrative commissions.

He began to write to his son about returning to Salzburg. This might have been welcome news to Anna Maria, but it was the last thing Wolfgang wanted. A return to Salzburg and his father would put paid for ever to his plan to marry Aloysia. Once back under his father's domineering influence, there would be no escape.

So Wolfgang began to stall, began to suggest that things might be beginning to look up a little, began to hint at possible opportunities to work. But then disaster, catastrophe. Something happened that was a mystery then, and remains a mystery to this day.

Here is what we know. Despite her new-found semi-optimism, things were not going well for Anna Maria. Her health was troubling her again. She wrote to her husband, 'All this long while, about three weeks, I have been plagued with toothache, sore throat and earache, but now, thank God, I am better. I don't get out much, it is true, and the rooms are cold, even when a fire is burning. You just have to get used to it.'

She tells Leopold she has run out of the 'black powder' and the 'digestive one', and if one of their friends is coming to Paris, she would appreciate a new supply.

Leopold is unsympathetic. 'My dear wife, do not forget *to be bled*. Remember that you are away from home … Perhaps you can get the black powder at some chemist's shop. It is called *Pulvis epilepticus niger*.'

It is as if Anna Maria knew that from now on she was going to receive no useful advice from her husband, nor was there any prospect of him sending money so she could return home to Salzburg. So she makes up her mind not to bother him any more with information.

The letters she now writes are generally cheerful, with no mention of her declining health. In a letter dated 12 June 1778, she begins by saying in an almost offhand way that she was bled the day before, so won't be able to write much today.

There follow descriptions of Paris, the location of their lodgings, a walk she has taken in the Luxembourg Gardens with a visit to the picture gallery there. 'I was frightfully tired when I got home,' she writes in the same sentence, giving it no import at all.

The rest of the letter concerns trivialities, the merits or otherwise of a newfangled device called a lightning conductor, how nature should be allowed to take its course, and houses should not be built next to mountains.

She is clearly trying to steer Leopold clear of the truth, that she was seriously unwell and did not know what to do about it. Only after she has signed off the letter tenderly, with 'I kiss you several thousand times and remain your faithful wife', then rather formally, 'FRAU MOZART', does she add below the signature, 'I must stop, for my arm and eyes are aching.'

It was the last letter she would write.

Anna Maria died shortly after ten o'clock on the evening of 3 July 1778. Within an hour of her death, Wolfgang would write a letter, a quite extraordinary letter, to his father. It is extraordinary because he leaves Leopold in no doubt that his mother is still alive. Right at the start, he writes: 'My dear mother is very ill.'

He then describes how, after she was bled, she felt quite well, but a few days later complained of shivering and feverishness, accompanied by diarrhoea and headache. She got worse and worse, and was seen by a doctor; 'But she *is* still very weak and *is* feverish and delirious.'[*]

He writes a lengthy passage about how our lives rest in God's hand, and when He decides to take a life to him, there is nothing anyone can do to prevent it. He then writes this: 'I do not mean to say that my mother will and must die, or that all hope is lost. She may recover health and strength, but only if God wills it.' These words were written with his mother's corpse on the bed close by.

At two o'clock in the morning of 4 July, four hours after his mother's death, he pens another letter, to a close family friend in Salzburg, telling him that his mother had died, and asking him to go and see Leopold and Nannerl and prepare them for the awful truth that will follow.

Not until 9 July, nearly a week after his mother died and five days after she was buried in the cemetery of Saint-Eustache, did he write to his father and inform him of his mother's death.

He owns up to the fact that he had deceived his father, but for the best motives, and hopes he will be forgiven. He clearly deliberately uses spiritual language calculated to appeal to his devout father:

---

[*] The italics are my emphasis.

My last letter of the 3rd will have told you that no good news could be hoped for. On that very same day, the 3rd, at twenty-one minutes past ten at night my mother fell asleep peacefully in the Lord. Indeed, when I wrote to you, she was already enjoying the blessings of Heaven – for all was then over. I wrote to you during that night and I hope that you and my dear sister will forgive me for this slight but very necessary deception. As I judged from my own grief and sorrow what yours would be, I could not bring myself suddenly to shock you with this dreadful news.

His language becomes even more pious, before he then describes her death:

Let us rather pray to Him, and thank Him for His goodness, for she died a very happy death. In those distressing moments, there were three things that consoled me – my entire and steadfast submission to the will of God, and the sight of her very easy and beautiful death which made me feel that in a moment she had become so happy; for how much happier is she now than we are! Indeed I wished at that moment to depart with her.

This is not, I believe, the authentic voice of Wolfgang. He is writing in a way calculated to please his father, and lessen any wrath his father might have towards him for being deceived.

Not only does it not sound like Wolfgang, but in the description of Anna Maria's death it is also clearly untrue. This becomes evident in a letter Wolfgang wrote fully three weeks later, again to his father, this time giving elaborate and intricate detail of the harrowing final days his mother suffered.

Wolfgang can only have hoped that the passage of time, however brief, would have calmed the initial impact of his father's, and his sister's, grief. For in this later letter, he spares them little. It is almost as if he wants them – his father especially – to understand what he has gone through, and to share some of it.

It is also clear from the opening words that he is attempting to leave them in no doubt that there was nothing he could have done to prevent his mother's death. This, to me, is clear evidence that he felt a sense of guilt. He was, after all, the only family member with her. All responsibility was on his shoulders. And yet she died.

In one of the longest letters he would ever write to his father, dated 31 July 1778, after generalities about mutual health and pious words about prayer (for his father's benefit again, no doubt), comes this stark sentence: 'First of all, I must tell you that my dear departed mother *had to die*.'

No doctor could have saved her, he writes. Her time had come. He promises his father he will give only a short account of how his mother died,

Left

Mozart's letter to a
family friend in Salzburg,
informing him of Anna
Maria's death.

but then proceeds to go into quite unsparing detail. In what clearly seems to
be a stab at his father, he addresses the question of whether she should have
been bled earlier, as Leopold had advised:

> *You think she put off being bled until it was too late? – Maybe that's true.*
> *She did put it off a little. But I share the opinion of some people here who*
> *advised her against being bled.*

This is close to open disagreement with his father, not a course of action he
is used to taking. He continues in the same independent vein:

> *[They] tried to persuade her to have an enema instead – but she didn't*
> *want it – and I didn't dare say anything, because I don't understand*

these things and consequently would have had to take the blame if the procedure hadn't been good for her.

He then goes into the pros and cons of enemas, and the technicalities of being bled. The surgeon decided to take not quite two platefuls of blood, because it was such a dreadfully hot day, but insisted it was very necessary.

But soon after she was bled, he writes, she began to have diarrhoea. More observations then about how foreigners who choose to drink the water in Paris always end up with diarrhoea. He himself was no exception, but managed to cure it by adding a little wine to the water(!).

Then back to his mother. He describes how he took control when she began to complain of headaches, insisting she stay in bed all day. She alternated between being hot and feeling chilly, so he administered some 'Antispasmodic Powder'.

In an apparent attempt to deflect criticism from himself, he blames his mother for the fact that it was so long before a doctor came:

> All this time I wanted to send for a doctor – but she didn't want one. When I insisted she told me that she had no confidence in French doctors – so I started looking for a German – but, naturally, I could not go out and leave her alone.

He at last found a German doctor, 'an elderly German of about seventy', whose attendance proved to be unreliable. He gave Anna Maria rhubarb powder stirred into wine, which shocked Wolfgang.

> I can't understand that, for it is said that wine increases your body heat – but when I said that, they all shouted – Not at all, what are you saying? wine doesn't make you hot – wine only strengthens the body. It's the water that creates the heat – and all the while the poor patient was desperately longing for a little fresh water – how much I would have liked to give her some – dearest father, you cannot imagine what I went through – but there was no other way, I had to leave her, in god's name, in the hands of the doctor.

It seems an unlikely scenario, the doctor insisting on giving Anna Maria a mixture of wine and water, when it was obvious to Wolfgang that it was fresh water she needed. More evidence, in my view, of Wolfgang trying to deflect any blame. Then, finally:

> Just put yourself in my position when [the doctor] quite unexpectedly said to me – 'I fear she will not live through the night'.

I say 'finally', but only so far as his mother is concerned. The letter continues for several more pages, but there is not another single mention of his mother's final illness or death. He details how he has been unable to compose, he regales his father about how he has fallen out with Baron von Grimm, and he rants against the French who treat him as if was still a seven-year-old, the age he was when they first saw him.

He finally signs off the letter with ten thousand kisses for his father, and an embrace for his sister, as if for all the world things are normal.

Within days he received an excoriating letter from his father:

> *I told you in May that she ought not to postpone being bled … Yet she put it off until June 11th … The day before this treatment she took far too violent exercise, and got home exhausted and overheated … she was probably bled too little, and finally the doctor was called in far too late … for she was already in danger.*

And just in case Wolfgang was failing to get the point:

> *You had your engagements, you were away all day, and as she didn't make a fuss, you treated her condition lightly. All this time her illness became more serious, in fact mortal – and only then was a doctor called in, when of course it was too late.*

Leopold then raises the stakes. He reminds his already fragile son how his birth nearly killed his mother (a reference to the placenta having to be forcibly removed), but ultimately he was responsible for her death in another way:

> *The unbreakable chain of Divine Providence preserved your mother's life when you were born … but she was fated to sacrifice herself for her son in a different way.*

In other words, Wolfgang might not have killed his mother when he was born, but he managed to kill her in the end. Leopold might have attempted to soften his words by using the third person, but one can only imagine the effect these words must have had on Wolfgang.

In fact this letter from Leopold crossed with the one from Wolfgang describing his mother's death, but if he hoped that his account would absolve him of any guilt in his father's eyes, he was swiftly disabused of the notion.

In a letter of 27 August, Leopold lays the blame for Anna Maria's death solely at the feet of his son, for forming a 'new friendship' with Aloysia and wishing to travel to Italy with her. Only to prevent that happening did his mother stay with him and accompany him to Paris, a trip that cost her her life.

It is cruel language for a father to use to his son, and it does not take much imagination to hear Wolfgang screaming out in frustration at his father's intransigence. To be accused of having in effect brought about your mother's death – at the second time of trying – is likely to have caused him an unending sense of guilt, to be borne for the rest of his life.

But something within Wolfgang now changed. To begin with, he went quiet on his father. Increasingly pleading letters from Leopold arrived in Paris asking why Wolfgang was not writing to him.

He implores his son to work harder, to try to win commissions. But it seems he finally gave up. He wrote to Wolfgang on 31 August announcing in triumphalist tones – 'thanks to my brave perseverance' – that he has persuaded Archbishop Colloredo to appoint Wolfgang konzertmeister on a salary of 500 gulden.

It was the last thing Wolfgang wanted: to be back in Salzburg in the employ of the detested prince-archbishop. He knew he had no choice but to accept, but this time it would be on his terms:

> I'm serious when I say that if the Archbishop doesn't allow me to take a
> trip every 2 years, I cannot possibly accept the Engagement … There's
> one other condition for my return to Salzbourg: I don't want to be only a
> violinist as I was before – I'm not a fiddler any more – I want to conduct
> from the piano – and accompany arias. It would have been a good thing
> if I could have had a written guarantee, specifying that I will be in line
> for the position of kapellmeister, otherwise I may have the honour of
> doing duties for two posts – but getting paid for only one.

This is a new, emboldened Wolfgang. He not only lays down conditions, he even criticises his father for not obtaining terms in writing. It is also a musician recognising his greatest strengths.

So Wolfgang prepared to leave Paris, 'a city I can't stand'. But even here he is doing it on his own terms. He informs his father that he will travel back via Munich, where he knows Aloysia Weber is working as a court singer.

This time it is his father who has no choice but to accept. Wolfgang is on his own, with no mother to keep him in line. Leopold has lost a level of control over his son, and he will never get it back.

Wolfgang left Paris on 26 September 1778, nearly twenty-three years old. For the first time on any of his travels, he is on his own. If it was a still immature Wolfgang who had arrived in Paris with his mother, from now on it is Mozart the man, and Mozart the musician.

15

Unlucky in Love

Mozart the musician came of age in Paris. He might not have been able to compose while his mother was in extremis, but he most certainly was composing both before and after.

A month after arriving in Paris, he composed a concerto for an extremely unusual combination of instruments, and whenever that happens it is a good idea to look for the person who commissioned it.

Adrien-Louis de Bonnières, Duc de Guînes, an army general and diplomat, was an accomplished flautist, his daughter Marie-Adrienne a harpist. He asked Mozart to compose a piece for the two instruments and orchestra, and the result was the beautiful Concerto for Flute and Harp (K. 299).

The piece is light and airy, elegant and expressive. It shows off flute and harp to perfection, which is all the more extraordinary since Mozart did not have extensive experience of writing for either of them as solo instruments. In fact he never used the harp again in any composition.

This might have had something to do with the fact that he was disappointed to find that Marie-Adrienne was scarcely able to play her part. In fact the whole experience left him wounded. The Duc brushed off Mozart's request for payment, passing the matter on to his head butler, who would pay no more than half the agreed amount. 'There's noble treatment for you,' Mozart wrote to his father.

Next he turned to a full-scale symphony, and the significance of this work is that he was not writing it at the behest of an aristocratic patron, but to be performed before an audience of the general public.

In writing about it to his father, his arrogance and his extreme dislike of all things French reveal a rather unattractive side to his character:

I am very happy with it, but whether others like it, I don't know – and to tell you the truth, it doesn't matter much to me, for who, after all, are these people who wouldn't like it? – I can vouch for a few intelligent French listeners who will be there. But the stupid ones, well, it won't be a big misfortune if they don't find it to their liking – but I do hope that even the stupid asses will find something they can like.

Writing again almost three weeks later, after the first performance, things had got a lot worse:

During rehearsals I was extremely worried because I had never heard a worse performance in all my life. You can't imagine how they bungled and scratched their way through the Sinfonie – twice in a row – I was truly worried – I would have liked to have one more rehearsal, but because they are always rehearsing so much stuff all at once, there was no more time. I had no choice but to go to bed with a troubled heart and a dissatisfied and angry mind.

He decided on drastic action – or at least that is what he told his father:

The next day I decided not to go to the concert at all. But then in the evening the weather turned nice, and I decided to go, but with the firm resolve that if things went as poorly as during rehearsal, I would walk straight up to the orchestra, snatch the violin out of the hand of Herr Lahousè, the first violinist, and conduct myself.

This is the new, emboldened Mozart, forging his own way as professional musician, and he wanted his father to know it. Having built up the tension and prepared Leopold for the worst, he delivers the good news:

The Sinfonie began … and right in the middle of the First Allegro came a Passage that I knew would please, and the entire audience was sent into raptures – there was a big applaudissement – and as I knew, when I wrote the passage, what good effect it would make, I brought it back once more at the end of the movement – and sure enough there they were: the shouts of Da capo. The Andante was well received as well, but the final Allegro pleased especially … I was so delighted, I went right after the Sinfonie to the Palais Royale – bought myself an ice cream, prayed a rosary as I pledged – and went home.

It is a beguiling image — the celebrated composer hurrying off on his own to eat an ice cream after the first performance of his most important

Left

Handwritten score
for Symphony in D
major, known as the
Paris Symphony.

symphony to date (the rosary line no doubt added to assuage his father's religious sensibilities).

The 'Paris' Symphony, as it has predictably become known, is a joyous and upbeat piece of writing, in the bright and brilliant key of D major. Mozart had scored it for a larger orchestra than he had used before, and it is full of unexpected turns and lively phrases, which demand vigorous playing from the whole orchestra.

He had suspected this was just the kind of music the Parisians wanted to hear, and he provided them with it. If they had known how he had castigated their musical tastes in that letter, they might have been less inclined to applaud so enthusiastically.

But here is what I find most extraordinary about the whole episode. All those passages I have quoted about the rehearsal and performance of the new symphony come in the *same* letter which began with the words, 'My dear Mother is very ill', and continues with 'They are giving me hope, but I don't have very much.' Words written with his mother lying dead on the bed just a few feet from him.

How was he able to detach himself from the appalling circumstances he was enduring, to the extent, even, that after describing the first performance of the symphony, he goes on to report that Voltaire, 'the godless Arch-culprit, has kicked the bucket like a dog'? And this is followed by a further page of small talk.

We cannot know. The most we can say is that this is the new Mozart, unencumbered by his father's influence, ruminating unbounded about anything that takes his attention. Mozart was a musician before he was a writer. If he wanted to express true emotions, he did so through his music. And that is what he was about to do, in the immediate aftermath of his mother's death.

He turned to the instrument of which he was master, and composed the Piano Sonata in A minor (κ.310).

This work is without doubt the most intense and deeply personal piece of music he had composed to date. It is the only instrumental work for which he chose the dark key of A minor, and the first of only two piano sonatas in any minor key.

It begins brightly enough, but the mood soon darkens. The main motif of the opening movement is a constantly descending phrase. It has a ring of despair to it. There is no let-up in pace as the movement drives relentlessly forward.

In the second movement Mozart takes us deep into his world, with a mixture of emotions. The opening is singing and expressive, but then we find ourselves confined in a windowless space, and when we think we have found some comfort, he destabilises and disturbs us with dissonant chords repeated mercilessly.

The final movement, brief and agitated, has a restless energy, and when in the middle section we think he has found light by switching to the major key, it is false hope. We are back in minor mode for a fiery ending.

Mozart the musician is now fully mature, and masterpieces will continue to flow from him. All this from the composer himself, without the overbearing influence of his father.

The transition to Mozart the man, alas, would be a little bumpier.

Under instructions from his father to return to Salzburg as quickly as he could, he dawdled, taking as much time as he possibly could. He was in no hurry to be back in his home city with his father. There was something else on his mind, and he was determined to act on it.

Throughout his stay in Paris, with all its ups and downs, the tragic loss of his mother, the success of his music, the woman he was in love with had stayed in his thoughts.

He wrote regularly to Aloysia's father, knowing his words would be passed on. Yet as far as we know, he wrote only one single letter to the woman herself, and it is a remarkable letter – not for what it says, but for what it does not say.

He wrote it on 30 July, a little under a month since his mother had died, and the day before the lengthy letter in which he finally informs Leopold of his mother's death. For some reason he chose to write it in Italian, possibly because that is the language of musicians, and certainly the content of the letter bears this out.

For the most part, it is professional advice on how best to sing an aria he had composed the previous year:

> Pay attention to the expression marks … think carefully about the meaning and the force of the words … put yourself with all seriousness into Androm-eda's situation and position! – imagine yourself to be that very person.

This is fascinating advice, and it is exactly what we might expect a singing teacher to write to his pupil. But it is hardly the sort of language a young man would use to the woman he is deeply in love with and hopes to marry. The letter is brief, and a model of politeness and courtesy. It is utterly devoid of any language that might be considered personal or intimate. Twice he refers to her as 'Dearest Friend', and describes himself as 'Your true and sincere friend'.

What it is not, by any stretch of the imagination, is a love letter. Nor does it have any of the humour he usually peppers his letters with, and certainly none of the earthy language he has used to his cousin Maria Anna, the Bäsle.

And that particular person, with whom he has had such a fun-filled, boisterous and intimate sexual relationship, is about to re-enter the story.

It is difficult to be absolutely certain about Mozart's motives and intentions at this particular moment in his life, since the only evidence we have to go on are his own, often convoluted and rambling, letters.

But we can state with certainty, I believe, that he is now travelling to Munich with the firm intention of proposing marriage to Aloysia Weber. What is slightly less obvious is why he decides to involve Bäsle. This is a young woman of roughly the same age as Aloysia. Both women are in their early twenties, and he is highly attracted to each of them.

"Mozart was a musician before he was a writer. If he wanted to express true emotions, he did so through his music."

But involve her he does. In December 1778, still on his unhurried return to Salzburg, he writes to her, imploring her to come to Munich. And in *this* letter, in total contrast to the formal and distant language of his letter to Aloysia, we are back in the familiar and comfortable Mozartian world of rhymes, puns, jokes, sexual innuendo and language that is sometimes downright pornographic:

Make sure you get to Munich before the New Year,
so I can look at you from afar and near
I will show you around town if you don't mind,
and if need be I'll clean your behind ...
Be sure to come even for a bit,
otherwise we'll be in deep shit.
I shall greet you high and nobly with pizazz
and put my personal seal on your ass
I will kiss your hands and have such fun
shooting off my rear-end gun.
I shall Embrace you with a smack
and wash you down front and back.
I shall pay up all I owed you from the start
and then let go a resounding fart,
and perhaps even drop something hard ...

P.S. Shit-dibitare, shit-dibitate,
the pastor of Rodempl,
he licked the ass of his kitchen maid,
to set a good example.

The only possible reason I can think of for his wanting his Bäsle in Munich with him was for moral support. Did he have a feeling deep down that a marriage proposal to Aloysia might not be totally straightforward? It is highly likely, since she certainly failed to respond to whatever advances he had made when he was with her, and her family, in Mannheim.

In case it should all go wrong, he would have a female there who would ease his pain, massage his shoulders, breathe reassuring words, offer moral – and, if necessary, immoral – support.

And come to Munich she did. Sadly, because the two of them are now together, we have no correspondence between them, so we cannot know if they resumed their sexual relationship. In fact, the only evidence we have of what actually happened at this crucial moment in Mozart's life comes from someone else who was there, recalling events many decades later.

Mozart duly turned up at the Weber family's residence in Munich, bearing a gift for Aloysia in the form of a newly composed aria. He was formally dressed 'in mourning for his mother in the French style, in a red jacket with black buttons'.[26]

But, in what must have been an excruciating moment for Mozart, when he entered the room Aloysia appeared not to know who he was. The family was there to witness her rejection.

How did Mozart react? According to the same witness, by defusing the situation totally. He went to the piano, and sang to his own accompaniment. This is the Mozart we know and have to love. He sang these words:

> Let the wench who doesn't want me
> kiss my ass.[*][27]

We are not told how the assembled company reacted.

From what we know of Aloysia, her rejection of Mozart is perhaps understandable, even if her method was somewhat cruel. She was now well established as a court singer in Munich, earning as much money as her suitor and his father combined. Why would she want to marry a Salzburg court musician on a low salary and without prospects, particularly when the spark of love was not there?

In fact Aloysia went on to marry a leading actor by the name of Joseph Lange. He was also an accomplished painter, and we owe to him the portrait of Mozart, sadly unfinished, painted just a year or two before he died, and considered to be the best likeness of any portrait (see page 233).

The Langes were for many years a power couple in the artistic milieu of Vienna. But the marriage was to end in separation, and after Lange's death Aloysia fell on hard times, her singing career over. She would then appeal to one of her younger sisters for financial help, and it appears this sister (the witness to Aloysia's rejection of Mozart) was happy to oblige. Aloysia often said in later life that she regretted rejecting him, and believed he loved her until the day of his death. Her sister appears not to have taken offence at this, which she might have considering she went on to marry Mozart herself. But that is to look ahead. Constanze does not properly enter our story yet.

Aloysia might have been deluding herself by believing Mozart continued to love her. In fact in a letter he wrote three years later, he vilifies her as 'lazy, coarse, deceitful, not to be trusted, false, malicious, and a Coquette'.

But it is certainly true that her rejection left him devastated. Even if he had seen it coming, he was unprepared for the effect it would have on him.

"Let the wench who doesn't want me kiss my ass."

Mozart's response to Aloysia's rejection.

---

[*] *Leck mir das Mensch im Arsch, das mich nicht will.*

Within days, on 29 December 1778, he wrote to his father:

Today I can do nothing but weep – I have too sensitive a heart ... in all my life I have never written anything as poorly as today. I simply can't write – my heart is on the verge of tears all the time!

At least he had his Bäsle to comfort him. 'My Bäsle is here – why? – to please me, her cousin.'

He could put it off no longer. He had to return to Salzburg, and to his father and sister. But he was dreading it, and he could not help but pour his bile into his letters to Leopold. In language reminiscent of his views on all things French, he writes:

I swear by my honour that I can't stand Salzburg and its inhabitants. I mean the native Salzburgians. I find their language – their manners – quite insufferable.

Mozart arrived back in his home city around 15 January 1779, after an absence of sixteen months. They had been the most dramatic months imaginable, and at the same time the most disappointing and frustrating.

On a musical level he had composed several big pieces, but his output had not been prolific. He had the consolation that some of the pieces – the 'Paris' Symphony in particular – had been well received.

But crucially, in not a single city had he been offered paid employment. This, in his father's eyes, was a remarkable failure, and Mozart knew he would have to account for himself.

On a personal level, things could hardly have been worse. His mother had died in Paris, in his care. That was something else he would have to account to his father for. And then, in mourning for his mother, he had been rejected by the woman he wanted to marry.

And now? He was returning to a city he loathed, to work for a man he loathed, in a lowly position and at a pitifully poor salary. It is probably not too much of an exaggeration to say that it was a broken young man who returned to Salzburg at the beginning of the year.

As is always the case when Mozart is with his family, we have scant knowledge of his activities. We know that he stayed in Salzburg for almost two years, and that it was the most mundane existence.

A rare entry by Mozart in a diary kept by his sister gives us an insight into this period, his use of repetition capturing perfectly the humdrum life he was now leading. The entry is dated 27 May 1780: 'At half past seven I went to Mass, or something like that. Then I was at the Lodronpalais,

Joseph Lange

k.k. Hof-Schauspieler
und *SENIOR.*

or something like that. Played cards at Countess Wicka's, or something like that.'[28]

And all the time he was employed as court organist by the detested Archbishop Colloredo, with a commitment to compose new works, in addition to court and chapel duties, at a salary of 450 gulden – not 500, as his father had promised.

At least he fulfilled that commitment to compose. He produced symphonies, concertos, and some of his most sublime church music. He wrote the Coronation Mass (K. 317), and the *Vesperae solennes de confessore* (K. 339), which contains the sublime 'Laudate Dominum'. He also composed the Sinfonia concertante in E flat (K. 364) for violin, viola and orchestra, the first piece of music written by anyone that put the viola on an equal footing with the violin. In this case the likely inspiration came from the fact that Mozart himself was a highly skilled viola player. He played the violin as well, as we know, but in this piece it is as if he is trying to show that the viola, with its deeper, more sonorous tone, can be just as melodic.

In the autumn of 1780 his sister Nannerl fell seriously ill with a severe bronchial infection. Leopold rose to the occasion, once again taking total control, supervising every meal and administering every form of medication.

The atmosphere inside the Tanzmeisterhaus must have been tense, to say the least. It is fair to assume Mozart spent as much time out of the house as he could. But we hear nothing of friends or musical colleagues, with whom he might have spent an evening relaxing, eating and drinking.

He must have been praying for something to turn up, something to rescue him from the banality of his existence. And it did, out of the blue.

A commission came from Karl Theodor, Elector of Bavaria, for a new opera to be put on in Munich. It was to be called *Idomeneo, rè di Creta*. As had happened before, Archbishop Colloredo had had rank pulled on him. He could not refuse the more senior elector.

Mozart was given six weeks' leave of absence to work in Munich on the new opera. He could not get out of Salzburg fast enough. He left on 5 November, once again waved off by his father.

Mozart's spirits soared the moment the carriage trundled out of Salzburg. We know this from the first letter he wrote home to his father three days later from Munich. He says himself:

> *How happy and relieved I felt when I arrived here – Happy because we met with no misfortune on the road, relieved because we could hardly wait to reach our destination.*

In true Mozartian style, he then gives a thoroughly comical description of just how uncomfortable the journey was:

> *I can assure you, none of us was able to sleep even one minute throughout the night, – the kind of carriage we had jolts your very soul out of your body! – and the seats! – hard as a rock! – from Wasserburg on I thought that I wouldn't get my rear end to Munich in one piece! – it was so sore – and I suspect fiery Red – between two stations I sat with my hands pressed against the seat holding my rear suspended in the air.*

This is the Mozart we have come to know and love. I have to say, of all the images we have of the sublime musician, none makes me smile more than

the sight of him, being jolted this way and that by a poorly sprung carriage, his hands clasped on the front of the seat, holding his bottom in the air to avoid it being bruised black and blue – or red.

It seems his father shared the joke. In a rare flash of humour, Leopold responded that, for his part, he would never travel by mail coach if he could avoid it, if only to spare his manhood: 'I prefer my two plum stones.'

In Munich the serious work began, and it was not easy. The libretto had already been written, the singers chosen. Mozart had to work with what he was given. But there was an enormous plus. The orchestra was one of the best in Europe, and most of the principal singers were known to Mozart.

He immediately set about tightening the plot and ordering rewrites of part of the libretto, even down to changing individual words and syllables, to make them more suitable to be set to music. He swiftly turned out passages for rehearsal. He was in his element. He was once more composing an opera, and working with musicians who, for the most part, he knew and respected.

Above

The Mozart family with a portrait of Mozart's mother on the wall, *c.* 1780, by Johann Nepomuk della Croce.

In December the elector himself attended a rehearsal, afterwards coming out with the priceless comment (which Mozart was obviously happy to pass on to his father): 'Who would have thought that such great things could come out of such a small head?'

What is more, Mozart now had the measure of his father. When he complains to Leopold that he has a heavy cold that he cannot shake off, his father at first offers sound advice: keep warm, drink no wine, take a little black powder before going to bed, have some footbaths.

But then Leopold talks about his own health, and Nannerl's. He writes about how sad he is on the eve of what would have been his thirty-third wedding anniversary. And, with total lack of sensitivity, 'If I had been with your Mother, I would like to believe, she would still be alive.'

This might once have thrown Mozart into a deep depression, the guilt demon weighing heavily on his shoulder. Now, though, he is his own man. He does not need to hear such language from his father:

> *I beg you, don't send me such sad letters anymore – because – right now*
> *I need a cheerful spirit, a clear head, and good inspiration for my work,*
> *none of which is possible when one is sad.*

He knows now that the only way to deal with his father is to be direct with him.

Nannerl was recovering from her debilitating illness, and father and daughter planned to come to the premiere of *Idomeneo* in Munich, along with friends from Salzburg. They arrived on 26 January 1781. The dress rehearsal took place the following day, Mozart's twenty-fifth birthday, and on the 29th Mozart's new opera had its premiere.

It was a triumph. Mozart had already written a dozen or so operas, and *Idomeneo* is rightly considered his first truly mature effort. In the decade that was left to him, he would compose ten more, including all his greatest, but it was *Idomeneo* that showed he was, at the age of just twenty-five, a master of the genre. In every aspect of his writing – orchestral colour, melodic line, the fitting of the music perfectly to the characters – he had come of age as an operatic composer.

Idomeneo was performed three times, after which Mozart could relax. He, his father and his sister did exactly that. The Munich Carnival was on, and they happily indulged in the festivities. There was partying, feasting and drinking of wine, and endless dancing.

On one occasion it appears Mozart picked up a prostitute, dancing with her in full view of his father, in what was almost certainly a drunken act of defiance. When Leopold later remonstrated with him, he claimed he had not recognised her for what she was, and even when he did

Left

A page from Mozart's
original score for
Idomeneo.

realise, he felt it only polite to continue in her company, as he explained
in a letter:

> *I could not simply walk away without saying why, and who would want*
> *to let such words fall to someone's face? And in the end, did I not return*
> *her to her seat and dance with others? … Anyway no one can say I saw*
> *her at any other time, or was in her house.*

But the revelries were soon to come to an end. Two months before the
premiere of *Idomeneo*, the entire Habsburg empire had been rocked by the
death in Vienna of the Mother of the Nation, Empress Maria Theresa. In
fact for a time the premiere itself was in doubt.

Now, in late January 1781, Archbishop Colloredo decided to move his
entire household – officials, clerks, cooks, valets, footmen – from Salzburg
to Vienna, in deference to the late empress and in expectation of the full
accession of her son, Emperor Joseph. There was a personal reason too. His
elderly father was seriously ill and unlikely to live long.

The prince-archbishop decided it was time his whole court was properly
in place. That meant summoning the Mozarts back home. Both had seriously
outstayed their leave of absence. Wolfgang had been given six weeks to mount
his opera in Munich; he had been away for four months. Both father and son
were on salaries, and Colloredo wanted them back where they belonged.

Well, not quite. He sent orders to Leopold Mozart to return immediately to Salzburg and resume his duties as deputy kapellmeister. Wolfgang
Mozart he ordered to travel straight to Vienna, to join his retinue there.

Mozart bade his father and sister farewell. They set out for Salzburg, while Mozart left on a direct route for the imperial capital. The journey was no more comfortable than his last one, as he wrote to his father: 'I had gone by mail coach … but by that time my ass and the various parts that lie around it were burning so badly I couldn't bear it any more.'

It would be the last flash of humour for some time. Mozart arrived in Vienna on 16 March 1781. He was to live there for the rest of his life. Over the next ten years he would produce his greatest works. But it would be a difficult decade for him, and the problems began from the day he arrived.

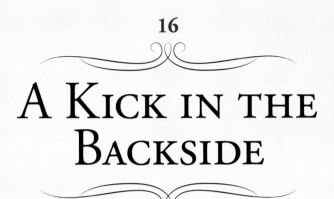

16

A Kick in the Backside

With a sore bottom, and 'dog-tired' from travelling all night, Mozart arrived in Vienna at nine o'clock on the morning of 16 March 1781. At four o'clock that afternoon he was performing for at least twenty persons 'of the highest nobility'. The following day he performed again.

Archbishop Colloredo was driving Mozart from the moment he arrived in Vienna, and Mozart resented it. In fact he resented every aspect of his new life in Vienna. The day after he arrived he wrote to his father bemoaning the fact that he had been given a room in the same building as the archbishop, unlike two other musicians who were lucky enough to be out of Colloredo's sight.

Being in the same building meant he was treated like one of the staff. At the lunch table there sat two valets, two cooks, a pastry chef and – 'little me'. He was made to sit below the valets, though above the cooks at least, indicating where a musician lay in the archbishop's esteem. Mozart's resentment of his treatment oozes from every word of this letter.

Using strong language, he goes on to accuse the archbishop of stealing money from his musicians, and says he has already made his mind up to do something about it:

Today we are to perform at Prince Gallizin's … I'll just have to wait and see whether I will receive some payment. If I get nothing, I will go to the Archbishop and tell him straight out: if he won't allow me to earn something on my own, he will have to give me some extra pay so I won't have to live off my own money.

This is fighting talk, dangerously so. One can only imagine Leopold sinking his head in his hands when he read the letter. His son was determined to get off on the wrong foot. Leopold could see disaster ahead. If his headstrong boy was using that kind of language out loud, he could soon be in serious trouble.

If he stopped to look at the letter carefully, though, one other factor could not fail to have struck him. The letter was a real departure from previous correspondence. No jokes, no puns, the paragraphs orderly and logical, no misspellings, the thoughts focused and organised. And that would remain true of subsequent letters. The language might be strong, but it accurately reflected Mozart's thoughts. He really had grown up.

Mozart had built up a head of steam the moment he arrived in Vienna, and over the ensuing days it intensified. To his father's certain despair, he was now beginning to be deliberately disobedient, to flout flagrantly the strict rules of the archbishop's household.

He complained about the seating arrangements at lunch. Why should he sit beneath valets, whose duties included lighting chandeliers and opening doors? Why should he not sit at the table of the illustrious Count Arco, the archbishop's chamberlain? (There is a name that will re-enter the story very soon.) His complaints were ignored.

Sadly none of Leopold's letters have survived – perhaps Mozart destroyed them in anger – but we can surmise from his replies the language Leopold used. To Leopold's mollifying suggestion that it tickles the archbishop's pride to have him around, he is withering:

> *What you are saying about the Archbishop is pretty much true. But of what use is it to me? – I cannot live on that – and believe me he won't let my* light shine *– what distinction is he really giving me?*

Within a week he took matters into his own hands. He was supposed to go to a certain nobleman's house under escort with other musicians. Once there, a lackey would announce their arrival and escort them into the aristocrat's presence.

Mozart was having none of it. He left late, arrived late, went straight upstairs, brushed past the lackey, entered the salon and walked straight up to the nobleman. The other two musicians, he reports, were cowering against a wall.

His letter went on to list a number of counts and countesses with whom he has dined – without the archbishop's permission – before bluntly informing his father of his ultimate aim, which must have seemed to Leopold to be not just unrealistic, but arrogant: 'My main goal right now is to meet the emperor in some agreeable fashion. I am absolutely determined that he *should get to know me.*'

Mozart was treading a dangerous path, alienating all those around him. Word was certain to reach the archbishop, his employer and paymaster. Back in Salzburg, Leopold fretted that his son's impetuous behaviour would cost him his job – a job that he, Leopold, had strived so hard to get for him. And if he lost his income, what then? How would he make enough money to live on?

Over the following weeks Mozart's anger and frustration simmered. Knowing the argument would hit home with his father, he detailed how the archbishop was actually causing him to *lose* money:

> *How much do you suppose I would get if I were to give a concert of my own? – The Archbishop is a great hindrance to me here, for he has done me out of at least a hundred ducats, which I would certainly have made by giving a concert in the theatre … But this arch-booby of ours will not allow it.*

And it is not long before Leopold read the words he must have dreaded his son would write, sooner or later:

Above

A view of eighteenth-century Vienna, looking out from the Belvedere Palace.

Were I to leave the archbishop's service, I would give a grand concert, take four pupils, and in a year I should have got on so well in Vienna that I could make a least a thousand thalers a year.

Leopold could not have been surprised. Leaving the archbishop's service had been on his son's mind since they were together in Munich. He must have heard it many times, brushing it off each time. Now he feared – dreaded – his son meant it.

Mean it he certainly did. Matters came to a head on Wednesday, 9 May. Mozart had a face-to-face meeting with the man he detested: 'I hate the Archbishop to the point of madness.' Insults were thrown in both directions.

Archbishop Colloredo shouted at Mozart that he was a knave, a slovenly fellow, a scoundrel, a lousy rogue, a cretin. Mozart – and we can only imagine the look of utter horror on Colloredo's face – gave back as good as he got.

Colloredo asked Mozart if he was threatening him, and if he was, there was the door, right over there: 'I don't want to have anything to do with such miserable scum any more – get out!'

At last, I said – and I don't want to have anything to do with you either … I'll give it to you in writing tomorrow.

Knowing his father would be shocked and appalled, he appealed rather touchingly to his sensitivity:

Now, dearest father, tell me whether I didn't say all these things rather too late than too early? – Listen, my Honour is worth more to me than anything else, and I know the same is true of you.

It is the culmination of weeks of insults and mistreatment. Mozart had taken so much, and had decided he would take no more. Without doubt it was the first time a subordinate had spoken to the archbishop in such a way. It was simply inconceivable that a mere musician – 'I didn't know I was a valet'* was how Mozart put it to his father – would stand face to face with a prince-archbishop and exchange insults.

But Mozart had done it. He had well and truly burned his boats. Or more accurately, he hadn't quite done so, but he was very soon about to.

The afore-mentioned Count Arco tried to mediate, initially refusing to accept Mozart's letter of resignation. He told Mozart he could not resign without first obtaining his father's consent. This must have infuriated Mozart, who was making his own decisions as a fully-grown man, but he

---

* *Ich wusste nicht dass ich Kammerdiener wäre.*

reported the count's words to Leopold, as well as his riposte that he knew his duty towards his father better than the count.

He pleaded with his father to understand why he had resigned, at the same time making it clear – in understated and conciliatory language – that whatever his father's view, the resignation would stand.

The trauma of all this was taking its toll on Mozart's health. He spared his father no detail:

> All the things this splendid servant of god dished out, had such a terrific effect on my body that in the evening I had to leave the opera in the middle of the first Act and go home so I could lie down – I felt quite hot and feverish – my body was trembling all over – and I staggered about in the street like a drunkard.

Leopold, predictably, was furious and unmoved. He sent his son what must have been a long and stinging letter – his letters have not survived, but we know from Mozart's reply the general tone of what his father had said.

Now we see just how far Mozart had come emotionally. He was not standing for his father's intransigence. He had stood up to the prince-archbishop, so he could most certainly stand up to his own father. He uses language to his father he has never used before:

> I don't know what to write first, my dearest father, because I have not recovered from my Bewilderment and, in fact, will not be able to do so ever, if you continue to think and write as you just did – I must confess that there was not a single sign in your letter by which I can recognise my father! – A father perhaps, but not the Best, the most loving father who would be concerned for his honour and the honour of his children – in other words, not my father.

Not my father. Leopold must have blanched when he read this. With these few short sentences he must have realised he had lost control over his son. Until now he had guided every aspect of his son's life. But that boy was now a man of twenty-five, alone in the imperial capital, and making his own decisions about his future.

There was more. Leopold had insisted that if Mozart went through with his threat to leave the archbishop's employ, he should return to Salzburg immediately, where he would be able to find work. And, although it was unspoken, Leopold would again be able to control his son's activities.

Once again Mozart was having none of it:

> In Salzburg – at least for me – there isn't a penny's worth of stimulation. There are many with whom I don't wish to associate – and most of the

"Mozart had taken so much, and had decided he would take no more."

others, well, they do not think that I am good enough for them; not ex-actly an inspiration for my talent! ... In Salzburg I long for 100 different forms of entertainment, but here – not a single one – for just to be in Vienna is entertainment enough.

Mozart was his own man in every respect. No one but he would decide his future, and his father had no choice but to accept that.

But then Leopold did something really underhand. He wrote to Count Arco behind his son's back to find out what was going on, and the count summoned Mozart to tell him. Mozart wrote to his father with details of that meeting. He did not actually castigate his father for what he had done – though he might reasonably have done so – but he left his father in no doubt that he stood up for himself, against both of them.

Mozart quotes Count Arco's words, which, knowing what we know now, have relegated the count's reputation to that of pompous shallow fool:

He told me then: believe me, you allow yourself to be dazzled too easily; – a person's fame is of short duration here – in the beginning one is given a lot of accolades, and one earns good money, that's true – but for how long? – after a few Months the Viennese will want something new.

The count decided to spare Mozart nothing, but again – as Mozart reports to his father – he was not taking the insults lightly:

The Archbishop thinks you are a thoroughly Conceited person. I believe it, I said, because that is how I behave towards him. I treat people the way they treat me – When I see that someone is contemptuous of me and puts me down, I can be as proud as a Baboon –

Another distinguished figure who most certainly had never been spoken to like that, certainly not by a lowly musician.

We get the impression that Mozart was enjoying himself. He really no longer cared whom he insulted. If he had made an enemy of the top man, the prince-archbishop, what did it matter if he upset his underling?

Mozart knew he was different from everyone else, even from his own father. He was blessed with genius. He had heard his father use that word since his earliest years, and he had come to accept it. He knew it was true. He had only to sit at the keyboard, and anybody, everybody, from kings and emperors down, would marvel.

There now occurred one of the most famous – notorious – moments in Mozart's entire life, one that has entered mythology. It is all based on a single sentence he wrote to his father in a letter of 9 June 1781.

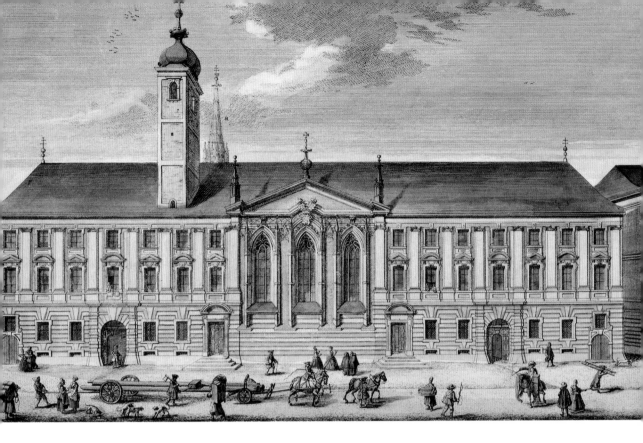

Above
Church of the Teutonic
Order, Vienna, where
the infamous kick in the
backside occurred.

A week after that meeting, Count Arco again summoned Mozart to come
and see him, on the pretext of wanting to show him a letter from his father.
Mozart came to the meeting armed with a formal letter of resignation, and
asked to be allowed to present it to Archbishop Colloredo himself. Count
Arco refused. And then this, with Mozart referring to himself in the third
person, as if even he cannot quite believe it happened to him:

> *Finally, as this fellow is forced to hand in his petition himself, instead of*
> *at least granting him access, you throw him out of the door and give him*
> *a kick in his Backside.*

We know it was not just a form of words, because later in the letter Mozart writes:

> *If he really thinks well of me, then let him persuade me with reason, but*
> *not throw words such as 'lout' and 'knave' at me, and then throw me out*
> *of the door with a kick in the ass.*

And in another letter four days later:

> *He could have advised me to forward my petition to the archbishop …*
> *he could have suggested any number of things – No – he throws me out*

Right
Statue of Mozart
in the Imperial
Palace Gardens,
Vienna, erected
in 1898.

of the door and gives me a kick in the backside – Well, that means in straightforward German that Salzburg no longer exists for me; except to find a good opportunity to administer to the Herr Count a kick in the ass in return, even if it should happen on a public street.

It has been called the most infamous kick in the backside in the history of art. Wolfgang Amadé Mozart was finally, once and for all, dismissed from Archbishop Colloredo's service with a kick in the backside from his chamberlain.

Leopold's son had, in effect, dismissed himself from service at court, in the process insulting to their faces the most important and influential people in his life.

Any hope of re-employment was out of the question. Not only that, he was refusing direct orders to return to Salzburg. Leopold was in despair. We know it from Mozart's letters to him, which are well written, thoughtful and rational. Leopold was dealing with a young man now, and a young man who knew his mind.

A point which his son was about to reiterate. Could things get any worse for Leopold? Yes, they could.

Mozart, by leaving the employ of the court, had to relinquish his room in the archbishop's residence. He was out on the street with nowhere to go.

Well, not exactly. Mozart knew exactly what he was doing. In fact he had taken action some weeks before. Buried deep in one of his letters was the sentence:

> I quickly gathered my belongings into my trunk – and old Mad. Weber was kind enough to offer me her home – where I now have a pretty room and am among helpful people who lend a hand with things one might need in a hurry, the sort of thing one just doesn't have when one lives alone.

Leopold was on to it immediately. He knew exactly what was going on. The life of the Weber family had changed dramatically since Aloysia rejected Mozart's proposal of marriage so coldly in Munich.

Fridolin Weber, the father, had died suddenly. Aloysia, as we know, had moved to Vienna where she was in demand as an operatic soprano and was now married to the actor and artist Joseph Lange. Frau Weber and her three unmarried daughters had followed Aloysia to Vienna, where they took an apartment on the second floor of the exotically named Zum Augen Gottes ('God's Eye') building, earning income by taking in lodgers.

Mozart had now moved in with them, and Leopold was nothing short of apoplectic. He had already lost control of every aspect of his son's professional life as a musician; he had failed to persuade him to return to Salzburg; now he was getting involved with young women again, and who could tell where that might lead?

To marriage, obviously, and a disastrous marriage at that. So thought Leopold. We know it, because it caused Mozart to respond to him, with a touch of facetiousness:

> What you're saying about the Weber family, I can assure you it's not what you think – I know I was a fool about Frau Lange, that is true, but that's the way it is when you are in love! – I really loved her, and even now she is not indifferent to me – it's lucky for me that her husband is a jealous Fool and won't let her go anywhere, so I see her very rarely – trust

me when I say that old Mad. Weber is a very helpful woman and that I cannot return her helpfulness proportionately, because I just don't have the time.

Leopold was not convinced, causing Mozart to write again:

Just because I am living with them, people assume I'm marrying the daughter; no one said anything about us being in love, they conveniently skipped that part. Their logic is: I take a room in this house, I get married – If I've ever thought about not getting married, it's definitely now! – The last thing I wish for is a rich wife, but even if I could make my fortune by marriage right now, I could not oblige, because I have too many other things on my mind – God has not given me my Talent so that I should hitch it to a woman and waste my Young life in idleness – I am just beginning to live; am I to bring bitterness into my life through my own doing? I have nothing against the state of matrimony, but at the moment it would be a disaster for me.

And he goes on, and on, and on, protesting too much. For he is being disingenuous: to say he has fallen in love might be putting it a touch too strongly. But he has developed a strong attachment to his former love Aloysia's younger sister, Constanze.

Leopold must have thrown his hands up in despair.

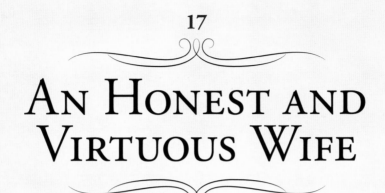

17

An Honest and Virtuous Wife

When I say that 'love' might be too strong a word, I am basing that on what Mozart himself wrote. He does use the word, true, but it comes in a short and rather pat sentence at the very end of a lengthy description which suggests affection rather than love.

It is possible he was deliberately downplaying Constanze's virtues, lest his father think he had once again become infatuated. But his description of her, I believe, sounds as though he meant it:

I must make you better acquainted with the character of my beloved Konstanze[*] – she is not ugly, but also not really beautiful; – her whole beauty consists of two little black eyes and a graceful figure. She has no great wit but enough common sense to fulfil her duties as a wife and mother …

And to nip in the bud any adverse reports that might have reached Leopold:

She is not extravagant in her appearance, rumours to that effect are totally false; – to the contrary, she is in the habit of dressing very simply … It's perfectly true that she would like to dress attractively and cleanly but not necessarily in the latest fashion – And most of the things a woman needs, she can make herself; indeed, she does her own hair every day; – she knows all about housekeeping and has the kindest heart in the world –

---

[*] Mozart varied his spelling of Constanze. To begin with she was Constanze; later he increasingly wrote her name as Konstanze.

And finally:

I love her and she loves me with all her heart – now tell me whether I could wish for a better wife?

Leopold must have been tempted to answer that. He could no doubt have named several young Salzburg women he would rather his son marry.

Mozart had been corresponding with his father for several months before he finally came out with that last sentence. He knew of the rumours reaching Salzburg. References to his amorous pursuits were buried in long letters about other matters – musical activities, aristocratic contacts – and always consisted of evasion and denial. This, written on 25 July 1781 and replete with double negatives, is a perfect example:

I am not saying that I am unsociable with the mademoiselle in the house, I mean the one I'm supposed to be married to already, I'm not saying I never speak to her – but I am not in love with her – Yes, I joke around with her and have fun whenever time allows, and that's only in the evening when I'm taking supper at home … If I had to marry every lady with whom I've been joking around, I would easily have collected 200 wives by now –

It seems likely his father accused him directly of truly unsavoury behaviour. Mozart was not afraid to confront the allegation head on:

I have too great a horror and disgust, dread and fear of diseases, in fact I like my health too much to play around with whores. I swear that I never had anything to do with a woman of that sort – If it happened, I would not have kept it from you.*

He leaves his father in no doubt, though, in a man-to-man sort of way, that he has physical needs which need to be sated:

The voice of nature speaks in me as loud as in any man, louder perhaps than in some big, robust brute of a fellow … I cannot think of anything more essential to me than a wife.

By December 1781 he had made up his mind to marry Constanze. He knew his father would take some convincing, but he was in no hurry. Suddenly he had become very busy.

In the first place, word had inevitably got out about how this young man from provincial Salzburg had stood up to the prince-archbishop – who was

Left

Constanze Mozart, 1782, painted by her brother-in-law Joseph Lange.

---

*Which gives credence to the supposition that he did no more than dance with the prostitute in his father's presence at the Munich Carnival.

in any case not a popular man – hurling insults back at him, and how he had then done much the same thing to his chamberlain.

He was already well known in certain aristocratic quarters as a remarkable young musician, something of a dandy, hair always immaculately dressed, clothes rather fine, very small of stature, with an instant grin and infectious laugh.

Mozart found himself increasingly in demand to perform in salons and halls, and indeed to have lunch with certain aristocratic ladies. He was good company, with none of the inbuilt snobbishness and class awareness of the Viennese. I can offer no direct evidence for this, but I am sure they would have been entranced by his Salzburg accent, his 'country' way of talking, his use of Bavarian dialect, words, expressions – much as a Londoner might enjoy listening to the lilt of a West Country accent.

Soon he was a regular guest in the highest salons in the city, and his hosts knew better than to patronise him, or underestimate his worth. One can imagine there was laughter at the prince-archbishop's expense at these gatherings, and jokes about the relative merits of musicians, when compared to valets and cooks.

And then, a glittering prize. He was commissioned to write a new opera. It would be his first work for the Vienna imperial court theatre. It was, as with *Idomeneo*, exactly what he needed, and it had arrived at exactly the right moment. It would not have come as a complete shock to him. He had been lobbying the director of German opera in the city, who was also a librettist, to commission an opera.

When it was announced that there was to be a royal visit from Russia later in the year – Grand Duke Paul, son of Catherine the Great, and heir to the Russian throne – the librettist, one Gottlieb Stephanie, sought out Mozart.

This is where we now have real evidence of Mozart the composer. From the very start, he takes control of the project. He has already worked enough on opera to know that it is the composer who must lead. No more will he allow others to dictate what he must do, or even influence it.

Nothing in opera is as important as the music, he believes, and so the libretto must be at the service of the music.

He spells it out to his father in no uncertain terms:

I would say that in an opera the poetry must be altogether the obedient daughter of the music. Why are Italian comic operas popular everywhere, in spite of the miserable libretti? Because the music reigns supreme, and when one listens to it all else is forgotten. An opera is sure of success when the plot is well worked out, the words written solely for the music, and not shoved in here and there to suit some miserable rhyme.

This is a wonderful insight into the thinking of a young composer, twenty-five years of age, who, in the following decade would compose the greatest operas yet written.

Time was short, and Mozart threw himself at the project. And here occurred a happy confluence of his professional and private life: the main female character in the opera, by coincidence, was named Konstanze. The first aria that Mozart set to music for her was '*Ach, ich liebte, war so glücklich*' ('Oh I was in love, and so happy').

Mozart was not going to let this go by. He sent a copy of the aria to his father, which had been written out by Constanze. It appears he did not tell Leopold it was his future wife who had written it, and Leopold could not have recognised her hand.

But it is a perfect example of how Mozart happily entwined his two lives. It is easy to imagine him working furiously on the score, Constanze at his side, breaking off to laugh and joke with her, share a coffee, no doubt a frequent kiss. The act of composition came so easily and naturally to Mozart that what might distract a lesser composer was all part of the process to him.

Just three weeks after receiving the libretto, Mozart had finished the first act. Then events intervened. The visit of the Russian Grand Duke was postponed, and it was decided not to stage the new opera until the following autumn. The pressure was off.

There is no doubt in my mind Mozart could have met the deadline, but even he was grateful for the extra time. The opera was to be called *Die Entführung aus dem Serail* (*The Abduction from the Seraglio*), and pandered to the fascination of Viennese aristocracy for all things Turkish.[*]

The plot concerned the attempt of the hero Belmonte to rescue his beloved Konstanze from Pasha Selim's harem. The rescue fails, but the magnanimous Pasha recognises true love and pardons the couple.

Musically the opera shows how easily Mozart could adapt to other styles. He uses a richer orchestration here than ever before, adding bass drum, cymbals, triangle and piccolo to give an authentic Turkish feel to the music.

The opera premiered on 16 July 1782 at the Vienna Burgtheater, the most prestigious of Vienna's state theatres, situated right alongside the Hofburg Palace, residence of the emperor.[†]

It was a huge success, and brought Mozart in the sum of 1,200 florins, three times more than his paltry salary in Salzburg.[‡] Now he really could tell his father that the move to Vienna had been a wise decision, and he was a man of some substance. In other words, fit to keep a wife.

---

[*] The Habsburg empire's largest trading partner was the Ottoman empire. Turkish customs – clothes, coffee, spices – permeated Vienna, as did the rhythms and sound of Turkish music. One of Mozart's most famous pieces for piano would be the *Rondo alla turca*, the third movement of his Piano Sonata No. 11 in A major (K. 331), written soon after the opera.

[†] It is likely that this is the opera that caused the emperor to say to Mozart, 'Too many notes, Herr Mozart', bringing Mozart's famous reply, 'Just as many notes as are required, Your Majesty, no more, no less', although I have seen it attributed to at least two other Mozart operas. Cited in *Die Mozart-Autographe der Staatsbibliothek zu Berlin*, Exhibition notes, Berlin 2006, by Roland Dieter Schmidt-Hensel, State Library Berlin, it has been subject to many slightly varied translations.

[‡] Approximately £30,000.

Above

The original Burgtheater, where *Die Entführung aus dem Serail* premiered in 1782.

The path to marriage was still not smooth, and it was made a lot bumpier by the fact that there was a rat in the pack. Leopold had an informer in Vienna, a man with a scurrilous tongue who kept him informed of his son's amorous goings-on. And how had this man described Mozart's intended bride? As a slut (*ein Luder*).

Mozart found out about it, or more likely Leopold threw the accusation back at him. On 22 December 1781 Mozart sat down to write his father a long and difficult letter. It took him four days, and was his attempt to rebut, point by point, the accusations his father had hurled at him.

The informer, Mozart knew full well, was that 'arch-scoundrel' Winter. Peter von Winter was a violinist in the Mannheim-Munich orchestra, a composer whose operas had met with some success, who happened to be in Vienna at the time, studying with Antonio Salieri.

We do not know why Winter took it on himself to keep Leopold informed. He was roughly the same age as Mozart. Maybe it was jealousy that Mozart had been awarded the valuable court commission for *Die Entführung*. Whatever the motive, he was making life for Mozart very difficult indeed.

He somehow found out that Constanze's family had made Mozart sign a pre-marriage contract, under which he promised to marry her within three years, or pay her 300 gulden a year compensation,[*] and he informed Leopold.

Leopold clearly challenged Mozart on this, and in response he feigned total ignorance of what his father meant:

> I am asking you to explain some words from your last letter to me: 'you probably will not believe that I know of a proposal that was made to you and to which you did not respond, at the time I found out about it'.

But he knew his father had seen through this, and so he wrote:

> I will make an honest confession to you, convinced that you will forgive me for taking this step because I know that if you had been in my situation you would have acted the same – The only thing I'm asking your forgiveness for is that I haven't informed you about this earlier.

Since Fridolin Weber's sudden death, a guardian had been appointed to look after his daughter's interests. This man, a financial administrator with the court theatre by the name of Johann Thorwart, had become alarmed at Mozart's intimacy with Constanze, and had expressed his misgivings to her mother.

It was his recommendation that Mozart should sign a pre-marriage contract, to establish whether his intentions were sincere.[†] Frau Weber acquiesced. So did Mozart. Without informing his father, he signed.

In his eyes, this was not a contract, but more 'the written assurances of my honourable intentions'. And he vented his anger against his father's informant:

> Certain busybodies and loud-mouthed gentlemen like Herr Winter must have given an earful about me to this guardian, who doesn't even know me at all, that he should be wary of me – that I had no secure income – that I was far too intimate with her – that I might probably jilt her – and that the girl would therefore be ruined, etc. All this made him smell a rat.

Mozart goes into great detail about how the guardian filled Constanze's mother's ears with scandalous lies about him. He then had a face-to-face meeting with the guardian, which did not go well, and the guardian advised Frau Weber to forbid all association between them.

---

[*] Approximately £7,500.

[†] Yes, a forerunner of the Hollywood pre-nup.

He tries to reassure his father by telling him Frau Weber is firmly on his side:

> *The mother told him: [my] entire association with [Constanze] consists in coming to their house and – I can't forbid him my house – he is too good a friend for that – a friend to whom I am obliged in many ways – I am satisfied and I trust him – you must work out an agreement yourself.*

But the guardian simply won't listen, and makes it a condition of the relationship continuing that Mozart sign a pre-marriage contract.

In a classic line, he says that signing the contract was the easiest thing he had ever had to do, because he knew he would never have to pay those 300 gulden, 'for I shall never forsake her'.

He saved his most powerful point until the end. Constanze herself would have none of it:

> *What did this heavenly girl do as soon as her father [i.e. guardian] had left? – She demanded that her mother give her the document – then said to me* – dear Mozart! I don't need any written assurances from you, I believe what you say – *and she tore up the writ – This gesture endeared my dear Konstanze to me even more.*

With a final flourish that Winter himself had advised him to drop all ideas of marriage, and take a mistress – 'You can afford it!' – he signs off the letter in the usually affectionate way, convinced he has put his father's mind at rest.

A vain hope. As far as Leopold was concerned, the pre-marriage contract was clear evidence of a conspiracy to entrap his son. His anger thoroughly aroused, and with no danger of understatement, he rants that both the guardian and Frau Weber 'should be put in chains, made to sweep the streets, and have boards hung round their necks bearing the words, "Seducers of Youth"'.

Mozart might have been set on making Constanze his wife, but it was going to be an uphill struggle getting his father to give their marriage his blessing.

At times, it was an uphill struggle even for the couple themselves. From Mozart's point of view, it was unthinkable that he could go ahead with marriage without his father's approval. For Constanze, she was aware her guardian was set firmly against it, and despite Mozart's reassurances in his letters, it was likely her mother was not fully supportive either.

Tensions between the couple were inevitable. Several times the engagement actually ended, and it was Constanze who broke if off each time. The most serious break came when Mozart displayed jealous anger at her high

"Tensions between them were inevitable. Several times the engagement actually ended."

spiritedness at a party that he had not attended. Constanze was at the house of Baroness von Waldstätten, and in a moment of high jinks both she and the baroness had allowed 'some Chapeaux' (*sic*) – a young rogue – to measure their calves with a ribbon.

To make matters worse in Mozart's eyes, Constanze had laughingly told her sisters what had happened *in his presence*, which was how he learned of it. He clearly flew into a rage, in effect accusing her of immoral behaviour, causing Constanze to retaliate, and in front of her sisters to call the engagement off.

Later on the same day, Mozart writes a letter to Constanze, which is a mixture of anger but also a plea for forgiveness. He begins by attempting to justify his anger, and administering what amounts to a lecture:

> *No woman intent upon her honour does that sort of thing – I do understand the* maxime *that when you are with others, you do as others do – but one has to think about certain related matters – whether it is a gathering of good friends and acquaintances? – whether you are a child or a young woman of* marriageable age *– but especially, whether you are already engaged to be married.*

Mozart has turned into his father. This is exactly the kind of language Leopold uses to him. He then pens a line that is thoroughly insulting to the baroness:

> *If it's true that the Baroness permitted the same thing to be done to her, well, that's something entirely different because she is a woman past her prime who cannot possibly excite anybody any more.*

Baroness von Waldstätten was thirty-eight.

He dispenses what amounts to fatherly, and rather absurd, advice. If Constanze positively could not resist playing along with the others, then she should have taken the ribbon and measured her calves herself. That, he rails, is what any honourable woman would have done in similar circumstances.

Having got it off his chest, he makes a valiant attempt at reconciliation:

> *But it's over now – and a mere acknowledgement of this unwise exhibition would have been enough to make everything all right and – if you don't take it amiss, dearest friend – would still make it all right – You can see from this how much I love you – I don't flare up like you – I think – I reflect – and I feel – If you, too, can feel – if you allow your feelings to come forth – then I know for sure that on this very day I can say to myself confidently: Konstanze is the virtuous, Honourable – sensible and truly beloved of that Trustworthy and well-meaning*
>
> *Mozart*

Despite the rather double-edged nature of those last few lines, it appears to have done the trick. The engagement was back on.

With all this going on, the turmoil of an on-off engagement, his father's obdurate refusal to sanction the marriage, Mozart is working flat out – 'I must just spend the night on it, that is the only way' – on his new opera, *Die Entführung*.

The opening, as we know, was a triumph, and this emboldens Mozart to address his father in more direct tones regarding his marriage. Buried in his words is an admission that he and Constanze have already consummated their relationship, therefore they have no option but to marry:

> *I must implore you, implore you for all you hold dear in the world: please give me your consent so that I can marry my dear Konstanze – Don't think it is only for the sake of getting married – if it were for that reason alone, I'd be glad to wait a little longer – However, I feel that it is absolutely necessary on account of my honour as well as that of my girl, but also on account of my health and peace of mind.*

His letter has crossed with another angry rejection from his father. He is all the more hurt because his father has not acknowledged the success of the new opera. No congratulations for that, nor thanks for the fact that – although fully occupied with the opera – he found time to compose a symphony hurriedly for the Haffner family in Salzburg at his father's request.*

Things were not going well on the domestic front in Vienna either. Constanze's mother was clearly no more in favour of the marriage than Mozart's father, and Constanze had fled from the family apartment to stay with her friend (and accomplice in the calf-measuring 'crime') Baroness Waldstätten.

Frau Weber resorted to extreme action, and threatened to call the police to have Constanze forcibly returned home. We know this because Mozart wrote to the Baroness in despair, asking for her advice on how to resolve the matter. (She might have been less inclined to give it, had she known of his unflattering comments about her age.)

The letter is undated – unusual for Mozart – and is, perhaps, a sign of his desperation. So, too, is this sentence: 'If such an action [calling the police] is legal here, I would know of no better way to avert it than by marrying Constanze tomorrow morning.'

Which is, pretty much, what he did. Mozart now decided to think the unthinkable, and act on it. It might not have been the very next morning, but on 2 August he and Constanze went to confession and took

---

*The 'Haffner' Symphony (K. 385) is today one of Mozart's best-known symphonies.

Right

St Stephen's Cathedral, Vienna, where Mozart and Constanze married.

Communion together. On the following day their marriage contract was signed and witnessed.

On 4 August 1782 Mozart and Constanze were married in St Stephen's Cathedral. Only a small group was present, and it seems at least one rift had been healed, or at least papered over. Constanze's mother and her younger sister Sophie were there, as well as the daughters' guardian who had caused so much trouble. Mozart's best man was a surgeon-barber whom he had known for many years, and a district councillor acted as witness.

It was, as Mozart wrote to his father three days later, an emotional scene: 'When we were joined together, my wife and I began to cry – everybody was touched by that, even the priest; – they all wept when they saw how deeply moved we were in our hearts.'

That evening Baroness Waldstätten, who had clearly acted – successfully – as mediator, put on a wedding feast, which Mozart described as 'more princely than baronial'.

He had finally taken matters into his own hands, and married his Constanze. It was the only way to quell disputatious voices, in both Salzburg and Vienna. It appears they had been quelled in Vienna; the same was not entirely true in Salzburg.

Two days after the wedding, Mozart received a letter from his father. The good news, if it could be so called, was that Leopold was resigned to his son's marriage. However, he still refused to give his blessing. Worse still, he made it clear he believed Mozart had lied to Constanze about the Mozart family wealth, and as a result she was only out to get her hands on it.

Mozart was incensed. He wrote calmly, but we can feel the fury in his words:

You are very much mistaken about your son if you think him capable of a dishonest deed –

My dear Konstanze, now, thank god, my wedded wife, has long known my situation and what I can expect from you – However, her friendship and love for me are so great that she gladly – and with the greatest joy sacrificed her entire future for me – and my destiny.

He remains polite towards his father, but the language is formal and without affection. At the end, he holds out the prospect of bringing his wife to Salzburg to meet her father-in-law and sister-in-law:

– and I wager – I wager – that you will rejoice in my happiness once you get to know her! – what else could possibly happen if in your eyes, just as in mine, a right-thinking, honest, virtuous, and amiable wife remains a blessing for her husband –

Well, those words come *almost* at the end. They are followed by a paragraph on how the new symphony, the 'Haffner', should be played – the outer movements 'as fast as possible' – as if, for all the world, the letter was nothing out of the ordinary.

Final proof, if it were needed, that Mozart has finally, at last, once and for all, broken away from his father. He was already his own musician; he is truly now his own man too.

Not that that is going to make things any easier, as far as relations with his father are concerned.

18

RETURN TO SALZBURG

As the year 1783 began, Wolfgang Amadé Mozart (as he most often called himself) could reflect with considerable satisfaction on his situation. There was no question about it; he was Vienna's most popular composer. The likes of Gluck and Salieri, both far senior to him in the Viennese musical hierarchy, could only watch. He was in heavy demand to perform in the salons of the highest nobility, and it was only a matter of time before new commissions – surely, soon, another opera – came in.

And he was a married man, living with his wife Constanze in a spacious apartment in the fashionable Hohe Brücke. He was approaching his twenty-seventh birthday. There seemed no reason why he could not look forward to a long and successful career.

Mozart, from the time of his arrival in Vienna, had cut an elegant figure, having first acquired a taste for smart clothes when he was presented as a child with formal court clothes by Empress Maria Theresa. He was a frequent guest in the highest salons, and he knew how to dress appropriately. Perhaps it was partly in compensation for his lack of height. He stood around five feet four inches in adulthood.

Perhaps, too, in compensation for his looks. There are no contemporary accounts remarking on his fine features. In fact the reverse is more often true. He was variously described as small, pock-marked, with a large nose, a head that was larger than would be expected on such a small body, protruding yet bright eyes. He did, though, have nice hair and refined hands.

He also seems to have had an unusually formed left ear. I say 'seems', because some thirty years after his death an anonymous artist drew an abnormally shaped ear, with a normal one alongside it. Under the normal one is written 'A normal ear' (*ein gewöhnliches Ohr*). Under the abnormal one the words 'My ear' ('*Mein Ohr*') are written, but the word 'Mein' has been crossed out, and 'Mozart's' written in.

The Mozart is almost certainly Franz Xaver Wolfgang, youngest son of the composer, who inherited considerable music talent. In the first substantial biography of his father, written nearly forty years after his death, the drawing of the abnormally shaped ear is reproduced, saying that it belonged to Franz Xaver, and that he inherited it from his father.

Given how rapidly the young Wolfgang Mozart's fame spread across Europe, it is surprising how few portraits of him there are done from life. I have reproduced the ones we know to be authentic (as far as that is possible) in this book, and they seem so varied one has to wonder if the artists were looking at the same individual.

By far the best-known portrait, and the one that is ubiquitous in Salzburg, on everything from chocolate and mugs to books and programmes of his music, shows him facing to the right, head half turned towards us, in neat wig, bright red jacket, and coloured ruff. (See overleaf.)

It is the single image by which we know Mozart best today. Yet it was painted from memory eighteen years after his death.

In 2008 an exciting discovery was made. A painting was unearthed, showing a similar-looking figure, facing to the left this time, in a red jacket with white ruff. He wears an elegant grey wig, and the large nose has a marked bridge.

All the evidence points to this being a portrait of Mozart painted in 1783, given what we know of his love for fine clothes. In September 1782 he wrote to one of his patrons expressing a desire for a beautiful red coat he has seen, which is worth it 'just for the buttons that I've been hankering after for some time … They're mother-of-pearl with some white stones around the edge and a beautiful yellow stone in the centre.' The patron promised to acquire it for him.

The description broadly matches the one in this portrait, and might well be the one that was painted from memory nearly twenty years later.

Perhaps to clinch it, this newly discovered portrait was owned by a descendant of Johann Lorenz Hagenauer, the Mozarts' landlord in Salzburg. It is painted in oils, measures nineteen inches by fourteen, and is now owned by an American collector who has insured it for £2 million.

Proof of the care Mozart took over his appearance comes in a letter he wrote to his sister Nannerl the previous year. His day begins early, with

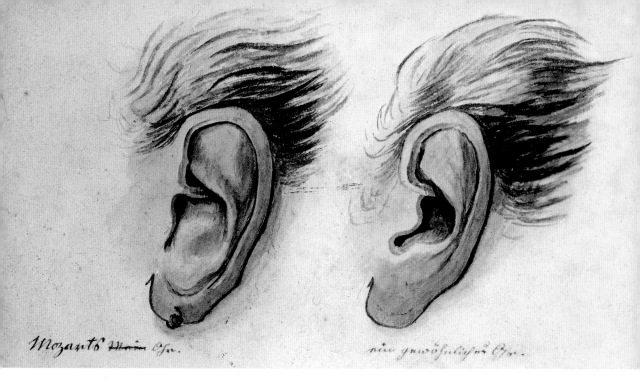

Mozarts ~~Horn~~ *Ohr.*   *ein gewöhnliches Ohr.*

considerable time spent on dressing properly. It gives a fascinating insight into his composing habits too:

> *At 6 o'clock in the morning I'm already done with my hair; at 7 I'm fully dressed; – then I compose until 9 o'clock; from 9 to 1 o'clock I give lessons – Then I Eat, unless I'm invited by someone who doesn't eat lunch until 2 or 3 o'clock as, for instance, today and tomorrow at the Countess Zizi and Countess Thun – I cannot get back to work before 5 or 6 o'clock – and quite often I can't get back at all, because I have to be at a performance; if I can, I write until 9 o'clock.*

On nights when he has to attend a performance, he tries to do a little composing before going to bed: 'Often enough I go on writing until 1 o'clock – and then, of course, up again at 6 o'clock –'

It is a long working day. But then, for Mozart, this is not work. He is doing what to him is as natural as breathing. How else, with all the trauma and tension of an on-off courtship, would he have been able to compose no fewer than three piano concertos, Nos. 11–13 (к. 413–15) during the winter of 1782–3?

The spur to this was the realisation that performing his own concertos at the piano, and directing the orchestra, was becoming increasingly popular with audiences, making theatre managements eager to book him. Over the coming years that would become one of the main sources of his income.

And what of the city in which he would now live out the remaining years of his life? At the crossroads of Europe, Vienna attracted travellers from

Above

Anonymous drawing of Mozart's 'unusually formed left ear'.

Overleaf

Left: The image by which we know Mozart best, painted from memory eighteen years after his death.

Right: A portrait of Mozart believed to have been painted in 1783.

the four corners of the continent. With them they brought their national customs, costumes, language and, most importantly for our story, music.

When words were not safe in a Europe soon to witness revolution and regicide in Paris, what was safe? Music. Who can say that music is seditious? And so different rhythms, exotic sounds, were to be heard on street corners in Vienna, as well as in theatres and salons.

A Bavarian by the name of Johann Pezzl, born in the same year as Mozart, gives us a vivid description of the Habsburg capital in the years 1786 to 1790 – exactly the years Mozart lived in the city – in his *Skizze von Wien* ('Sketch of Vienna'). No city, not even London, could rival its diversity:

> *Here you can often meet the Hungarian, striding swiftly, with his fur-lined dolman, his close-fitting trousers reaching almost to his ankles, and his long pigtail; or the round-headed Pole with his monkish haircut and flowing sleeves; both nations die their boots – Armenians, Wallachians and Moldavians, with their half-Oriental costumes, are not uncommon – The Serbians with their twisted moustaches occupy a whole street – The Greeks in their wide heavy dress can be seen in hordes, smoking their*

long-stemmed pipes in the coffee-houses on the Leopoldstädter Bridge – And bearded Muslims in yellow mules, with their broad, murderous knives in their belts, lurch heavily through the muddy streets – The Polish Jews, all swathed in black, their faces bearded and their hair all twisted in knots, resemble scarecrows – Bohemian peasants with their long boots; Hungarian and Transylvanian waggoners with sheepskin greatcoats; Croats with black tubs balanced on their heads – they all provide entertaining accents in the general throng.[29]

And as for languages, Vienna was a veritable Tower of Babel. Pezzl notes that the 'native' languages of the Austrian Crown Lands are German, Latin, French, Italian, Hungarian, Bohemian, Polish, Flemish, Greek, Turkish, Illyrian, Croatian, Wendic, Wallachian and Romany.

As for music, well, it is as natural to foreigners as it is to the Viennese themselves:

One cannot enter any fashionable house without hearing a duet, or trio, or finale from one of the Italian operas currently the rage being sung and played at the keyboard. Even shopkeepers and cellar-hands whistle the popular arias … No place of refreshment, from the highest to the lowest, is without music. Bassoonists and clarinettists are as plentiful as blackberries, and in the suburbs at every turn one alights upon fresh carousing, fresh fiddling, fresh illuminations.[30]

Mozart was in the right place at the right time. He represented a new musical generation. Gluck, kapellmeister of Vienna – the most senior musical post – was sixty-six years of age when Mozart came to Vienna.

Salieri, who would succeed him as kapellmeister, was only five and a half years older than Mozart, but it was if he belonged to an older generation. He had none of the wit and sparkle of his young competitor, who could out-play and out-compose him too.

Neither of these illustrious musical names posed a threat to Mozart when it came to receiving invitations to perform in the salons of the nobility. And as far as improvisation contests – a popular form of salon entertainment whereby two pianists would compete to ascertain who was the more accomplished at improvising on a given tune – were concerned, Mozart had already seen off the competition.[*]

---

[*] Two decades later Beethoven would defeat one of Europe's most celebrated pianists, Daniel Steibelt, in an improvisation contest, and refuse to take part in any more.

Mozart could charm and impress the aristocracy, and he soon proved he could fill a theatre. Pezzl does not name the 'Italian operas currently the rage' that he refers to in his *Skizze*, but it is more than likely that these are the great operas that Mozart would go on to write with Lorenzo Da Ponte as librettist.

But that is to look ahead. In the immediate future he had to address the problem of his continuing alienation from his father, and his promise to bring his new bride to Salzburg to meet his father and sister.

Constanze became pregnant within weeks of their marriage. This provided Mozart with a convenient excuse not to follow through immediately with that promise. In fact he came up with a number of excuses, one following another as each was rejected in turn by his father.

First, in October, it was the fact that the most profitable season for musicians was about to begin. The nobility were due to return to the city from their summer residences, and would be resuming music lessons. Even if he and Constanze came to Salzburg in November, they would have to be back in Vienna by December, and how hard it would be for them to leave Leopold after such a short time(!).

Then it was the cold weather and the adverse effect that would have on his pregnant wife. Everyone, he said, was urging him to wait until spring.

More important than anything was the sheer volume of work he had, which he clearly thought would impress his father:

> I'm so busy these days that at times I don't know whether I'm coming or going any more – the entire morning, until 2 o'clock, is taken up with music lessons; – then we eat; – and after lunch I have to grant my poor stomach a short hour of digestion; only the evening is left for composing – and not even that is sure, because I am often asked to take part in a concert.

Finally, with spring soon to give way to summer, he uses an excuse so unlikely that we have to wonder how he ever thought his father would fall for it:

> Now we wish for nothing more than to be fortunate enough to embrace you both very soon – but can that be in Salzburg? – I think not, unfortunately! – For some time now certain thoughts have been running through my head … and that is whether the archbishop will have me arrested when I come back to Salzburg.

He is seriously suggesting to his father that he fears being arrested if he sets foot in Salzburg, and his reasoning is that although the archbishop dismissed him from service, he never received the dismissal in writing. Maybe that was deliberate, he suggests, so they could arrest him later.

Leopold wasn't taken in by any of this, and must have felt his son was setting out to goad him still further by ending practically every letter he now writes with both his and his wife's names, and sometimes more:

most obedient children
W.A. Mozart,
Man and wife
are one life.

most obedient children
Konstanze and Mozart
My wife is now entering her 91st year.[*]

M.C. et W.A. Mozart

your most obedient children
W. et C. Mozart

W. et C. Mzt

Then, on 17 June 1783, at last a genuine reason not to leave Vienna immediately for Salzburg. A son was born to Mozart and his wife, and thereby hangs a legend.

Decades later Constanze recounted how her husband was working on his String Quartet in D minor (K. 421) on the night of his son's birth, and was actually composing the *Minuet and Trio* at the moment of birth. We have no reason to doubt it. Composing was Mozart's way of breathing.

In writing to Leopold and congratulating him that he had now become a grandfather, Mozart first provides some totally superfluous information about how his wife's breasts have become very swollen, he fears she will develop milk fever, and without consulting him a wet nurse was brought in.

More rambling about the merits of feeding a newborn water rather than milk, as if he is delaying getting to the point. Then he drops a bombshell. He and Constanze have named the boy Raimund Leopold after his godfather. Not Leopold Raimund. In other words, Mozart has not asked his father to be godfather.

Mozart goes into a tortuous – and frankly unbelievable – explanation of how this happened. The first person he informed of the safe delivery of his child was his landlord, a certain baron by the name of Raimund Wetzlar, 'who is a good and true friend'.

Wetzlar came straight to the apartment and offered himself as godfather.

---

[*] A rare flash of humour in his letters, reversing his wife's age.

I couldn't refuse him – and so I thought to myself, well, I can still call the boy Leopold – and just as I was thinking it – the Baron said with the greatest delight – Ah well, now you have a little Raymund – and he kissed the child – so what was I to do – well, I had the boy baptised Raymund Leopold.*

What was he to do? Leopold must have thought there was an easy answer to that. Just tell this baron that the child's grandfather would be godfather, as was customary for a newborn, and his first name would, naturally, be Leopold. By all means give him Raimund as a second name.

But the deed was done. Mozart was presenting his father with a fait accompli, and a most hurtful one at that. It did not look good for a future reconciliation.

Mozart keeps his father informed of the baby's progress, stating that he is the spitting image of himself, which everyone remarks on, and that pleases Constanze because that is what she has always wanted.

He also reverts to classic Mozart language, albeit this time sparing his father's blushes: 'The baby is quite lively and healthy, he has a tremendous amount of things to do such as drinking, sleeping, crying, p------, sh------, and spitting up etc.'

As the weeks pass, the baby becomes stronger and Constanze's recovery is on track, and it becomes harder for Mozart to delay the promised trip to Salzburg. Leopold's letters are lost, but it is obvious from his son's replies that Leopold is becoming more and more exasperated with the excuses and delays.

Still Mozart persists with the most absurd excuse of all, and he blames it on friends who are filling his head with fear. 'If you so much as set foot in Salzburg, you'll never get out again'; 'you cannot know what this evil malicious prince[-archbishop Colloredo] is capable of'; 'you don't know what kind of tricks they have up their sleeve'.

Mozart writes out these fears in a letter, together with the advice he has been given that they should all meet up in some third place – not in Salzburg or Vienna.

Another furious and sceptical reply from his father, and Mozart has one last attempt to put the whole thing off, or at least arrange a meeting somewhere completely different, such as Munich. There is a decided tone of authority to his letter, dated 12 July 1783:

Have I ever given you the impression that I have no desire or eagerness to see you? – certainly not! – what is true is that I have no desire to see

---

* Mozart as usual cavalier with his spelling of proper names.

Salzburg or the archbishop – so pray, tell me who would be the one who gets fooled if we met at a third place? the archbishop and not you – *I hope I don't need to tell you that I care little about Salzburg and nothing at all about the archbishop and that I shit on both of them.*

This time his father must have fired off a real broadside, because before the month was out he and Constanze were on the road to Salzburg – without Raimund. They left their six-week-old baby in the care of a foster mother.

This might seem to us a strange decision, unless perhaps the infant was unwell. Wouldn't a major motive for the trip be for baby Raimund to meet his grandfather and aunt? What must Leopold and Nannerl have thought when Mozart and his wife arrived without their baby? And surely the couple themselves, newly parents, must have felt the absence of their newborn acutely?

We cannot know any of this for certain, since Mozart does not mention the decision in a letter. Similarly there is scant information about the visit to Salzburg, for the simple reason that when the family was together, no letters were being written.

Most of what we know comes from entries Nannerl made in her diary, and for the most part these are brief and formal. Other information comes from Constanze herself, recalling events forty years later.

We know enough, however, to be able to say that the visit was hardly a successful one. If reconciliation was its purpose, it fell far short of achieving it.

"I care little about Salzburg and nothing at all about the archbishop and I shit on both of them."

Mozart

Mozart and his wife arrived in Salzburg on 29 July 1783. It was the first time Mozart had set foot in his home city for nearly three years.

We have no information on how the initial family reunion went, but we can assume it was frosty, or at least cool. Relations between father and son had to all intents and purposes broken down. Mozart was arriving home with a wife his father had fought tooth and nail to stop him marrying.

Similarly, Nannerl had taken her father's side over the marriage. She had added postscripts to her father's letters, accusing Mozart of forsaking family obligations for a woman who was unworthy of him, and who she accuses in harsh language of being an interloper. Along with her father, she too had refused to give her blessing to the marriage.

Constanze herself had tried more than once to repair things. She wrote to Nannerl ahead of the wedding asking for her friendship, but was rebuffed. She tried again, a week before the wedding, and was rebuffed again.

Constanze did not conceal her hurt. 'All that I deserve is that for the love of God you should suffer me as you do all the others.'[31] Still to no avail. Fully a year later Constanze and her husband arrive in Salzburg.

Constanze was by now thoroughly upset at the refusal of the Mozarts – father and daughter – to accept her. And she gave a telling anecdote, again many decades later, of how the hurt affected her husband.

One night the family, all four of them, were singing the quartet from Mozart's opera *Idomeneo*. At this point in the opera Idomeneo's son is having to take leave of his father, who is behaving irrationally towards him.

Wolfgang, his wife recounts, 'burst into tears and left the room and it was some time before he could be consoled'.[32] Leopold and his daughter were witness to this, and still relations were not repaired.

Musically, at least, as this incident reveals, the family was united. All four were highly accomplished musicians (something of an understatement as far as one of them is concerned), and there was by all accounts much music-making in the Tanzmeisterhaus. It is likely that during this stay Mozart composed his three piano sonatas, K. 330–32, and Nannerl will have been the first to play them.

Musical activities reached their peak with the performance of Mozart's newly composed Mass in C minor (K. 427). This was performed in St. Peter's Abbey on 26 October with Constanze herself as first soprano soloist.

Significantly the performance did not take place in the cathedral, and although many of Mozart's former musical colleagues at court took part, Archbishop Colloredo himself stayed away. So much for Mozart's fears he might be arrested if he set foot in Salzburg.

The Mass in C minor is a mighty work, and it must have left both performers and audiences stunned with its sheer depth and complexity. Yet Nannerl, in her diary, simply records that it took place, and that her sister-in-law had sung.

Similarly, after Mozart and Constanze left Salzburg the following day, Nannerl wrote the briefest entry in her diary: 'At half past 9 o'clock my brother and sister-in-law departed.'[33] In fact this farewell was their last. They would never see each other again.

Right to the last, relationships remained unrepaired. As she and her husband left, Constanze asked her father-in-law if she might take as a memento one of the many gifts her husband had received on his earlier travels. Leopold refused.

The stay in Salzburg had lasted for a little under three months, and it must have been painful from start to finish. Even a tragedy, totally unexpected, failed to bring the family any closer together.

While in Salzburg, Mozart and his wife received the dreadful news from Vienna that their baby son, Raimund Leopold, had died. All they were told was that he suffered from intestinal cramps and died on 19 August 1783, at the age of just two months and two days.

No letters regarding this have survived, so we cannot know the effect it had on the family. Did Leopold castigate his son for leaving the baby behind in Vienna? Did he regret never having had the chance to see his grandson? We can only surmise.

We can be sure of one thing: that little Raimund's death went no way towards healing the cracks in the family relationships.

What strikes me as even more extraordinary is that we have no evidence of how Wolfgang and Constanze themselves were affected by their son's death. Nannerl wrote nothing in her diary. Close friends – musical colleagues, certainly – were frequent visitors, yet none (as far as I am aware) has left any account.

Even Mozart himself is practically silent on the matter. Once back in Vienna, he and his wife must have been fully informed as to what had happened, and why the child could not be saved. Yet there is not a word from him in letters to his father for almost two months, and even then it is the briefest reference, buried towards the end of a letter which is mostly about various opera librettos. Just before his farewells, Mozart writes: 'We are both very sad about our poor, bonny, fat, darling little boy.' And with just those few words, Mozart and Constanze's first child passes into history.

But sadness certainly did not dull Mozart's creative genius. He was about to embark on his golden years, creating his greatest works. It began as soon as they embarked on the journey from Salzburg back to Vienna.

The couple stopped off in Linz, where Mozart was invited to give a concert at the Linz theatre four days after arriving. But he had forgotten to bring a symphony with him. So he dashed one off 'at breakneck speed, for it has to be finished in time'.

In under four days he completed his Symphony No. 36 (к. 425), known, for obvious reasons, as the 'Linz'. It is one of his finest, and is just the beginning of an extraordinary burst of creativity.

Mozart is a composer who does not have to wait for the Muse to inspire him. He composes because he *has* to, and often for mundane reasons. He has agreed to give a concert in Linz, he has no symphony, so the easy answer (easy for him) is to write one.

This would remain the pattern for the rest of his life. Musically he is approaching his zenith. In his private life too, he and Constanze are soon to experience joy.

That difficult, awkward, tense – but necessary – visit to his father and sister in Salzburg is behind him. The way forward is clear.

19

PATERNAL PRIDE

The new year, 1784, it is not an exaggeration to say, brought a new life for Mozart, both musically and at home. Constanze was soon pregnant again. 'She finds it difficult to remain seated for long, because our future son and heir gives her no peace,' he writes.

Early in the year they moved into a spacious apartment in a brand-new building on the Graben, named the Trattnerhof after its owner. The building housed a large hall in which concerts could be given, and this was one of the factors that helped Mozart make an inspired decision, a radical departure from the norm.

It was usual for a composer or performer to hire one of the court theatres for a benefit concert, but he could not expect to be offered more than a single date in a year. This was unlikely to bring in much money; in fact it could even result in a loss. He hit on the idea of using not court theatres with all their formalities and conditions, but rather unconventional – and smaller – venues such as the Trattnerhof and the Mehlgrube (a restaurant with an adjoining ballroom, built on the site of a former flour store).

Being Mozart, he could offer something extra that no other musician in Vienna could: he would perform his own piano concertos. From the subscribers' point of view, this would represent true value for money – something they could not get elsewhere. From his point of view, it meant he could control every aspect of the concert, and therefore reap maximum profit.

He decided to put on three subscription concerts at the Trattnerhof, and again, being Mozart, he decided to compose three *new* piano concertos, one for each of the concerts.

In the space of a year he composed no fewer than six new piano concertos, Nos. 14–19 (к. 449–51, 453, 456 and 459). During 1784 he presented a series of three subscription concerts at the Trattnerhof. The following year he gave a series of six concerts at the Mehlgrube.

In addition to this he performed privately in aristocratic salons at least eighteen times in 1784, and five times in 1785. In the period of winter 1782–3 to April 1786 he composed no fewer than fourteen piano concertos.

After performing one of these concertos (probably No. 14), he wrote to his father:

The first concert on 17th of this month went very well – the hall was filled to the brim; – and the New Concerto that I performed won extraordinary applause; wherever I go now people speak in praise of that concert.

He was the toast of Vienna. There was no one else who could touch him, or even come close.

Add to this the personal joy of the arrival of a son. On 21 September 1784, Constanze gave birth to a boy and he was named Karl Thomas. Once again friends noted how like his father the baby looked.

But something had to give, and it was Mozart's health. In August he went to the Burgtheater to see the new opera by Paisiello. Just a week before Karl Thomas was born, he wrote to his father that at the performance he sweated so profusely that his clothes were drenched. He looked for his servant, who had his overcoat, but there was an order forbidding servants to enter the theatre by the main doors. So Mozart had to go out into the cold night air to find him.

The result was that he developed rheumatic fever. For four days running, at the same hour each day, he had a 'fearful attack of colic, which ended each time with vomiting'.

It must have made for a difficult few weeks in the Mozart household. Constanze was in the last stages of pregnancy; at the same time her husband was seriously ill with rheumatic fever. All this at a time when he was fully stretched with concert performances, not to mention salon recitals and teaching.

Mozart goes into no further details in his letters, but it appears he recovered – he was not the only one, apparently many in Vienna came down with the same illness – and his wife was safely delivered of a healthy boy.

Within a short time, Mozart decided he would make use of the income he was now generating. The subscription concerts were proving to be a huge

success. In the space of three years, his earnings had more than tripled from just over 1,000 florins to nearly 4,000.[*]

With a growing family, an ever increasing number of pupils coming to see him, not to mention musical colleagues, publishers, copyists, as well as servants, he felt the need for a larger apartment. A week after Karl Thomas's birth, and with his own health still fragile, he moved the family into a much larger apartment in the Domgasse, in the shadow of St Stephen's Cathedral.[†]

---

[*] From approximately £25,000 to £93,000.

[†] The only location in Vienna now preserved to his memory.

It was a hugely prestigious address, and the apartment had a ceiling of stuccoed marble. The rooms were large, and there was space enough in the main salon for a chamber ensemble to play before an audience. Mozart's stock rose with the aristocracy among whom he now moved so freely. But he had not sat down and done his sums.

The rent was three times more than he had paid in the Trattnerhof. He now had to find 460 florins per month.* That is a large sum of money by any standards. On top of that, he had a wife and growing child to support, as well as a retinue of servants. To have servants might seem to us today to be an unnecessary extravagance, but given the circles in which he moved, it was to be expected.

To compound matters, he started spending money liberally. He bought a new fortepiano with a specially constructed pedal attachment. He owned several other musical instruments. He also had his own carriage. In preparation for a trip to Munich he had six pairs of shoes made, which his father found rather excessive. The trip was ultimately cancelled.

For relaxation he bought a billiard table – billiards was one of his favourite hobbies – and he also apparently kept a horse, though it's not entirely clear for how long. As he himself said: 'One must not make oneself cheap here – that is a cardinal point – or else one would be ruined for ever. Whoever is the most *aggressive* has the best chance.'

He soon began to feel the pinch. He had to borrow money to pay for the cost of making manuscript copies of three earlier piano concertos, which he would offer to the public by subscription. To increase their profitability, he reduced them to just piano plus four instruments, meaning they could be performed in a salon without the need to hire a full orchestra.

The results, to his surprise, were disappointing, and there now began a cycle that was soon to become a pattern.

The loan was short-term, and he needed to borrow from someone else to pay it off. He turned to his patron and good friend Baroness Waldstätten, the same lady who had allowed her calf to be measured along with Constanze's, and who threw the wedding feast for him and his new bride. He was, as the saying goes, borrowing from Peter to pay Paul.

---

* Approximately £11,500.

It has been speculated that Mozart gambled heavily.[*] Certainly gambling was prevalent at every level of society, and it is more than likely that Mozart put money on a game of billiards or cards, but how much and how often is impossible to say. It is likely he did not bet substantial amounts of money, or it would most probably have been remarked on. But the occasional flutter? More than likely.

What most certainly was remarked on was his predilection for smart clothes, stylish furniture, and the best in food and wine. These extravagances, together with his now seriously high rent, are enough to account for his sudden need to borrow.

A sign of his standing in Viennese society was his application to join the Freemasons, which was accepted in glowing terms. He was admitted to the Zur Wohltätigkeit ('Beneficence') Lodge as an Apprentice Mason on 14 December 1784 with these words:

> *Favourite of a guardian angel. Friend of the sweetest muse. Chosen by benevolent Nature to move our hearts through rare magical powers, and to pour consolation and comfort into our souls. You shall be embraced by all the warm feelings of mankind, which you so wonderfully express through your fingers, through which stream all the magnificent works of your ardent imagination!*[34]

In a very short time he was promoted to Journeyman, and soon achieved the highest rank, Master Mason. His fellow Masons understood exactly what they were getting, and the kudos he would bring to their organisation.

To become a Freemason was a good career move for a freelance musician, but there is no doubt Mozart was genuinely enthusiastic about it. He was soon composing pieces of music for ceremonial occasions at his Lodge, and he was later described as 'a diligent member of our Order'.

Another composer resident in Vienna, Joseph Haydn, whom Mozart had come to know well, also became a Freemason. He joined another Lodge two months after Mozart. And, somewhat surprisingly, someone else was about to join *both* Lodges. All the more surprising since this individual did not live in Vienna, and did not even intend staying in the city for long. But he had impeccable credentials, and so his membership was fast-tracked.

Yes, Leopold Mozart had decided to come to the imperial capital to visit his son and daughter-in-law, and his baby grandson.

---

[*] Uwe Kraemer, '*Wer had Mozart verhungern lassen?*' ('Who let Mozart starve?'), an article published in Musica 30, June 1976.

The invitation had come from Mozart and his wife. In fact Mozart had repeatedly urged his father to come and visit them, but had always been rebuffed. Yet now Nannerl, somewhat to her father's surprise, had married and moved away from Salzburg. Leopold was alone.

As for Mozart, he was extremely keen for his father to see the degree of luxury in which he and his family lived, and to see for himself just what an impact his son was having on musical life in Vienna.

So, at last, Leopold accepted the invitation. He wrote to Mozart that he would bring a former music student with him, a sixteen-year-old boy who was a violinist, keyboard player and budding composer – almost as if that would keep the visit more professional than personal.

It did not begin well. Leopold and his young companion left Salzburg in heavy snow and freezing temperatures in the first week of February 1785. Predictably Leopold caught a severe cold on the journey. He was now three months past his sixty-fifth birthday, and a chilly, uncomfortable journey was exactly what he did not need.

To make matters worse, his son was so busy he barely had time to greet his father, and had even arranged for him to attend a concert on the very night he arrived. The frantic pace did not let up. Leopold, exhausted, wrote to Nannerl:

> We never get to bed before one in the morning and never get up before nine. We dine at two or half past the hour. The weather is horrible! Concerts every day and unending teaching, music-making, and composing. Where am I supposed to go? If only the concerts were over! It is impossible to describe the confusion and commotion.

His health was not improving. He thought he had shaken off the cold he caught on the journey, but it was persisting. He had a pain in his left thigh and came to the conclusion that it was rheumatism. His remedy was some burr-root tea in bed in the morning, and not getting up until one o'clock.

Leopold was his old difficult and curmudgeonly self. Mozart and his wife had every reason to regret the day they ever invited him. So how did they handle him? With a stroke of genius, by killing him with kindness. They had allies in the form of Constanze's mother and younger sister Sophie. They treated Leopold like a lord and he loved it.

For a start, they took Leopold to lunch at Frau Weber's. This was the woman Leopold had insulted time and again in his letters, accusing her of trying to trick his son into marriage. There is no question that she would have known of Leopold's insulting attacks on her. The lunch could have been a disaster.

Instead, this is how Leopold wrote about it to his daughter:

I must tell you that the meal, which was neither too lavish nor too stingy, was cooked to perfection. The roast was a fine plump pheasant, and everything was excellently well prepared. We lunched on Friday … but there was no thought of a fast-day. We were offered only meat dishes. A pheasant as an additional dish was served in cabbage and the rest was fit for a prince. Finally we had oysters, most delicious glacé fruits and (I must not forget to mention this) several bottles of champagne.

Leopold was so impressed he even let his strict Catholic adherence to fish on Fridays lapse – and confessed as much to Nannerl! You can just see the Webers running around after him, helping him to food, and more food, replenishing his glass, making sure he wanted for nothing. Leopold had never been treated like that, and he clearly relished every moment.

It did not end there. Constanze's sister Sophie took it upon herself to look after Leopold, as he struggled with his various ailments. She gave him lunch, and when he felt too unwell to attend any of his son's concerts, she stayed with him until late in the evening.

Constanze played her part also, in what was clearly a well-organised strategy. She made sure Leopold had his fill of little Karl, now five months old. Karl played his part to perfection too, bringing untold joy to his grandfather. He wrote to Nannerl:

Little Karl is the image of [Wolfgang]. He seems very healthy, but now and then, of course, children have trouble with their teeth. On the whole the child is charming, for he is extremely healthy and laughs when spoken to. I have only seen him cry once and the next moment he started to laugh.

The strategy was working so well that Leopold even found himself being won over by the woman he was not so long before prepared to stop at nothing to prevent his son marrying, a woman he was quite prepared to label a slut.

Instead he remarked on what a sensible and frugal house she kept. He even – who would have thought this possible? – included her when he signed off a letter to Nannerl: 'Your brother, your sister-in-law … and I kiss you millions of times.'

Leopold was also, just as his son intended, impressed with the grandeur of the apartment, and particularly admired the fine furniture. It seems Mozart gave him no inkling of any money problems.

Leopold was won over; the strategy had worked. But to Mozart, what mattered most was to show his father just what he had achieved musically in

"Leopold found himself being won over by the woman he was prepared to stop at nothing to prevent his son marrying."

the city that was the European capital of music: the concerts he was putting on, the aristocracy that were coming to see him. He wanted his father to hear what they were saying about him.

It is not an exaggeration to say his aims were not only fulfilled but surpassed.

Leopold went to the Mehlgrube to hear his son perform a brand new piano concerto. When I say brand new, I mean it. With the performance just an hour, or even less, away, Leopold watched in awe as Mozart supervised a group of copyists writing out the parts. In other words, he was still composing, or at the very least orchestrating it. In fact, Leopold wrote to Nannerl, telling her that because her brother was supervising the copyists, he did not even have time to play through the rondo, the second movement.[*]

Despite all this, 'the concert was magnificent and the orchestra played splendidly'. If this had been a small piece, it would still have been remarkable. In fact it was Mozart's Piano Concerto No. 20 in D minor (K. 466), one of the longest and most intense of all his piano concertos.[†]

Leopold always knew his son had a God-given talent, but this was beyond anything he had expected. It was a revelatory moment. And his own ego was suitably flattered when important people flocked to him afterwards to congratulate him on his son's achievement. He confessed to being overcome with emotion.

Even the emperor himself, 'when your brother left the platform, waved his hat and called out "Bravo, Mozart!"' There could be, in Leopold's eyes, no higher accolade.

It did not end there. The following Saturday evening, no less a musical personage than Joseph Haydn was guest at Mozart's apartment to hear three new string quartets performed.[‡]

After the performance Haydn came up to Leopold and said: 'Before God and as an honest man I tell you that your son is the greatest composer known to me either in person or by name. He has taste and, what is more, the most profound knowledge of composition.' We can easily imagine Leopold swelling with pride at what has gone down as one of the most prescient remarks in musical history.

---

[*] Still one of the best-known movements of any of Mozart's piano concertos.

[†] Beethoven, Brahms and Clara Schumann were among those who wrote cadenzas for it.

[‡] These – K. 458, 464 and 465 – together with three earlier ones – K. 387, 421 and 428 – would be dedicated to Haydn and are known today as Mozart's 'Haydn Quartets'.

Left

Mozart's String Quartet No. 19 in C Major (K.465), one of six quartetts dedicated to Haydn.

It is worth pausing for a moment to contemplate what must have gone through Leopold's mind during that visit, perhaps as he lay awake at night alone with his thoughts.

Everything he had dreamed of for his son during all those tours so many years ago had borne fruit. True, he had never found employment at a European court, and the only employment he had ever had, thanks to his father's efforts, was at the court in Salzburg, and he had managed to get himself dismissed from that.

But here he was now, in the Habsburg capital, living comfortably, dressed in finery, lauded by the highest in the land, writing and performing music better than anyone before him. And Leopold, an accomplished musician, was well qualified to be judge of that.

Could there possibly have been an element of guilt, buried deep within? Guilt that he had held his son for so long in check, trying too hard to get him paid employment, fighting him over his desire to leave Salzburg? On the evidence he was witnessing in Vienna, his son surely could have made a comfortable living earlier in his career.

And Constanze. She was clearly a good wife to Wolfgang. She looked after him, making it possible for him to work at the pace he needed to, protecting him where necessary. Maybe Leopold had been a little harsh in his opposition to her.

He must have thought, too, of his own wife, and all that she was missing. How he must have longed to tell her what their son had achieved.

And, lastly, might there not have been just a touch of envy at the back of his mind? Proud though he so obviously was of his son's mastery of music, it must surely have been difficult to acknowledge just how far the son had eclipsed the father. Added to that, what had become of his hopes that Wolfgang would keep his ageing parents in luxury?

Here Leopold was now, on a short visit to his son in Vienna, soon to return to an empty house in a city he loathed, earning a living as best he could with his position at court and his music pupils. Things had not turned out the way he had envisaged.

In the light of day, though, amid the bustle of his son's busy life, he could at least bask in reflected glory. One other thing had happened to him in Vienna, and this was perhaps the most unexpected development of all. It appears he might have fallen just very slightly in love.

And the object of his affection? His son and daughter-in-law's great friend Baroness Waldstätten. She, too, must have been in on the conspiracy to kill him with kindness. She invited Leopold out to her house in Klosterneuberg, sending her carriage and horses to pick him up.

In a letter to his daughter he referred to the baroness as 'this woman of my heart'. He will certainly have known that she was separated from her husband. But we can probably be fairly sure that even if he did lose his heart, he took away with him no more than a warm glow of appreciation.

Leopold remained in Vienna for a little over two months, at the end of which he was physically exhausted but emotionally content. His son, permanently exhausted, shared his contentment. The relationship between father and son had finally been repaired.

On 25 April 1785, Mozart and Constanze accompanied Leopold to the nearby village of Purkersdorf, where the road forked. They had lunch together. Afterwards they said their goodbyes, more warmly than any of them had thought possible.

Leopold boarded a coach to Linz on his way home to Salzburg. Mozart and Constanze boarded another coach back to Vienna.

Father and son had taken their final farewell.

20

WOMANISER, CRIMINAL AND GENIUS WITH WORDS

A **truly colourful character** now enters our story, an individual whose name would surely be lost to history were it not for his connection to Mozart. He was born Emanuele Conegliano in the small town of Ceneda (now Vittorio Veneto), north of Venice.

He was Jewish by birth, but his father converted himself and his family to Roman Catholicism so he could marry a Catholic woman. Emanuele was baptised a Catholic and, as was the custom, he took the name of the bishop who baptised him. If Monsignor Lorenzo Da Ponte could only have known of the exalted status his name would one day hold in the annals of musical history!

At the age of twenty-four the bishop's namesake was ordained a priest, and proceeded to lead a life not entirely compatible – at the same time not entirely unknown – to his calling. He moved to Venice, where he made the acquaintance of a certain Giacomo Casanova (yes, that one), whose behaviour in the field of sexual conquests he was keen to emulate.

The older man clearly gave him instruction, because he then – it was alleged – took up residence in a brothel in Venice and organised entertainments for the clients there. It was further alleged he pimped the prostitutes, living off their immoral earnings, and also abducted a respectable woman. This might or might not have been his mistress, with whom he had two children.

For these alleged crimes he was arrested and charged. He was brought to trial, found guilty on all counts and banished from Venice for fifteen years.

Right

Lorenzo Da Ponte
wrote the librettos
for Mozart's most
popular operas.

He found his way to Vienna, where a letter of introduction secured him a meeting with a composer in his early thirties who was making a name for himself. No, not Wolfgang Mozart but Antonio Salieri. Da Ponte put himself forward to Salieri as a poet and writer. Salieri was sufficiently impressed to help him obtain the post of librettist to the Burgtheater, which involved overseeing all librettos for the theatre. Da Ponte was suddenly very busy. He had fallen on his feet.

'Modesty' is not a word that could ever be applied to Da Ponte. This is what he thought of the librettos that fell onto his desk:

> *What trash! No plots, no characters, no movement, no scening* [sic]*, no grace of language or style! Written to produce laughter, anyone would have judged that most were written to produce tears. There was not a line in those miserable botches that contained a flourish, an oddity, a graceful term, calculated in any sense to produce a laugh. So many agglomerations of insipidities, idiocies, tomfooleries!* [35]

It would be so much better if he wrote the librettos himself. He would show them how to do it:

> In mine, one would find, at least here and there, some clever turn, some smart quip, some joke. The language would be neither barbarous nor uncouth. The songs would be read without annoyance! Finding an attractive subject, capable of supplying interesting character and fertile in incident, I would not be able, even if I tried, to compose things as wretched as those I had read![36]

And so he wrote librettos himself, for Salieri and several other composers of opera. The resulting operas all flopped.

A chance meeting at the home of Baron Wetzlar changed his life. For this was the same Raimund who was landlord to Mozart and had stood as godfather to his first-born. And so Mozart met the man who was to write the librettos for his greatest operas.

Not that Mozart was immediately filled with confidence. How could you ever trust an Italian? His father, with whom he had toured Italy so many times, would know exactly what he meant:

> We have a certain Abate [Abbot] da Ponte here as a text poet; – he has an incredible number of revisions to do at the theatre – he also has to do per obligo – a whole New libretto for Salieri – which he won't be able to finish for 2 months – He promised to write me something New after that; – but who knows whether he will keep his word – or even wants to! – You know, these Italian gentlemen, they are very nice to your face! – enough, we know all about them! – and if he is working with Salieri, I'll never get a text from him.

But he was wrong. It was, from every practical point of view, an unlikely collaboration. Da Ponte was seven years older than Mozart, or to put it in a more significant way, when they started working together one was well into his thirties, the other in his late twenties. When lives, on the whole, were shorter than they are today, this was a significant difference.

One had led a thoroughly colourful life, ranging from holy orders to debauchery and a criminal trial. The other had virtually no experience of the world outside the rarefied realms of music. For one, the state of marriage was fortuitously denied to him by his priestly calling, allowing him to indulge his preferred, more libidinous, tastes. The other was happily married with a son.

They were different nationalities, speaking a different native language. Potentially most damaging of all, each doubted the other's abilities. We have seen Mozart's words to his father. Da Ponte too had his misgivings. He recognised Mozart's musical genius – 'gifted with talents superior, perhaps, to those of any other composer in the world', he wrote much later in his *Memoirs*[37] – but he doubted his stagecraft.

To put it bluntly, though, they needed each other. Mozart's operas hitherto had not been the unconditional successes he had hoped for. By far the best received, *Die Entführung*, had not brought him either greatly enhanced fame or much fortune. It was his piano concertos that were responsible for that. And as for Da Ponte, he could point to nothing.

One crucial quality, however, they shared. It was not apparent to those who knew them, and it was not immediately apparent to the two men themselves. They thought along similar lines. The fact that they were both outsiders in the imperial capital gave them a certain bond, a mutual mistrust of authority. It also allowed them to see that the rigid hierarchy of aristocratic life in Vienna meant nothing. The high born were every bit as capable of corruption, deceit, jealousy, intrigue, infidelity and mischief as the lowest on the streets.

If they were to collaborate, it was inevitable something radically different would emerge – something 'edgy', as we would say today, even dangerous, taking as targets a previously untouchable layer of society.

To say that something radical *did* emerge is an understatement. The genius was to make it a comedy. It seems it was a shared genius. Da Ponte, naturally, claims credit for the initial collaboration. 'I went to Mozart … and asked him whether he would care to set to music a drama I should write to him.'[38]

Then, he gives credit to the composer: 'In conversation with me one day, he asked me whether I could easily make an opera from a comedy by Beaumarchais – *Le Mariage de Figaro*. I liked the suggestion very much, and promised to write him one.'[39]

The result would change the face of opera. From the opening bars of the overture, a low rumble in strings and bassoons, the audience knew they were hearing something different. And in the very first scene, a servant is mocking his master. This might be comedy, but it is a reversal of the norm. That sort of thing did not happen in real life, and it was an insult to the aristocracy – who would make up most of the audience – to allow it to happen on stage. And Mozart's music, note for note, perfectly captures this. Revolutionary stuff, both in music and ideas.

Predictably the censor, under orders from the emperor, had tried to ban it. Da Ponte, naturally, claims credit for persuading the emperor to pass it as entertainment. And what entertainment! Da Ponte's perfect verse allows Mozart to rise to exquisite musical heights. This is like nothing he has written for the stage before.

The sophisticated audience will have been amused and beguiled, and at the same time shocked, from the first scene onwards. The two most sympathetic characters are women – Susanna and the Countess – and it is they who carry the opera.

The Countess's aria at the opening of Act 2, '*Porgi, amor*' ('Grant, love, some comfort'), in which she laments her husband's infidelity, is heart-stoppingly beautiful. Again, in Act 3, it is Countess Almaviva who moves in a single aria, '*Dove, sono*' ('Where are they, the beautiful moments'), from reflecting sadly on her lost happiness – accompanied by a doleful oboe – to renewed strength as she determines to overcome her misery.

Then again, it is the two women together who sing the sublime '*Sull' aria*' ('On the breeze'), conspiring together in their plan to trap the Count in his infidelity.*

This is real life, real emotions, remarkable in itself in opera up until this time, and even more remarkable for having been expressed by female characters. The mould had been broken. As Professor Jane Glover says, 'Mozart and Da Ponte had finally held the mirror up to the audience: "This", they were saying, "is all about you."'[40]

Le nozze di Figaro premiered at the Burgtheater on 1 May 1786, with Mozart leading the performance from the keyboard. It was produced nine times in all before the end of the year, with thirty-eight performances over the next five years.

That is substantial, particularly when the number of encores for particular numbers in the first year is taken into account. But it is not exceptional, not the triumph for which Mozart hoped. It also did not earn him a great deal of money.

The combination of Mozart and Da Ponte had worked better than any other collaboration either of the two men had had, however, and it was not long before a commission came in for a new opera from them, this time from Prague. Da Ponte immodestly claims credit for choosing the subject which, he says, 'pleased Mozart mightily'.[41]

Da Ponte was extraordinarily busy at the time, working on two other librettos for two different composers. He set aside morning and afternoon

> "*Da Ponte's perfect verse allows Mozart to rise to exquisite musical heights, like nothing he has written for the stage before.*"

---

* It is this aria that brought Mozart to a wider audience when it was used in the hugely successful film *The Shawshank Redemption*, playing across a prison courtyard to transfixed inmates. The narrator says: 'I have no idea to this day what those two Italian ladies were singing about … I'd like to think they were singing about something so beautiful it can't be expressed in words, and it makes your heart ache because of it.' [*The Shawshank Redemption* (Columbia Pictures, 1994), Frank Darabont (dir.)] A perfect encapsulation of Mozart's art.

for them, evenings for Mozart. He must have written the libretto for Mozart with a permanent smile on his face. The subject was the greatest lover in history, the Italian version of Don Juan, *Don Giovanni*. Da Ponte was, of course, able to draw on his own amorous experiences, in which he happily continued to indulge while in the process of writing:

> *I sat down at my table and did not leave it for twelve hours continuous – a bottle of Tokay to my right, a box of Seville to my left, in the middle an inkwell. A beautiful girl of sixteen – I should have preferred to love her only as a daughter, but alas …! – was living in the house with her mother, and came to my room at the sound of the bell. To tell the truth the bell rang rather frequently, especially at the moments when I felt my inspiration waning. She would bring me now a little cake, now a cup of coffee, now nothing but her pretty face … Sometimes she would sit at my side without opening her lips, or batting an eyelash, gazing at me fixedly, or blandly smiling, or now it would be a sigh, or a menace of tears.*[42]

'But alas …!' Da Ponte was showing his writing skills even in his *Memoirs*. Just two words, some dots, and an exclamation mark. Less is more. As we would say today, he was learning on the job. Which is somewhat surprising, given that the libretto he produced was much darker than Mozart might have expected, beginning and ending as it does with violent death, and involving the truly chilling reappearance of the murdered man as a ghost.

Given Da Ponte's predilections, Mozart might have expected another comedy replete with amorous entanglements. Maybe Da Ponte was reflecting on his own life, and considering the punishment that might lie ahead for him if he continued his libidinous ways. He gives us no indication either way in his *Memoirs*, merely congratulating himself on completing his three commissions on time, as if the other two – long forgotten – are in some way the equal of *Don Giovanni*.

Mozart once again rose to the musical challenge, depicting characters more complex than in any of his previous operas. The setting this time, despite the Italian title, is Vienna itself, and specifically the Graben, the wide central thoroughfare with many small streets radiating off it, where Mozart and his wife had first lived, and which was the haunt of most of the city's three thousand prostitutes.

If *Le nozze* held up a mirror to the Viennese, *Don Giovanni* reflected its subjects even more explicitly, both in location and habits. Far from parody, which might allow its targets an indulgent smile, this opera was warning them that if they continued their debauched lifestyle, they risked being consumed by the flames of hell, the fate of the *Don* himself.

There is, though, both light and shade. In one of the most serene moments in any Mozart opera, when Giovanni seduces Zerlina, Mozart writes a duet of exquisite tranquillity and beauty, '*Là ci darem la mano*'. Giovanni uses every ounce of charm he possesses. Zerlina at first tries to resist, but then melts completely. The aria demonstrates, as Professor Glover succinctly and perfectly puts it, 'Mozart's own understanding of gentle conquest'.[43] 'Gentle' is the operative word.

Then, during a party at Giovanni's house, as Zerlina realises she is about to be seduced again, she lets out a scream. Legend has it that in rehearsals Mozart achieved the desired effect by pinching soprano Caterina Bondini's bottom. Given what we know of the mischief lurking so close to the surface of Mozart's character, I can well believe it.

The opera was premiered in Prague on 29 October 1787, after two postponements, the first because it was not ready, the second due to a singer's illness. Constanze later recounted that her husband was working on the overture up until the last minute. He was writing it during the night ahead of the first performance, she keeping him awake with liberal supplies of coffee. The orchestra apparently played the overture at sight.

Mozart himself reported: 'Some of the notes fell under the desks, it is true, but the overture went remarkably well on the whole.'

So did the entire opera. One critic noted that

> *Prague had never yet heard the like. Herr Mozart conducted in person. When he entered the orchestra he was received with threefold cheers, which again happened when he left it … The unusually large attendance testifies to a unanimous approbation.*

Prague loved Mozart, and had for some time. His earlier opera *Le nozze di Figaro* had triumphed there. When he returned to the city to complete work on *Don Giovanni*, he wrote to a friend:

> *Everyone was hopping about with sheer delight to the music of my 'Figaro' … 'Figaro'. Nothing is played, blown, sung, and whistled but – 'Figaro'. No opera is seen as much as – 'Figaro'. Again and again it is – 'Figaro'. It's all a great honour for me.*

There were no question marks over *Don Giovanni*. Prague took the opera to its hearts. To this day, visit the city of Prague and you will find it still proudly boasts of having commissioned Mozart's most perfect opera, of appreciating his worth as an operatic composer far more quickly and readily than Vienna.

It is an accurate assessment, for Vienna did not entirely take *Le nozze* to its heart, and the same was true of *Don Giovanni*. When word of its success in Prague reached the Habsburg capital, it was decided to put it on at the Burgtheater, but no slot could be found for seven months.

It finally premiered in Vienna on 7 May 1788, with some alterations. Emperor Joseph II himself wrote, without even seeing it, 'Mozart's music is certainly too difficult to be sung'[44] (too many notes?). Da Ponte apparently told Mozart that the emperor had remarked that the opera was 'not the food for the teeth of my Viennese'. To which Mozart replied, 'Let us give them time to chew it.'

A countess who at least saw the opera remarked the music was 'learned', and 'little suited to the voice'. An archduchess, again without seeing it, wrote to her husband, 'In the last few days a new opera composed by Mozart has been given, but I was told that it did not have much success.'[45]

The critics praised the music but condemned the work as a whole. 'Is such magnificent, majestic and powerful song really stuff for ordinary opera-lovers, who only bring their *ears* … but leave their *hearts* at home?' wrote one. Another: 'The beauty, greatness and nobility of the music for *Don Juan* [*sic*] will never appeal anywhere to more than a handful of the elect. It is not music to everyone's taste, merely tickling the ear and letting the heart starve.' And this from a later critic in Berlin: 'Whim, caprice, pride, but not the heart created *Don Juan* [*sic*].'[46]

Reviews can hurt. They hurt today; they hurt then. Although *Don Giovanni* was performed fifteen times during 1788, Mozart's finest, most complex, most dramatically and musically perfect opera fell out of the repertory in Vienna for the remainder of its composer's life.

Paradoxically, given its reception, Mozart actually earned quite good money for *Don Giovanni*. Maynard Solomon estimates that proceeds from both Vienna and Prague productions brought him in around 1,275 florins.[*] But the fact it was not an out-and-out success meant no further opera commission came to Mozart until late in 1789.

This was to be the final collaboration between Mozart and Da Ponte, and by general consent among musicologists, it was their least successful. The plot of *Così fan tutte* is frankly absurd. Even the most loyal Mozart aficionados do not attempt to relate it to real life.

Two young men are engaged to their sweethearts. An older friend challenges them to test their fiancées' love by appearing in disguise and each attempting to seduce the other's fiancée. Absurd, yes, and also immoral.

For this reason Vienna's director of Italian opera and kapellmeister Antonio Salieri[†] had turned it down. Opera was created to portray nobler ideals than that. Much later Constanze herself confessed she did not much admire the plot, and Beethoven dismissed it as trivial and unsuited both to the high art of opera and the musical genius of Mozart.

Così is a long opera, running without cuts (which is rare) to around four hours, but it contains a moment of heart-stopping beauty. As the two young men set off to sea at the end of Act I scene 1, the two female characters, Fiordiligi and Dorabella, joined by their fiancés' friend Don Alfonso, wish them a safe journey with the trio '*Soave sia il vento*' ('May the winds be gentle'). The beauty of this is enhanced by the relatively unusual combination of soprano, mezzo-soprano and bass voices.

The opera premiered successfully, but further performances were abruptly interrupted by the sudden death of the emperor, Joseph II. Vienna went into official mourning, and all the theatres were closed.

Mozart and Da Ponte would not work together again. In fact the emperor's death spelled the end of Da Ponte's career in Vienna. Those who had

> "*It is not music to everyone's taste, merely tickling the ear and letting the heart starve.*"
>
> One of numerous harsh reviews for *Don Giovanni*.

---

[*] Solomon, *Mozart, A Life*. The amount approximates to a little short of £32,000.

[†] He had succeeded Gluck as kapellmeister after Gluck's death in 1787.

been jealous of his collaborations with Mozart conspired against him, and he was dismissed from court service. His life then took some colourful turns.

He had in his pocket a valuable letter of recommendation from the late emperor to his sister in Paris, a certain Queen Marie Antoinette. Da Ponte set off for Paris where the French Revolution was taking its violent course, only to learn while travelling that the King and Queen of France had been arrested.

He diverted his journey round Paris and headed for the Normandy coast, his new target being London. There, he took what employment he could, including teaching Italian, and even setting up as a purveyor of fruit and vegetables, effectively a grocer, before landing a job more suited to his talents – librettist at the King's Theatre.

But increasing debts and finally bankruptcy forced him to flee to the United States, where he settled (still unmarried) with his mistress and children, once again setting up a grocery store and teaching Italian.

At the age of seventy-nine he became a naturalised American citizen, and five years later founded the New York Opera Company, which would one day, after many vicissitudes, become the Metropolitan Opera.

Da Ponte had made his mark in the United States, and when he died in New York at the age of eighty-nine, an enormous funeral ceremony was held for him in the old St Patrick's Cathedral, centre of Roman Catholicism in the city. One can imagine that would have pleased him. Even more he would have been truly gratified to know that his name – his adopted name – would forever be associated with the greatest composer who ever lived. But I doubt it would have surprised him.

⌣⟶

Let us return to the year 1787, which began with the triumphant success of *Le nozze* in Prague, continued with the premiere of *Don Giovanni*, and also saw the composition of a substantial number of chamber works, including the String Quintet No. 3 in C (K. 515); *Ein musikalische Spass* ('A Musical Joke') (K. 522),[*] and his single most popular chamber piece, *Eine kleine Nachtmusik* (K. 525).

In April he received a visit in the Domgasse apartment from a lad of sixteen, short (like himself), thickset, unruly hair, unkempt clothes, with a guttural accent from the Rhineland. He introduced himself as Ludwig van Beethoven.

---

[*] At the end of which the instruments fall apart, wrong notes everywhere. It is not known what inspired Mozart to write this. We can assume he heard a musical ensemble play, they were simply not up to it, and he parodied them.

Mozart bade the boy play, and Beethoven began with a piece by Mozart, naturally. Mozart waved it away, saying he had obviously learned it for the occasion, and invited him to play something of his own.

Beethoven asked Mozart for a tune, any tune, and he would improvise on it. Mozart obliged, and Beethoven proceeded then to give the most remarkable display of improvisation Mozart had witnessed.

He walked into the adjoining room, where Constanze was entertaining friends, and said, 'Watch out for that boy; one day he will give the world something to talk about.'[47] He agreed to take Beethoven on as a pupil, but Beethoven received word from Bonn that his mother had fallen seriously ill, her life was in danger, and he should return to Bonn immediately.

Thus the two great musicians, one at the height of his fame, the other beginning to make his way, met just this once. Oh, to have been a fly on the wall at that encounter! And what if Beethoven had taken lessons with Mozart? Might Mozart the perfectionist have rounded the sharp corners, smoothed the rough edges of Beethoven's music? Possibly. We shall never know.

The year ended well for Mozart. In December Emperor Joseph finally gave him paid employment. He was appointed Imperial Royal and

Chamber Composer, a position made vacant by the death of Gluck. It was only part time, requiring Mozart to compose no more than dances for the annual ball in the Redoutensaal in the imperial Hofburg Palace. It paid modestly, just 800 florins a year[*] – Gluck had been paid 2,000 florins – but it was employment.

In fact, being only part time and with such a huge reduction in salary, it was close to being an insult, even if he was so much younger than Gluck and working only part time. But that was not how Mozart saw it. He wrote triumphantly to his sister Nannerl, 'You probably don't know that His Majesty, the Emperor, has taken me into his services. I am certain that you welcome this news.'

At last he should have been able to report to his father that he had secured paid employment at court. But it was not to be. Six months earlier he had received the shocking, devastating news that his father had died.

---

[*] Approximately £20,000.

21

THE FINAL, AND GREATEST, SYMPHONIES

*L*eopold had begun to complain about his health the previous autumn. He had humming noises in his head. 'Sometimes it lasts the whole day. I never have it in the morning when I get up. Who can tell where it comes from? It isn't in the blood. Perhaps it is wind; perhaps it comes from the digestion, or a weakness of the nerves.'

In January he wrote that his health was still not as good as it should be, and he hoped the spring weather would improve it. But his condition worsened, and Nannerl left her family in St Gilgen to come to Salzburg to care for her father. She spent two months with him, before having to return to her family at the end of April.

In early May the doctor diagnosed 'blockage of the spleen', and Leopold – ever the pessimist – informed a friend he was dying. Yet in what would be his final letters to both his daughter and son, he assured each of them he was rapidly recovering and would keep them informed if things became worse again.

It therefore came as a severe shock to them when they learned that on 28 May 1787 Leopold had died. Both suffered guilt from not having been with their father at the end, and both resented the fact he had not kept them informed about just how ill he was.

Mozart also had his own problems. Shortly before Leopold's death, he had faced the inevitable and realised he could no longer afford the rent in the Domgasse. He moved with his family into a small and much less expensive apartment in the Landstrasse suburb, on the other side of the river Wien and beyond the city wall.

This had occasioned Leopold's last mention of his son in a letter. It was written to Nannerl, and it showed that Leopold still considered his son incapable of managing his own affairs: 'Your brother now lives on the Landstrasse, No. 224. He writes, however, no reasons for that. Nothing! Unfortunately I can guess the reason.'

Which made it all the more wounding for his son that in his will his father left all his money to Nannerl, with proceeds from the Tanzmeisterhaus in Salzburg to be divided between them.

Or possibly not. Nannerl put the apartment and its contents up for auction, and Mozart said he wanted none of it, bar a single payment of 1,000 florins.* It was proof, if proof were needed, that Mozart was finally – *finally* – free of his father, the man who for so many years had dominated his life in every aspect.

One particularly sad effect of Leopold's death was that it drove his children even further apart. Relations between brother and sister were already strained because of Nannerl's continued disapproval of her brother's marriage and her refusal to accept Constanze as a sister-in-law.

Letters between them following their father's death exhibit no closeness or offering of mutual comfort. Later in the year Mozart signs off a letter to Nannerl with the words, 'A thousand farewells'. Only two letters followed, one warning her not to expect prompt replies from him due to stress of work, the other, final one, apologising for failing to congratulate her on her name-day.

There is no doubt it was antipathy towards Constanze, and resentment of her brother's breaking away from their father over the question of marriage, that caused the break between brother and sister.

Nannerl retained that antipathy to the end. In her will she left six items of jewellery that had come down in the family for generations, and should rightly have gone to Constanze, to her son. In an echo of her father's refusal to give Constanze a parting gift at the end of the visit to Salzburg, she could not bring herself to leave them to Constanze in her will, let alone give them to her as a gift.†

The two Mozart children, one an incomparable musical genius, the other an extremely talented musician, who had toured Europe together as children, confiding in each other, sharing, laughing, crying together, never healed their rift.

---

* Approximately £25,000.

† In fact her son remedied this, shortly after his mother's death.

As we have seen, 1787 was a triumphant year for Mozart musically, but in his personal life it seemed to have been one problem after another. His own health was causing him difficulties again. He complained of rheumatic pains, headaches and toothache. Then the move to the suburbs, and the death of his father. In swift succession he also lost two friends.

For Constanze, too, life was not easy. In the autumn of the previous year she gave birth again, but the baby boy had lived for only one month. She became pregnant again quickly, giving birth at the very end of the year. Thus while Mozart was worried about his own health, organising a move to the suburbs, then dealing with his father's death – not to mention composing – Constanze's pregnancy was progressing.

It would be the couple's fourth baby. Only one child had lived beyond two months. Karl Thomas was now three years of age, a toddler of boundless energy whose father worked day and often night, and whose mother was increasingly weighed down by yet another pregnancy. The fate of this new child must have been constantly on their mind. Would they lose this one?

A daughter was born to the Mozarts on 27 December 1787. After three sons there must have been joy and renewed hope that a daughter had been born. Why else would they have adorned her with no fewer than six names – Theresia Constanzia Adelheid Friedericke Maria Anna, the last two after Mozart's mother?

Mozart decided the family should move yet again – their third move in little over a year – this time further out of the city, to a lodging that had a garden. Theresia Constanzia would have the best start in life that her parents could give her.

Less than two weeks after the move, Theresia died of an intestinal disorder, bringing more sadness to the family. She had lived just six months.

I believe it is the mark of true genius that when external circumstances are bleak, creativity may not only continue, but soar. In a new lodging, mourning the death of a daughter, even describing himself as being frequently beset by black thoughts, Mozart experienced an extraordinary burst of creativity.

In a few short summer months he composed several chamber pieces, as well as his greatest symphonies. These were Nos. 39–41 (к. 543, 550 and 551). These symphonies were not commissioned, which meant that no one would pay him for them, and there was therefore no financial incentive.

Yet they are monumental works, four movements each, complex and intense. The last of them, No. 41, was given the name 'Jupiter', not by the composer, but probably by an impresario. It is not known why for certain, but it is likely the impresario recognised it as something not of this world.

The final movement of the 'Jupiter' builds to a five-part fugue, which is the most complex passage of symphonic writing Mozart ever created. But to describe it like that, reducing it to musical form, is to lose the sheer intensity of it. I always sense an air of despair in it, as if Mozart was somehow in a hurry, sensing this might be his last word on the symphonic form. As indeed it would prove to be, though of course he could not have known that.

There was a practical reason for Mozart turning to the symphonic form at this particular moment in his life. The novelty, for Viennese audiences, of coming to see Mozart perform his own piano concertos had worn thin, and so the subscription concerts, which had proved so successful and lucrative for him, had dwindled and then all but ceased.

His Piano Concerto No. 25 in C (κ. 503), which was composed in 1786, was the last concerto he had written to perform at a subscription concert. It was therefore natural that he would turn to another form, namely the symphony.

It was a risk, not least because Austria was now at war with Turkey. It was common practice for the aristocracy to help finance their country's wars. Attending concerts was now considerably lower down on their list of priorities than it would normally be.

There was also the fact that an orchestral concert was expensive to stage, and it lacked the allure of virtuosity at the keyboard. In fact these three symphonies did not reverse Mozart's fortunes. Far from it. It is believed he never heard the 'Jupiter' – indisputably his greatest symphony – performed in his lifetime.

We are left, then, to marvel at the genius that could compose three such great and enduring works, with unhappiness around him and his own mood decidedly dark, for little reason other than the creative impulse that demanded they be written.

We know for certain that Mozart was not earning good money, because round about this time he began writing what would become a series of letters to a friend. They are the most extraordinary letters, which have coloured our understanding of the final few years of his life, and at the same time – regrettable though it might seem – have gone some considerable way to diminishing our respect for him as an individual.

Here was a man, respected and admired throughout Europe as the outstanding musician and creative genius of his generation, with friends in high places, who, as a result of certain extravagances, was finding it hard to make ends meet.

Given the esteem in which he was held, there were ways of dealing with this. Discreetly. Maybe some private meetings, a few words spoken, an understanding come to, the promise of a dedication on the title page of a new composition.

Yet, as far as we know, this did not happen. Mozart selected a friend and instead of discretion, wrote him what can be described only as a series of begging letters. Intense begging letters, pleading extreme poverty. Fortunately for posterity, for our understanding of Mozart, the friend kept the letters. Perhaps unfortunately for Mozart.

⁓

This is where Mozart reaped the benefit of being a Freemason. The friend he approached, a textile merchant by the name of Michael Puchberg, was a fellow Freemason. Over the course of the next three-and-a-half years Mozart wrote twenty-one letters (at least) to Puchberg, each time asking for a loan or giving reasons why, for the moment, he was unable to pay money back.

To begin with, he stresses their friendship and 'brotherly love', a clear reference to their membership of the Masons. He asks for just a small amount, which he will soon be able to repay.

But as the months pass, the tone of the letters changes. Puchberg has lent him money, and been patient about repayment, but not in the sort of sums Mozart is asking for. His tone becomes anxious:

I have to admit that it is not possible for me right now to pay back the money you lent me. Instead, I must beg you to be patient a little longer! – I am indeed very troubled about the fact that you are not in a position to help me out in the manner I had wished! – My circumstances are such that I will have to borrow money no matter what. But, good Lord, whom can I trust? – No one but you, my dearest friend.

It is not long before anxiety turns to desperation:

Oh, God! The situation I am in, I wouldn't wish it on my worst enemy; and if you, my best friend and brother, forsake me, I, hapless and blameless as I am, *will be lost.*

A measure of Mozart's desperation is the fact that Puchberg was not the only person Mozart appealed to for loans. He borrowed from several others, including an official in the Ministry of Justice whose wife was one of his pupils. This couple, Franz and Magdalena Hofdemel, will make a dramatic re-entry into our story at its very end.

But Puchberg was by a long way Mozart's greatest creditor. Mozart asked him for a total of 4,000 florins over the three-and-a-half year period. In all, he received loans of 1,415 florins, paid in fifteen instalments of small amounts.[*]

---

[*] Approximately £100,000 asked for, £35,375 received. It seems that the full amount was eventually repaid by Constanze in the years following her husband's death.

As well as essential expenditure such as rent, and general living expenses such as food and clothes, Mozart's expenditure rose again when he enrolled his son Karl Thomas in a prestigious boarding school. On top of this there were the costs of moving home several times, more furniture and decorating, continual music copying – and, apparently, he was still keeping a horse and his own coach.

Given the fall in his income and the scale of his outgoings, it is clear Mozart was living beyond his means. Maynard Solomon has estimated that in the final five years of his life, Mozart earned somewhere between 14,315 and 20,140 florins.[*] This was not even close to being enough to cover his costs.

What was he to do? He took a bold decision, which must have surprised those close to him, just as it does us today. He decided to undertake a major tour, alone, to Berlin, Prague, Dresden and Leipzig, in the hope of finding paid employment and earning money.

He told Constanze he expected to be received by the King of Prussia in Berlin, and the Elector of Saxony in Dresden. Neither was a realistic prospect. If she expressed surprise at his decision, he used as a clinching argument the fact that one of the most senior aristocrats in the city, Count Lichnowsky,[†] was leaving for Berlin and had offered him a seat in his carriage.

She will surely have drawn attention to the fact that her health was not good. She had just become pregnant again, for the fifth time in a little over six years, and the consecutive pregnancies had taken their toll.

But he left early in the morning of 8 April 1789. He probably felt some guilt about leaving his wife, because within hours of his departure, in fact while Lichnowsky was sorting out a change of horses, he was writing to her in the most loving terms:

> *Dearest little wife of my heart, a few quick words – How are you? – Are you thinking of me as often as I am thinking of you? I look at your portrait every few minutes – and cry – half out of joy, half out of sorrow! – Please look after your health, which is so dear to me, and stay well, my darling! – I am writing this with tears in my eyes.*

But things did not continue quite like that. For the first couple of weeks he writes almost every other day. But then for a whole month there is nothing.

"Given the fall in his income and the scale of his outgoings, it is clear Mozart was living beyond his means."

---

[*] Solomon, *Mozart, A Life*. The amounts approximate to between £357,000 and £502,000 in total, or between £70,000 and £100,000 a year.

[†] Beethoven's future patron.

Constanze is obviously concerned. Her letters to him are lost, but after a month's silence he writes to her, clearly responding to her concerns by suggesting that no fewer than four letters he has written must have gone astray: 'I wrote to you from Leipzig on April 22nd, from Potsdam on the 28th, again from Potsdam on May 5th, from Leipzig on the 9th.' He turns the tables on Constanze by pointing out that he spent seventeen days in Potsdam '*without any letters*': 'The strangest thing of all is that we both found ourselves *at the same time in the same sad situation.*'

In the same letter he casually mentions a soprano he has known for years, Josepha Duschek. In Dresden he accompanied her on the piano while she sang arias from *Le nozze di Figaro* and *Don Giovanni*. She was alone; her husband had not travelled from Prague to be with her.

Josepha followed him to Leipzig, which he describes to Constanze as a stroke of luck. It is clear from his response to her that she has accused him of forgetting her, and possibly of more. He reacts with righteous indignation, spiced with dirty talk typical of years gone by; but this time, it feels forced, as if he were trying to capture the past:

> *Oh, how glad I shall be to be with you again, my darling! The first thing I shall do is to take you by your front curls. For how on earth could you think, or even imagine, that I had forgotten you? How could I possibly do so? For even* supposing *such a thing, you will get on the very first night a thorough spanking on your dear little kissable arse, and this you may count upon.*

And four days later, he gives an extraordinarily graphic account of the sexual frustration he feels at being away from her:

> *Spruce up your sweet little nest, because my little rascal here really deserves it. He has been very well behaved but now he's itching to possess your sweet —— Just imagine that little rascal, while I am writing he has secretly crept up on the table and now looks at me questioningly. But I, without much ado, give him a little slap – but now he is even more ——* * *He is almost out of control – the scoundrel.*

It is not difficult to imagine Constanze, sceptical about the lost letters in the first place, pregnant and unwell, reacting with frustration, even anger, when she read his words. Particularly since, in the same letter, he prepares her for bad news as far as the financial success of the trip goes:

---

* On both occasions '——' represents words crossed out in the original letter, whether by Mozart or someone else is not clear.

My dearest little wife, when I return, you'll have to be content with seeing me rather than money ... my concert in Leipzig did not bring much, just as I had predicted, therefore I made a 32-mile round-trip almost for nothing.

But was it almost for nothing, and had his 'little rascal' really been well behaved? To put the question bluntly: did he have a sexual relationship with Josepha Duschek, while both of them were away from their spouses?

As with his cousin, the Bäsle, we can only examine the evidence and reach our own conclusion. Certainly his behaviour on the trip points to it. *Four* letters went astray? Is that really credible? According to his account to his wife, it was almost as though he met up with Josepha by accident, or good fortune. Could it instead have been elaborately planned? He knew her well from years gone by. Could he have contacted her, even, to set up the trip and the meeting? It is easy to believe he was somewhat fed up with things in Vienna. There was not much work for him, he had financial problems, his wife was pregnant yet again and, predictably, unwell. Oh, to get away from it all!

Was he capable of such behaviour, at least of being unfaithful even if not of plotting an entire trip? There were some who clearly thought so. After his death, it seems there were no holds barred.

A newspaper, *Der heimliche Botschafter* ('The Secret Messenger'), admittedly something of a scandal sheet, wrote that 'Mozart unfortunately had that indifference to his family circumstances which so often attaches to great minds.'[48] An obituarist wrote, 'In Vienna [Mozart] married Constanze Weber and found in her a good mother and a worthy wife, who tried to deter him from many follies and debaucheries.'[49]

Those closer to him seemed to concur. A biographer who knew him well in his final years, wrote, 'Mozart was a man, therefore as liable to human failings as anyone else. The very characteristics and strength which were needed for his great talent were also the origin and cause of many a blunder.' He added, 'He loved [Constanze] dearly, confided everything to her, even his petty sins – and she forgave him with loving kindness and tenderness.'[50]

More ominously, Constanze's second husband Georg Nissen took these words verbatim and included them in his biography of Mozart, adding a direct quote from Constanze: 'One must forgive him, one must make things good for him, because he was so good.' And in Nissen's own words: 'As a man he may have had many weaknesses ... He was high-spirited and pleasure-seeking, even in his youth.'[51] These words must have had Constanze's approval.

Constanze's younger sister, Sophie, recalled that 'to keep him from relationships of a hazardous kind, his wife patiently took part in everything with him'. Mozart's pupil Hummel denied the stories, at the same time as confirming them: 'I declare it to be untrue that Mozart abandoned himself to excess, except on those rare occasions on which he was enticed.'[52] And Mozart's later biographer, Otto Jahn, heard from one of Constanze's sisters that 'Constanze was not always patient, and there were occasional violent outbreaks.'[53]

None of this, of course, proves the case one way or another. If I were forced to make a judgement, I would say that the circumstantial evidence, indeed the circumstances, were so propitious that it would have taken a stronger man than Mozart to resist.

What we do know is that Mozart returned to Vienna on 4 June, having earned very little from the trip, certainly having had no meetings with rulers or any job offers, to find his heavily pregnant wife in such poor health that she needed urgent medical attention.

Immediately he resumes writing begging letters to Puchberg, and the tone is desperate:

> Oh God! instead of thanking you, I come to you with new requests! – instead of paying off my debts, I come asking for more. If you can see into my heart, you know how anguished I am about this. I probably won't need to tell you once again that [Constanze's] unfortunate illness is slowing me down with my earnings ... fate is against me ... it's now up to you, my one and only friend, whether you will or can lend me another 500 gulden?[*] I would suggest that until my affairs are settled I'll pay you back 10 gulden a month, then (as matters will turn around in a couple of months) return the whole sum to you with whatever interest you may wish to charge and, at the same time, acknowledge myself as your debtor for life.

Constanze was dangerously unwell. In one of his letters to Puchberg, Mozart describes her as resigned to her fate, whether that be recovery or death. He may have been exaggerating a little, since we know Constanze went on to live for another fifty years.

But she had suffered a ruptured varicose vein, which gave her intense pain in the foot. According to Mozart the bone itself was in danger, though it is not clear exactly what he means by that.

The family physician, Dr Thomas Franz Closset, recommended that Constanze should take the sulphur baths in the spa town of Baden, south of Vienna. More expense for her husband.

"Mozart was a man, therefore as liable to human failings as anyone else."

Mozart biographer

---

[*] Approximately £12,500.

Constanze returned to Vienna to give birth, and there must have been unalloyed joy when a daughter was once again born to the couple. She was named Anna Maria, again after her paternal grandmother.

Anna Maria lived for just one hour.

All this personal trauma at a time when Mozart was working on his opera *Così fan tutte*, as well as the exquisite Clarinet Quintet in A (к. 581). His creative juices were still in no way dimmed.

Mentally, though, he was in an increasingly fragile state. It was not helped by Constanze's health deteriorating once again. On doctor's advice, she returned to Baden. Mozart writes yet another begging letter to Puchberg, in a tone almost of exasperation:

> *My wife is slightly better. She already feels some relief, but she will have to take the baths sixty times – and later in the year she will have to go there again. God grant that it may do her good.*

More worryingly, relations between the couple were deteriorating. The tension was getting to them both. Health concerns following another infant death and money problems, with she in Baden, and he in Vienna.

It is clear that Constanze, who must have been in some despair down in Baden, has reproached him for not writing to her. He does not take the criticism lightly, and again turns the table on her:

> *DEAREST LITTLE WIFE!*
>
> *I trust that you have received my letter. Well, I must scold you a little, my love! Even if it is not possible for you to get a letter from me, you could write all the same. For must all your letters be* replies *to mine? I was most certainly expecting a letter from my dear little wife – but unfortunately I was mistaken. Well, you must make amends and I advise you to do so, otherwise I shall never, never forgive you.*

It was one of the least loving letters he had ever written to her.

Mozart is clearly dejected, anxious about his career, worried about his finances, concerned for his wife's health. It has been suggested that at this point in his life Mozart was perilously close to a total breakdown.[54]

Predictably his own health began to suffer. He complains of not being able to sleep, of catching a chill from walking too much and becoming over-heated. Good enough reasons to ask Puchberg for yet *another* loan, even 'the *smallest* amount'. It is as if he has lost all moral scruples about pleading for money. He is, possibly, at the lowest ebb in his life, and is about to descend even lower.

On 20 February 1790, Mozart's most high-ranking patron, Emperor Joseph II, died at the age of forty-eight. It was totally unexpected and the Habsburg empire went into deep mourning.

True, Joseph had never given Mozart the full-time employment he – and his father – had wanted so much for him, but he had encouraged and even applauded him. Now Mozart would have to start from scratch in building a relationship with the emperor's successor, his brother Leopold.

To say that it started poorly would be an over-statement. It never started at all. For the new emperor's coronation in Frankfurt, Vienna's leading musicians were invited, including Haydn and Salieri. Mozart was ignored, we do not know why – possibly a combination of his relative youth, his unpredictability, his scant adherence to formality and custom. Whatever the reason, he was hurt by the omission.

With little thought for Constanze he went anyway, borrowing money to finance the trip, determined to make his presence felt. He never got near to the emperor, and the few recitals he gave earned him practically nothing. He returned to Vienna even more in debt.

While he was away, though, Constanze, partially recovered from illness, took matters into her own hands. She negotiated a loan of 1,000 florins[*] against their furniture, which was enough to cover her husband's debts, and leave some money to live on. It was to be paid over two years at 5 per cent interest, which was manageable.

She also decided they would move, yet again, into a first-floor apartment in the centre of the city, with a more manageable rent. There was a room large enough for Mozart to teach in, and for a small chamber ensemble to play in. With perhaps undeserved consideration, she made sure there was a courtyard below for his carriage and horse.

Mozart was overjoyed at his wife's efforts, and determined to keep working hard, almost as if that alone would bring its own reward. There was renewed optimism in the Mozart household. Marital relationships seemed to be repaired. Within a short time Constanze was pregnant again.

The renowned London impresario, Johann Peter Salomon, invited both Haydn and Mozart to come to London, where he promised them a glittering reception. Mozart refused to go. He would not leave Constanze, and she could not accompany him because of her pregnancy.

Haydn accepted, and on the evening before his departure he had dinner with Mozart. Afterwards, Mozart walked Haydn, whom he called 'Papa', to his carriage. He implored the older man (Haydn was fifty-eight) to take care on the long journey, otherwise the two of them might never meet again.

Mozart was right. But it was he who would not live to see Haydn's return.

---

[*] Approximately £25,000.

22

A Stranger Knocks

Given that he did not live to see the end of it, the year 1791 was an *annus horribilis* for Mozart, but an *annus mirabilis* for humanity. He began the year with a burst of creativity. In January he composed his first piano concerto for three years – perhaps the form that came to him most naturally, or at least the form he most enjoyed, since it united him at the keyboard with an orchestra – No. 27 in B flat (к. 595), which he performed himself in March.

He followed this with three songs celebrating spring and a collection of dances for the Redoutensaal (the concert hall in the Hofburg). He composed a string quintet (к. 614), as well as other smaller works. No matter what else was going on in his life, there simply was, for him, no alternative to creating music.

Also – and this would certainly have pleased his father – he applied to the Vienna Municipal Council for the post of assistant kapellmeister at St Stephen's Cathedral, and on 9 May it was approved. He had employment. But his father's joy would have been severely diluted by the fact that it was unpaid.

Mozart would have responded to that by pointing out that the job carried with it a guarantee that when the present incumbent died (he was fifty-two, but had been in ill health for some years), he was guaranteed to succeed as kapellmeister, on a salary of 2,000 florins.* In the event, the incumbent would outlive him.

---

* Approximately £50,000.

Constanze's health was still a worry, and her pregnancy was not helping. Her foot was causing her serious problems. She found it difficult to walk and could not climb stairs. Mozart arranged for her to return to the spa in Baden. She left on 4 June, and took young Karl (aged six) with her.

Over the following weeks, Mozart went down to Baden several times to join his wife and son. The visits were brief, and it was on one of these that he composed one of the shortest, yet most heart-stoppingly beautiful pieces of music he was ever to compose. It was for a local schoolteacher and choirmaster, to thank him for arranging for Constanze to have ground-floor accommodation so she would not have to climb stairs. Inspiration for Mozart did not have to be divine.

The piece of music was a motet, just a few minutes long, with the title *Ave verum corpus* (K. 618). Lucky schoolteacher, lucky choir. Lucky us.

For much of the time, though, Mozart was alone in Vienna, exactly what he needed to work on an exciting new project that had, as it were, come out of nowhere. For some years Mozart had known a colourful character by the name of Emanuel Schikaneder, a man of many parts. He was immersed in the world of theatre, turning his hand to a variety of roles – manager, writer, actor, singer, composer, even dancer.

Since 1789 Schikaneder had managed the suburban theatre, the Frei-haus-Theater an der Wieden.* In the early summer of 1791 he came to Mozart with the idea for an entirely new opera, which he would of course write himself and in which he would sing one of the leading roles.

This would be a new kind of venture for Mozart. He would not be working for one of the court theatres, beholden either to royalty or to the aristocracy. The Theater an der Wieden was entirely different from the Burgtheater and other imperial theatres. It was self-contained in a large complex of buildings, which included apartments, shops and gardens. The theatre was enormous and could seat a thousand people.

The audience, by and large, would be made up of local residents, from both inside and outside the complex. This would not be a sophisticated aristocratic audience, such as might attend the Burgtheater. They would be middle and working class, 'ordinary' people. They would not want anything too complex or subtly satirical. First and foremost, they would want to be entertained, to be made to gasp and laugh. And in their own language, German.

Mozart seemed never to hesitate when the offer of composing an opera came along. He relished the chance to work with both orchestra and voices,

---

* He would later go on to own and manage the Theater an der Wien, where Beethoven would premiere many of his works, including his opera *Fidelio*.

and enjoyed all the many facets of opera production and the world it created in the mind.

Schikaneder's plan appealed to him too. He was a fellow Freemason, and had the idea of a fantasy based around the Masonic ideals of virtue, courage and clemency, all wrapped in the quest of the lead character for emotional fulfilment while undergoing trials and rituals.

The number three, which holds a special place in Masonic ritual, permeates the opera: three ladies, three boys, three slaves, three temples, three chances. Mozart's overture begins with three chords, which recur at important moments. He chooses as his home key E flat major, which has three flats and is used in Masonic music so frequently it is known as the Masonic key.

Schikaneder's libretto, as far as we know, was entirely original. He gave his work the title *Die Zauberflöte* ('The Magic Flute').

Mozart threw himself into the project, and thereby – possibly – hangs a tale. Schikaneder provided Mozart with a small garden house in the complex near the theatre building. Mozart spent the days in this house, working. Did he also spend the nights in it, or nearby, and not on his own?

Certainly rumours circulated to that end, during and afterwards. It was said he became very close to two of the singers, Barbara Gerl who played Papagena and Anna Gottlieb who sang Pamina.

It was Anna Gottlieb who made that appearance at the unveiling of the statue to Mozart in Salzburg, declaiming that she was the first Pamina. In newspaper interviews occasioned by her reappearance she hinted strongly that she had been more than that, that she had been involved romantically with Mozart.

Of Barbara Gerl, Mozart's biographer Otto Jahn stated that 'contemporaries affirmed that this very pretty and attractive woman had completely entangled Mozart in her coils'.[55]

Also, at the time Mozart was working on *Die Zauberflöte*, it was strongly rumoured in musical circles that he was conducting an affair with Magdalena Hofdemel, the piano pupil who was the wife of the man Mozart had written to pleading for a loan.

This would end in tragedy. On the day of Mozart's funeral, Franz Hofdemel attacked his wife with a razor, slashing her face and hands. He then cut his own throat. He died, but she survived. Magdalena was pregnant at the time. Vienna was soon awash with reports that the child was Mozart's, even that Hofdemel had poisoned Mozart in revenge. Both stories swiftly evaporated. The fact that Mozart had died in debt to Hofdemel (among others), and that he himself had accrued huge gambling debts, may have been contributory factors.

"Mozart seemed never to hesitate when the offer of composing an opera came along."

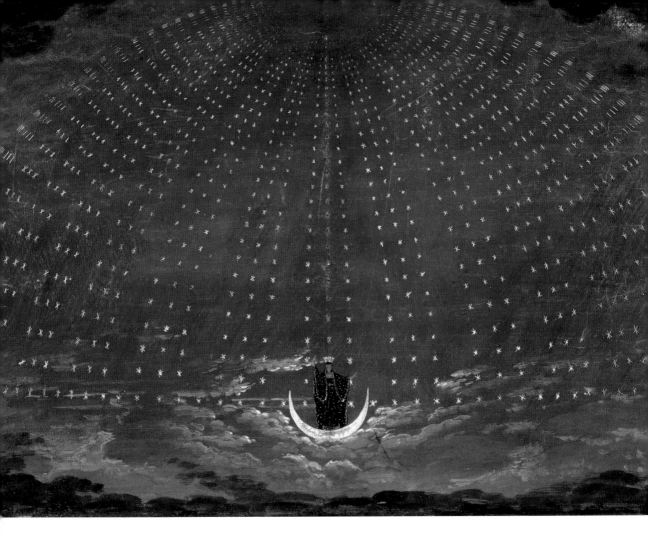

Above

The arrival of the Queen of the Night. Stage set for an 1815 production of *Die Zauberflöte*.

It is clear that down in Baden Constanze had her suspicions about what Mozart might be up to. Her letters to him have not survived, but it seems he is responding to her suspicion that he might not be spending nights at home when he writes, with a wry sense of humour:

> *And where did I sleep? – at home, of course – in fact, I slept very well – although the mice kept me pretty good company – and I had a first-rate argument with them.*

And he adds a postscript to the letter which almost goes too far in its protestations of love:

> *– catch – catchbis – bis – bis – bs – bs – lots of little kisses are flying through the air for you – – – bs – here is one more tottering after the others –*

Only days later there is a tone almost of desperation in his letter, as if he is trying too hard to convince her of his love:

You can't imagine how slowly time has been passing without you! – I cannot describe to you what I feel, but there's a sort of emptiness – which hurts somehow – a certain longing that is never fulfilled and therefore never stops – it's always there – and even grows from day to day … not even my work gives me joy any more.

No joy in his work? Yet he was composing the most joyful, optimistic, exuberant opera he ever composed. Maynard Solomon interprets these words as guilt over his infidelities. They may be. If they were, we can only be certain that feeling did not infuse his work.

He was in the midst of writing *Die Zauberflöte* when there occurred something truly strange, that has given rise to legend and intrigue ever since.

A stranger knocked on the door of Mozart's apartment in the Rauhensteingasse, with a letter offering him a commission to compose a Requiem Mass. The letter was unsigned. The man refused to identify either himself or the person on whose behalf he was acting, and warned Mozart not to try to find out the identity of either of them.

In the months that followed, as Mozart struggled to complete the work with his health failing, the stranger pursued him, demanding to know – on behalf of his client – where the Requiem was, to the extent that Mozart, in despair, believed he was writing the Requiem for himself – in other words, foreseeing his own death.

It is a story that has been told powerfully and many times since.[*] It originated with Mozart's early biographer Niemetschek, whose primary source was Constanze herself. Significantly, Constanze did not witness the episode at first hand, since she was in Baden. Nor, of course, did Niemetschek.

In essence the story is true, though in all probability it unfolded a little less melodramatically than Niemetschek recounts. The stranger was certainly unknown to Mozart, but it would not have taken Mozart long to establish who the writer of the letter was, not least because he was another Freemason. His name was well known in musical circles.

Count Franz Walsegg was an aristocratic landowner who lived in a castle around fifty miles south-west of Vienna. He was also a keen music lover who invited chamber ensembles to play for him in his castle.

---

[*] Perhaps most famously in the 1984 film *Amadeus*, based on Peter Shaffer's 1979 play, which portrayed the mysterious messenger as the ghost of his father, still giving him orders from beyond the grave.

The Count had tried his hand at composing, and found it rather more difficult than he had imagined. He then had the brilliant idea of inviting composers to write pieces for him, and then pay them to allow him to publish the compositions under his own name.[*]

The musicians who played for him were well aware of this arrangement, even if his friends and colleagues were not. It seems the count thought he was fooling the musicians too. One of them recounted years later that, after they had played a piece, the count would ask them to guess who had written it. They knew perfectly well it was written by someone else, but they guessed his name to flatter him.

In February 1791 Count Walsegg's adored wife died at the age of just twenty. The count was only twenty-eight himself, and would never remarry, though he lived for another thirty-six years.

Such was his grief that he decided to commission a Requiem Mass to be composed especially for her. And, as he had become used to doing, his intention was to claim the piece as his own work. He would certainly have known of Mozart, since the tenant in one of his Vienna properties was none other than Michael Puchberg, recipient of Mozart's begging letters. Puchberg would have known how to find Mozart, and thus the elaborate ruse began.

Once Mozart had established who the anonymous benefactor was, we need not be too shocked that he entered into the ruse. Mozart would have known that Count Walsegg paid well for the privilege of passing off other composers' work as his own. Why should Mozart complain? It would bring money in when he most needed it, and it no doubt appealed to his sense of fun. Fooling an aristocratic audience who thought they knew about music? Why not?

The biggest problem Mozart had was actually finding the time to put pen to paper. A Requiem was, by its nature, a large work. The sacred text was established, and could not be deviated from.

He set to work immediately. Hardly had he begun, than another substantial commission came in.[†] He was asked to write a new opera as part of the ceremonies for the new emperor in Prague in early September (compensation for not having been invited to the coronation in Frankfurt perhaps?). He was presented with a suitable libretto, already written, centring round the notion of a forgiving and benevolent emperor. The title was *La clemenza di Tito*.

---

[*] Something Count Waldstein had done in Bonn with a teenage Beethoven.

[†] This commission might have come before the commission for the Requiem. The chronology is not entirely clear.

It is tiring just to imagine the workload Mozart has taken on. He was working flat out on *Die Zauberflöte*; he had accepted a commission to compose a Requiem Mass for orchestra, soloists and choir; and he had agreed to compose an entirely new opera for the emperor's coronation, which needed to be ready in a matter of weeks.

It was not just a heavy workload, it was punishing, and Mozart, inevitably, would pay the price.

In his domestic life too, things were hardly peaceful. Constanze returned to Vienna and on 26 July she gave birth to a son. He was christened Franz Xaver Wolfgang. He was the couple's sixth child, and a brother for Karl Thomas. The parents' joy must have been tempered by the fear that Franz might not live for long, like his four unfortunate siblings.

A decision was then taken that might seem extraordinary to us today. Mozart needed to travel to Prague to oversee rehearsals for *La clemenza di Tito*, and it was decided that Constanze would accompany him. It meant putting Karl into a kindergarten, away from his parents at the age of six. It also meant they would have to leave their newborn son, just a month old, in the care of Constanze's mother and her sister Sophie.

Who exactly made the decision, whether Mozart or Constanze, or both, and whether they were agreed on this course of action, we do not know. Did Constanze willingly leave her baby behind, or was the decision forced on

her? Maynard Solomon suggests that Mozart's infidelities while Constanze was in Baden might have persuaded her she needed to be with him to prevent any more misbehaviour. It seems a drastic decision, in any case.

La clemenza di Tito premiered on 6 September at the National Theatre in Prague, with Mozart directing from the keyboard. The newly crowned emperor and empress – the coronation had taken place on the same day – were guests of honour.

As soon as the opera was launched, Mozart needed to get back to Vienna to supervise the opening of *Die Zauberflöte*, which was scheduled for 30 September. But his health was suffering.

'While he was in Prague Mozart became ill and was continually receiving medical attention,' wrote Niemetschek, his source, as always, the person who was closest to Mozart: his wife Constanze. 'He was pale and his expression was sad, although his good humour was often shown in merry jest with his friends.'[56] That irrepressible Mozart humour always just below the surface.

There was no time to be ill. As soon as they could, Mozart and Constanze rushed back to Vienna. It is probable, therefore, that Mozart was not aware that *La clemenza* had been very poorly received, though word must have reached him in Vienna. The empress, no less, in remarkably candid language, dismissed it as 'German piggery' (*porcheria tedesca*). 'The gala opera was not much and the music very bad so that almost all of us fell asleep,' she wrote.[57]

A second performance played to a half-empty theatre, and the theatre manager who had commissioned it later petitioned the authorities to be reimbursed for his losses. Niemetschek himself put the opera's relative failure down to the surfeit of entertainment on offer to celebrate the coronation – dances, balls and amusements.

The same was most certainly not true of *Die Zauberflöte*. Mozart directed the opening night from the keyboard, and it was a roaring success. The cavernous Freihaus-Theater was full to capacity. The locals flocked to see it, night after night.

If Mozart was close to exhaustion, his wife was suffering too. The whirlwind trip to Prague had taken its toll. At the end of the first week of October, Constanze went down to Baden again, this time taking baby Franz Xaver with her, as well as her sister Sophie to help look after him.

She was gone for only a week, but Mozart kept her up to date with a letter every other day. *Die Zauberflöte* continued its triumphant progress:

> *I've just come back from the opera – it was full as ever – The Duetto* 'Mann und Weib' *and the Glockenspiel in the first act had to be repeated as usual – the same was true of the boys' trio in the 2nd act, but what really makes me happy is the* Silent applause! *– one can feel how the opera is rising and rising.*

And that mischievous sense of humour bursts through, despite the fact that he must have been exhausted and drained. There is always time for a practical joke, based around the fact that Papageno on stage mimes playing the glockenspiel:

> *When Papageno's aria with the Glockenspiel came on, I went backstage because I had an urge to play the Glockenspiel myself – So I played this joke just when Schikaneder came to a pause. I played an arpeggio – he was startled – looked into the scenery and saw me – stopped as well*

and did not go on singing – I guessed what he was thinking and played another chord – at that he gave his Glockenspiel a slap and shouted 'shut up!' – everybody laughed – I think through this prank many in the audience realised for the first time that Papageno doesn't play the Glockenspiel himself.

It is a beguiling image, the composer of one of the most popular operas ever written, not taking himself, or his opera, too seriously.

So here we have Mozart, a newly composed opera running (if sporadically) in Prague, a newly composed opera running night after night in Vienna, turning again to the Requiem Mass he has been commissioned to compose. How then does he also find time to compose one of the best loved of all his compositions, the bright and cheerful Clarinet Concerto in A (K. 622), for the clarinet virtuoso Anton Stadler? We can only marvel.

After the week's rest in Baden, which she so badly needed, Constanze can hardly have been surprised on returning to Vienna to find her husband utterly exhausted. He had not stopped working, every day, from dawn until late at night.

Added to that it appeared that his morale had plummeted. He had become despondent and pessimistic. The letters, telling of boisterous practical jokes, had not told the whole truth.

Constanze later told Niemetschek that to try to cheer her husband up, she had taken him for a carriage ride in the Prater. They were sitting alone, when Mozart began to speak of death, and declared that the Requiem he was writing was for himself.

'Tears came to the eyes of this sensitive man,' she told Niemetschek. She then quoted her husband as saying, 'I feel definitely that I will not last much longer. I am sure I have been poisoned. I cannot rid myself of this idea.'[58]

Niemetschek duly published her words, and a conspiracy theory was born that lives to this day.

23

THE TASTE OF DEATH ON MY TONGUE

Constanze tried to take control. She urged her husband to put the Requiem aside, to stop work on it. It was making him unnecessarily depressed. For a time he obeyed, working on a small cantata for his Masonic Lodge. It was the last work he completed.

But he was anxious to return to the Requiem. He was aware he needed to complete it in order to receive full payment. There was also the musical imperative. He had begun it; he simply had to bring it to fruition.

In mid November 1791 his health unexpectedly deteriorated. His limbs became swollen, he was subjected to sudden uncontrollable vomiting. Soon he became immobile. He was confined to bed. His wife and sister-in-law Sophie made him a night-jacket that he could put on from the front, his body being so swollen that he could not turn in bed. They also made him a quilted dressing-gown that he could wear when he got out of bed. He was really looking forward to wearing it, Sophie said. In fact he was never able to get out of bed again.

He continued to work on the Requiem, but soon he was unable to hold a pen. In the room, along with his wife and Sophie, were three friends, singers who had performed in *Die Zauberflöte*. They sang through the parts of the Requiem he had composed. When they reached the first bars of the *Lacrimosa*, Mozart began to weep violently and they had to stop.

There also was Franz Xaver Süssmayr, a composer who had studied with Mozart. He had become close to the Mozarts, accompanying Constanze on her visit to Baden ahead of giving birth to Franz Xaver. Mozart trusted him to copy out parts, and he accompanied both Mozart and his wife to Prague for the premiere of *La clemenza di Tito*, helping Mozart to complete it in time, to the extent of working on it with him even in the carriage en route to Prague.

Now, in the final days of Mozart's life, Süssmayr wrote on manuscript paper the notes Mozart spoke and the sounds that came from his mouth. Mozart composed, with Süssmayr's assistance, as far as the *Lacrimosa* at the end of the *Sequentia*. Parts of the *Offertorium* are in Mozart's hand, and Mozart was able to give instructions for later passages. After Mozart's death, Süssmayr would complete the Requiem, having been entrusted to do so by Constanze.

Sophie has left a vivid account of Mozart's final hours. His condition was so bad on the night of 4 December that Constanze believed he would not live through the night. She implored her sister to stay with him the next day.

Sophie recounts how she entered his room, and he immediately said:

Ah, dear Sophie, how glad I am that you have come. You must stay here tonight and see me die.

She protested, reassuring him. But, she said, he could not be persuaded:

Why, I already have the taste of death on my tongue. And, if you do not stay, who will support my dearest Constanze when I am gone?[59]

What followed, according to Sophie, was a catalogue of errors. First, in response to Constanze's pleas, she rushed out to St Peter's to find a priest, 'but for a long time they refused to come and I had a great deal of trouble to persuade one of those clerical brutes to go to him'.[60]

Nissen, Constanze's later husband, suggests Mozart's antipathy towards the clergy was well known by them, and the reason no priest came was because 'the sick person himself did not send for them'.[61] Revenge, in other words. Mozart thus did not receive the last rites, which probably would not have troubled him.

Of rather more practical use to Mozart was a doctor, but Sophie had no more luck there. She tried to find Dr Closset. After a long search she found him at the theatre, but he refused to come until the play had finished.

Sophie rushed back to the Rauhensteingasse, to find her sister inconsolable. Süssmayr was at Mozart's bedside. The score of the Requiem was on the bed cover. Mozart was struggling to explain to Süssmayr how he wanted him to complete it, mouthing the sound of the timpani.

Dr Closset finally came to the apartment and prescribed *cold* (Sophie's italics) compresses on Mozart's burning head. These gave him such a shock that he lost consciousness.

The two sisters give different accounts of Mozart's last moments. According to Constanze, after the doctor had left, Mozart asked what he had said. She answered with a soothing lie, but he said, 'It isn't true. I shall die now, just when I am able to take care of you and the children. Ah, now I will leave you unprovided for.'

And as he spoke those words, according to Constanze, 'Suddenly he vomited – it gushed out of him in an arc – it was brown, and he was dead.'[62] Constanze told Niemetschek she crawled into the bed beside his body, as if to try to catch his illness and die with him.

Sophie's account is more gentle. Even though the cold compresses had caused Mozart to lose consciousness, the doctor said he should continue to be given them. Sophie accordingly applied a damp towel to his forehead. Mozart immediately gave a slight shudder and a very short time afterwards died in her arms.

Above

Mozart's last days. Painting by Henry O'Neill.

Right

The house where
Mozart died on the
Rauhensteingasse.

Mozart's death was recorded as having taken place at fifty-five minutes past midnight on Monday, 5 December 1791. He was thirty-five years and ten months old.[*]

Word of Mozart's death quickly spread through the city. The following morning a crowd gathered in the Rauhensteingasse outside the Mozarts' apartment, waving handkerchiefs up at the windows. Close friends were allowed in to pay their respects at Mozart's bedside. His body lay on view for the whole of that day and the morning of the next.

---

[*] John O'Shea, in his *Music and Medicine* (J. M. Dent & Sons, 1990), gives probable cause of death as 'chronic renal failure exacerbated by terminal infection, probably broncho-pneumonia with, perhaps, streptococcal throat infection'.

One of Mozart's most supportive patrons, Baron van Swieten,[*] took over arrangements for the funeral. He decided, in consultation with Constanze, that Mozart would have a third-class funeral, the cheapest form of funeral available. Legend has it that Mozart was given a pauper's funeral and his body thrown in a paupers' grave. It is not true.

Three forms of paid-for funeral were available: first, second and third class, as well as an unpaid-for pauper's funeral. Most Viennese chose third class, since it cost a mere 8 florins 56 kreuzer, against 110 and 40 for first and second class.[†] It was the custom in any case, after Joseph II had simplified the whole burial system in the interests of economy and hygiene, to the extent of banning headstones and recommending sacks instead of coffins. Both Constanze and van Swieten can have had no doubt Mozart himself would not have objected to this.

At three o'clock on the afternoon of 7 December Mozart's body received a ritual blessing in a small side chapel of St Stephen's Cathedral. It was then taken by hearse via the Grosse Schullerstrasse to the cemetery in the village of St Marx, outside the city. Neither Constanze, nor anyone else, accompanied it. This, again, was normal.[‡]

There, Mozart's body, which had been sewn into a linen sack, was removed from the coffin and placed in a 'normal simple grave',[§] alongside five or six other bodies. No one attended the interment. Mozart therefore has no grave, no headstone or memorial plaque, and the precise location of his body is not known.[¶]

It was not long before recriminations began among Mozart's somewhat belated admirers, and their principal target was Constanze. Why had she not arranged a more elaborate funeral? Why had she not accompanied her husband to his final resting place? Why had she not ensured that there was a grave where admirers of her husband could pay their respects?

Later, through her second husband, the Danish diplomat Georg Nissen, she defended herself. None of Mozart's friends or musical colleagues accompanied the body because that was the custom, that the hearse would make its way unaccompanied to the cemetery for burial.

---

[*] And a future patron of Beethoven.

[†] Approximately £225, £2,750 and £1,000.

[‡] By contrast, for Beethoven's funeral thirty-five years later, twenty thousand people lined the streets of Vienna as the cortège passed through the streets.

[§] *Allgemeines einfaches Grab.*

[¶] A memorial to him was erected in the Musicians' Quarter of Vienna's Zentralfriedhof in 1859.

Right

Mozart's two surviving
sons: Franz Xaver
Wolfgang Mozart (left)
and Karl Thomas (right),
1798, by Hans Hansen.

As for her own absence, she was prevented from following 'the mortal remains of her inexpressibly beloved husband'[63] because she was unwell and because of the 'severe' winter weather. There is no indication in any eyewitness accounts of Mozart's death that Constanze was unwell – distraught, yes, but not unwell – and the weather on that day is reported to have been fine, albeit with a December chill.

It also seems to be the case that Constanze did not visit the cemetery until seventeen years after his death. According to the late Emperor Joseph's new regulations, after ten years graves were raked over and the plots reused. There would have been nothing for her to see. The cemetery itself was closed nearly seventy years later.

Constanze's reputation continues to suffer because of the way she handled her husband's funeral. The full facts – like Mozart's final resting place – will never be known. We can surely assume with a fair degree of certainty that Mozart would have raised no objections to any aspect of the way in which his funeral and burial were handled.

We can be equally sure he would have vented his anger, no doubt with choice scatological language, on members of the medical profession and the Church.

When Mozart died, Constanze was left a widow at the age of twenty-nine, with a seven-year-old son and a four-month-old baby. Mozart had left no will, and because he had been in employment at St Stephen's Cathedral for less than ten years, she was not entitled to a pension.

In the face of real financial hardship, Constanze went into action. In the first place she petitioned the emperor for a pension, even though she knew she was not entitled to it. She pointed out her late husband's loyalty to the court, and how cruel it was for him to have been taken from the world 'at that very moment when his prospects for the future were beginning to grow brighter on all sides'.[64]

The court not only awarded her one-third of Mozart's salary as Imperial Royal and Chamber Composer, but backdated it to the beginning of the year. This meant she would receive just over 265 florins a year,[*] the court being careful to point out that this was granted as a special favour and was not to be seen as a precedent.

She also organised memorial concerts of her husband's music, which raised money, and she embarked on a campaign to publish as many of his

---

[*] Approximately £6,625.

works as she could. Whatever criticisms might attach to Constanze surrounding the immediate aftermath of Mozart's death, there is no question that she worked tirelessly to promote his name and music.

She continued to do so, indeed all the more so, after she married Nissen in 1809 and moved to Copenhagen. It was his intention to write a full-length biography of his wife's first husband, collecting and collating all available material, and Constanze furnished him with letters, documents and, of course, priceless stories and anecdotes, which only she could have known.

To undertake the enormous task ahead of him, Nissen, with his wife Constanze, returned to Salzburg. There was clearly no more appropriate place to write the biography than in the city of Mozart's birth, the home of his family. That must have brought mixed emotions to Constanze. She was returning to the city in which her first husband's father and sister had been so unwelcoming when she arrived there as a new bride all those years ago.

But more sadness loomed. Nissen died suddenly in 1826. Constanze was a widow again. His vast biography, with unrivalled access to the true character of Mozart provided both by the composer's wife and sister, was completed after his death and published posthumously.

Wife *and* sister – for Constanze was not the only Mozart living in Salzburg. Nannerl, having left the city after her marriage more than forty years earlier, was once again living there. It had not been a happy marriage. Her husband, already twice a widower with five children and fifteen years older than her, was domineering and uncaring, her stepchildren unruly and unaccepting of her.

She bore her husband three children of her own. In effect there were two families living in the same household. It was not a happy existence. As well as the tensions, Nannerl had grown unhappy living in a village on the banks of a lake. Beautiful it might have been, but it was lonely and isolated.

Nannerl's husband at least did her the favour of dying at the age of sixty-five in 1801. After his death, Nannerl lost no time in packing up her things and moving back into the city of her birth, Salzburg.

It was there, twenty years later, that she received a visit. Her brother's son, her own nephew, Franz Xaver Wolfgang, now thirty years of age, knocked on her door. Wolfgang, as he preferred to be known, had inherited his father's musical talent – to a degree – and was on a concert tour of Europe, in which he performed his father's music on the piano.

He and Nannerl had never met, and there was an instant bond between them. Soon Wolfgang became a regular visitor to his aunt. He relished learning more about the father he had never known and who was now famous throughout Europe. He knew of his father's childhood genius and the many tours he had undertaken. Now he was able to hear about them from the very person who had accompanied him.

Nannerl, for her part, was overjoyed to see at first hand that the musical gift had been passed on. She wrote:

> *In my seventieth year I had the great joy of meeting for the first time the son of my dearly beloved brother. What delightful memories were invoked by hearing him play just as his father had played. These memories are treasured by his aunt.*[65]

My dearly beloved brother. Remember, relations between brother and sister had become severely strained with, in the end, practically no communication between them. Wolfgang, by invoking such dear memories of his father, in effect helped to repair relations between brother and sister.

Of more practical importance, Wolfgang spoke lovingly of his mother, the difficulties she had faced, the efforts she had taken to keep his father's memory alive, to promote his music. He also told her Constanze, and her husband Nissen, were embarking on a huge project to produce the definitive biography of his father.

The natural consequence of this was that Nannerl began to see Constanze through different eyes. Her attitude to her sister-in-law inevitably mellowed.

With timing that could hardly have been bettered, as this transformation was occurring, Constanze and her husband arrived in Salzburg to work on the biography. There, in the same city as them, was the one person who could provide them with unique insight into their subject's childhood.

Thus, for the first time for forty years, the two women who were closest to Mozart met. It was as if the past, with its animosity and tensions, melted away. Nannerl was only too pleased to relate all she could of her brother's childhood, and their tours together. Another family rift had at least to some extent been healed, even if never fully.

When she was in her mid-seventies Nannerl's health began to decline. Who would look after her, care for her? Constanze, naturally. Most distressingly, Nannerl slowly lost her sight. She was able to continue to play the small piano in her apartment. But then she lost the use of her left hand. This woman, such a child prodigy that in her earliest years she was considered a finer musician than her brother, would play no more.

Nannerl died, reconciled with those closest to her, on 29 October 1829 at the age of seventy-eight.

Constanze lived on for another twelve-and-a-half years, and they were far from lonely. She did not marry again, but two of her sisters, Aloysia and Sophie, came to live in Salzburg with her.

There had always been a certain amount of tension between Constanze and her elder sister Aloysia. Inevitable, really, given that Aloysia was her husband's first love. After rejecting him, Aloysia had gone on to a glittering career at the Vienna Court Opera. Mozart had maintained contact with her, writing several songs for her, and accompanying her at recitals. She also sang the role of Donna Anna at the premiere in Vienna of *Don Giovanni*.

Her personal life had been less successful. Her marriage to Joseph Lange had broken down; soon her singing roles dried up and her career stuttered and finally ended. She came to live in Salzburg with Constanze because she had fallen on hard times in Vienna, and needed financial support. Constanze willingly gave it to her, even if she had been less than pleased to learn that Aloysia had earlier told a visiting English couple, Vincent and Mary Novello, founders of the music-publishing firm, that she believed Mozart had continued to love her to the day of his death. She added that she greatly regretted rebuffing his proposal of marriage, which she blamed on their two fathers.

Her regret must surely have been compounded by the knowledge that her sister was now living comfortably on the proceeds of her husband's musical legacy, and that it was Constanze's name, rather than her own, that would forever be associated with the name of Mozart.

Constanze, for her part, was prepared to let bygones be bygones. Her youngest sister Sophie came to live with her after the death of her own husband. Here were the two women who were present at the moment of Mozart's death. What memories they shared.

Constanze outlived Aloysia by almost three years. She died at the age of eighty, fifty-one years after her husband. Sophie died four-and-a-half years after Constanze.

Neither of Mozart and Constanze's two surviving sons inherited their father's genius. The elder, Karl Thomas, attempted a career in music, but at the age of twenty-six gave it up to become a financial officer in the Austrian accounting department in Milan. He died in 1858 at the age of seventy-four.

Franz Xaver Wolfgang, who was less than five months old when his father died, inherited a degree of musical talent. He became an accomplished pianist, performing his father's works. He composed too, though not in great quantity or anything of notable quality. In fact he seems to have given up composing altogether in his early thirties, though he continued to make a career by performing.

Throughout his life Wolfgang admired the father he had never known. He died just three days after his fifty-third birthday. His tombstone bore the epitaph: 'May the name of his father be his epitaph, as his veneration for him was the essence of life.'

Neither son married or had children, and thus the Mozart line died out. There was not before, and has not been since, another Wolfgang Amadeus Mozart.

AFTERWORD

I can think of no other composer of whom we can say that we know practically everything there is to know about their life from letters. The simple reason? No other composer travelled as much as Mozart did.

In all, as man and boy, Mozart took seventeen journeys through Europe, a total of 3,720 days, amounting to ten years, two months and two days, which (excluding his years as baby and toddler) in turn equates to nearly one-third of his life.

From the first journey to the last, letters flew back and forth. On the earliest journeys, the letter writer was Leopold Mozart, with his son adding postscripts. Later, when he travelled on his own, he wrote home practically every week, sometimes more than once a week.

These later letters are far from hurriedly scribbled notes; often they are several pages long, going into the minutiae of his life. For the musicologist, these provide invaluable insight into Mozart's musical career – performances, commissions and, most importantly, his compositional process.

The same is true of his private life. We would know practically nothing about the grim process of his mother's death or the tortuous affair of acquiring a wife and the deterioration of his relationship with his father if he had not made time to sit down and write detailed letters to his father.

For that reason, the most important source material for the Mozart biographer is these letters. Sadly, though, they provide us with only one half of the conversation.

Leopold Mozart, recognising his son's extraordinary musical gifts early on, determined one day to write his biography. For that reason he preserved all the letters his son wrote to him. Similarly his wife was under instructions to keep all letters from the early journeys. The biography never materialised, but the letters survived.

The same cannot be said of Leopold's letters to his son. Mozart destroyed very nearly all of them, or at least that is the presumption. Given that these letters were most often from a difficult and obstructive father – particularly where marriage plans were concerned – it is more than likely that after reading them and responding to them, the last thing Mozart wanted to do was keep them.

But respond he did, often in a line-by-line rebuttal of his father's accusations. From these replies we can accurately discern what Leopold had written.

The first collected edition of the letters in English, *The Letters of Mozart and His Family*, was by Emily Anderson (Macmillan, 1966).[*] While her translations were welcomed by Mozart scholars, with deference to the sensibilities of the age she felt it necessary to sanitise much of Mozart's crude expressions and toilet humour.

This was fully rectified by Robert Spaethling, Bavarian-born Professor Emeritus of German at the University of Massachusetts, Boston. In 2000 he published an entirely new translation of Mozart's letters (in the US, W.W. Norton; in the UK, Faber and Faber).

A native German speaker, with a Bavarian dialect similar to that of Salzburg, he rendered Mozart's usage of slang, and his eccentric spelling, into a comparative form of English.

This volume, *Mozart's Letters, Mozart's Life*, instantly became the standard reference work for Mozart's letters. I acknowledge my debt to it. With very few exceptions, my direct quotations are from it, with an occasional anglicisation of American spelling and idiom.

Spaethling includes only letters written by Mozart himself. For quotations from Leopold's letters (those, at least, that have survived) I have used Emily Anderson's earlier edition. A more modern edition of letters from both father and son, as well as letters from other principal correspondents, with essential notes and biographical material, is *Wolfgang Amadeus Mozart, A Life in Letters*, edited by Cliff Eisen, translated by Stewart Spencer, Penguin Classics 2006.

Amid the welter of books on Mozart, one that I found particularly useful was *Mozart's Women* by Jane Glover. Professor Glover is currently Felix Mendelssohn Emeritus Professor of Music at the Royal Academy of Music in London, having been the Academy's Director of Opera for eight years. She is also Music Director of Chicago's Music of the Baroque.

Professor Glover is a renowned Mozart scholar, and has conducted his music with major orchestras and opera companies around the world. She published *Mozart's Women* in 2005 (Macmillan), taking a look at the composer's life from a novel angle. Meticulous in its research, and based on a

---

[*] She was also the first to publish a collected edition in English of Beethoven's letters (Macmillan, 1961).

lifetime of immersion in Mozart's life and music, it is also a thoroughly good read. It is particularly strong on the female characters in Mozart's operas.

Full-length biographies I consulted include *Mozart: A Life* by Maynard Solomon (HarperCollins, 1995), *Mozart, A Cultural Biography* by Robert W. Gutman (Secker and Warburg, 2000), and *Mozart, The Early Years 1756–1781* by Stanley Sadie (Oxford University Press, 2006).

The late American musicologist H. C. Robbins Landon published *1791, Mozart's Last Year* (Thames and Hudson, 1988), *Mozart, The Golden Years 1781–1791* (Thames and Hudson, 1989), *Mozart and Vienna* (Thames and Hudson, 1991). All were useful to me in the writing of this book.

An essential reference work is *The Cambridge Mozart Encyclopedia*, edited by Cliff Eisen and Simon P. Keefe (Cambridge University Press, 2006).

What is certain is that there will be a whole new raft of publications to mark the tercentenary of Mozart's birth in forty years' time. The world will be as keen to know about this musical genius as it is today, and has always been.

Who can tell what original documents might have come to light by then? Maybe some of Leopold's letters to his son will prove not to have been destroyed. Autograph manuscripts might be sitting in someone's loft as I write this.

There is always a danger that biographies like mine – like all the books I have listed above – will become outdated, or in certain aspects prove to be wrong. That, though, is not a reason for not writing them in the first place.

We can be grateful that we know as much about this great artist as we do, and can only hope that future generations might be able to know more about him than we know today.

⌐⌐

This book is dedicated to the Emmy Award winning television documentary maker James Black. James was a lifelong lover of Mozart's music. At the time that he became ill with dementia, he had completed a six-part television series on Mozart's life that was soon to be put into production. His illness, and death in 2014, prevented this. His widow Nula is in talks to revive the series.

Nula helped James for many years with his research on Mozart, just as my late wife Bonnie helped me for many years with my research on Beethoven. James and Bonnie, we are certain, would be elated to know that Nula and I are now married.

POSTSCRIPT

The city of Salzburg is today 'Mozart city'. Fly into Salzburg and you land at W. A. Mozart Airport. The city's university is the Universität Mozarteum Salzburg. The house where he was born and the apartment in which his family later lived are museums dedicated to his life. On any day of the year (including Christmas) they are full of visitors – tourists, school groups, Mozart enthusiasts. They claim to be two of the most visited museums in the world.

Souvenir shops bristle with Mozart memorabilia, from emblazoned T-shirts and mugs to boxes of Mozart chocolates in all shapes and sizes. The boxes, that is. The chocolates are always round, made of dark chocolate, marzipan and nougat, covered in gold or silver foil with a portrait of the composer, and universally known as *Mozartkugeln* (Mozart balls).

All of which would rather surprise Mozart, since he, like his father, loathed the city, and the city thoroughly disliked him.

Not everyone approves of the way the city has used Mozart's name to such overwhelming commercial effect. In 2007 Salzburg Council commissioned a local artist to create a temporary installation that could stand alongside the statue in the Mozartplatz.

Instead of making a separate work of art, he created an installation covering the much revered statue – top to bottom – in shopping trolleys to protest against the commercialisation of the city and its heritage. His work did not find favour with Salzburgers. Such was the outcry at the defamation of the city's famous son that the trolleys were removed six months prematurely.

There is not a night of the year when Mozart's music cannot be heard in the city of his birth, from the most exclusive setting of the annual Salzburg Festival to the humblest abode. The same is true in Vienna, where music students, dressed in Mozart wigs and his famous red jacket and breeches, hand out leaflets for the day's performances; though only one building bears witness to his ten-year residency in the city.

Ultimately, as the people of Salzburg, and indeed Vienna, will readily admit, Wolfgang Amadeus Mozart belongs to the world.

NOTES

1. *The Travel Diaries of Vincent and Mary Novello*, quoted in Glover, Jane, *Mozart's Women* (London: Macmillan, 2005)

2. Solomon, Maynard, *Mozart, A Life* (London: Hutchinson, 1995)

3. My extracts from Leopold Mozart's letters are from Anderson, Emily *The Letters of Mozart and His Family* (London: Macmillan, 1966)

4. Gutman, Robert W., *Mozart, A Cultural Biography* (New York: Harcourt, 1999)

5. ibid.

6. ibid.

7. Niemetschek, Franz, *Life of Mozart*, trans. Helen Mautner (London, 1956)

8. ibid.

9. Lever, Évelyne, *Marie Antoinette: The Last Queen of France,* trans. Catherine Temerson (London: Piatkus, 2001)

10. Sadie, Stanley, *Mozart: The Early Years 1756–1781* (Oxford: Oxford University Press, 2006)

11. Eisen, Cliff, *New Mozart Documents* (London: Macmillan, 1991)

12. *Nannerl Mozarts Tagebuchblätter*, ed. Geffray, Geneviève (ed.), with Angermüller, Rudolph, quoted in Sadie, *Mozart: The Early Years*

13. *The Leisure Hour* (London 1882), quoted in Sadie, *Mozart: The Early Years*

14. Diary of Father Beda Hübner, quoted in Sadie, *Mozart: The Early Years*

15. From Friedrich Melchior's *La Correspondance littéraire, philosophique et critique*, quoted in Glover, *Mozart's Women*

16. My extracts from Mozart's letters are taken from Robert Spaethling's *Mozart's Letters, Mozart's Life*, the first in which the translations attempt to reproduce in English Wolfgang's often ungrammatical and misspelt German. See Acknowledgements.

17. Solomon, Maynard, *Mozart: A Life* (London: Hutchinson, 1995)

18. Burney, Charles, *Music, Men and Manners in France and Italy, 1770*, ed. H. Edmund Poole (London, 1974)

19. Rousseau, Jean-Jacques, *The Confessions, Book 7*, trans. J. M. Cohen (London: Penguin, 1953)

20. Johann Adolf Hasse, quoted in Sadie, *Mozart: The Early Years*

21. Eisen, Cliff, *New Mozart Documents*

22. Riesbeck, Caspar, *Travels Through Germany in a Series of Letters* (London, 1787)

23. Reviews collected by Christian Daniel Schubart (1739–91), quoted in Gutman, *Mozart, A Cultural Biography*

24. My extracts from Anna Maria Mozart's letters are also from Anderson, *Letters of Mozart and his Family*

25. Solomon, *Mozart: A Life*; Wolfgang Hildesheimer, *Mozart*, trans. by M. Faber (Oxford: Oxford University Press, 1985); Gutman, *Mozart, A Cultural Biography*

26. Nissen, Georg Nikolaus von, *Biographie W. A. Mozart's* (1828), quoted in Sadie, *Mozart: The Early Years*

27. Gutman, *Mozart, A Cultural Biography*

28. *Nannerl Mozarts Tagebuchblätter,* quoted in Glover, *Mozart's Women*

29. Landon, H.C. Robbins, *Mozart and Vienna* (London: Thames and Hudson, 1991)

30. ibid.

31. Nissen, *Biographie W. A. Mozart's,* quoted in Glover, *Mozart's Women*

32. ibid.

33. *Nannerl Mozarts Tagebuchblätter,* quoted in Glover, *Mozart's Women*

34. Solomon, *Mozart: A Life*

35. *Memoirs of Lorenzo Da Ponte*, trans. Elisabeth Abbott, ed. Arthur Livingston (New York: Dover Publications, 1967)

36. ibid.

37. ibid.

38. ibid.

39. ibid.

40. Glover, *Mozart's Women*

41. *Memoirs of Lorenzo Da Ponte*

42. ibid.

43. Glover, *Mozart's Women*

44. Solomon, *Mozart: A Life*

45. ibid.

46. ibid.

47. Recounted in Otto Jahn: *W.A. Mozart,* 3rd ed. by H. Deiters, 1889-1891; Eng. trans. by P. D. Townsend, 1891

48. Nissen, *Biographie W. A. Mozart's*

49. Friedrich Schlichtgroll, *Mozarts Leben* (Götha, 1793), facsimile edition of the reprint (Graz 1794), ed. Joseph Heinz Eibl (Kassel: Bärenreiter, 1974)

50. Benyovszky, Karl, *J. N. Hummel: Der Mensch und Künstler* (1934), quoted in Solomon, *Mozart: A Life*

51. Nissen, *Biographie W. A. Mozart's*

52. ibid.

53. Jahn, Otto, *The Life of Mozart* (3 vols.), trans. Pauline D. Townsend (London: Novello, 1882)

54. Solomon, *Mozart, A Life*

55. Jahn, *The Life of Mozart*

56. Niemetschek, *Life of Mozart*, trans. by Mautner

57. ibid.

58. ibid.

59. Nissen, *Biographie W. A. Mozart's,* quoted in Glover, *Mozart's Women*

60. ibid.

61. ibid.

62. ibid.

63. ibid.

64. ibid.

65. Gärntner, Heinz, *Constanze Mozart: After the Requiem* trans. by R. G. Pauly (Milwaukee: Amadeus Press, 1986)

INDEX

Page numbers in *italic* refer to illustrations

ACKNOWLEDGEMENTS

I was asked to write this book by Sam Jackson, Managing Editor of Classic FM. When I pointed out to him that there were already very many biographies of Mozart in existence, he said he believed that a new account of the great composer's life, written in an accessible and readable style, would appeal to Classic FM's five and a half million listeners. I hope the result meets his expectations.

As with my Beethoven and Strauss biographies, it was a joy to work with Elliott & Thompson, Classic FM's publisher. Lorne Forsyth, Chairman, and his team have become friends. Olivia Bays, Director, was once again my editor. I was about halfway into the book, when the decision was made to bring publication forward by a whole year to meet the 225th anniversary of Mozart's death in December 2016. This made huge demands on all aspects of production and resulted in a period of intensive writing, with the manuscript being completed in a matter of weeks. I am thus more than ever grateful to Olivia, as well as Pippa Crane and Jill Burrows, for spotting many repetitions and inconsistencies, as well as highlighting passages that needed clarification or expansion. The book is immeasurably better for their careful work. Pippa also sourced the illustrations, while designer James Collins worked at great speed to prepare the book for publication, and cover designer Tash Weber created a beautiful jacket. My thanks to them, and to the entire team at Elliott & Thompson.

Picture Credits

Page x: kevinjeon00/
    iStock images
Page 3: Wolfgang Sauber
    via Wikimedia Commons
    (https://creativecommons.org/
    licenses/by-sa/4.0/legalcode)
Page 5: Everett – Art/
    Shutterstock.com
Page 9: Anibal Trejo/
    Shutterstock.com
Page 10: Andreas Stiasny
    via Wikimedia Commons
    (https://creativecommons.org/
    licenses/by-sa/3.0/legalcode)
Page 13: Getty Images
Page 21: North Wind Picture
    Archives/Alamy Stock Photo
Page 29: Imagno/Getty Images
Page 43: Liam White/
    Alamy Stock Photo
Page 52: The Art Archive/
    Alamy Stock Photo
Page 55: Chronicle/
    Alamy Stock Photo
Page 61: akg-images
Page 65: Heritage Image
    Partnership Ltd/
    Alamy Stock Photo
Page 72: akg-images
Page 87: DeAgostini/
    Getty Images
Page 91: Everett – Art/
    Shutterstock.com
Page 96: DeAgostini/
    Getty Images
Page 104: canadastock/

Shutterstock.com
Page 105: canadastock/
    Shutterstock.com
Page 105: QQ7/Shutterstock.com
Page 108: Imagno/Getty Images
Page 109: Imagno/Getty Images
Page 117: Richard Bartz
    via Wikimedia Commons
    (https://creativecommons.org/
    licenses/by-sa/2.5/legalcode)
Page 124: INTERFOTO/
    Alamy Stock Photo
Page 127: Authenticated News/
    Getty Images
Page 132: Hubert Berberich
    via Wikimedia Commons
    (https://creativecommons.org/
    licenses/by/3.0/legalcode)
Page 144: akg-images
Page 147: DeAgostini/
    Getty Images
Page 153: DeAgostini/
    Getty Images
Page 159: The Art Archive/
    Alamy Stock Photo
Page 167: Granger Historical
    Picture Archve/
    Alamy Stock Photo
Page 171: DeAgostini/
    Getty Images
Page 172: Vladimir Mucibabic/
    Shutterstock.com
Page 176: akg-images
Page 181: DeAgostini/
    Getty Images
Page 191: Imagno/Getty Images

Page 193: Heritage Image
    Partnership Ltd/
    Alamy Stock Photo
Page 201: DaveLongMedia/
    iStock images
Page 205: Johann Werfring
    via Wikimedia Commons
    (https://creativecommons.org/
    licenses/by-sa/3.0/legalcode)
Page 214: World History
    Archive/Alamy Stock Photo
Page 219: Rama
    via Wikimedia Commons
    (https://creativecommons.org/
    licenses/by-sa/2.0/fr/legalcode)
Page 223: INTERFOTO/
    Alamy Stock Photo
Page 226: The Art Archive/
    Alamy Stock Photo
Page 233: The Art Archive/
    Alamy Stock Photo
Page 246: Pictorial Press Ltd/
    Alamy Stock Photo
Page 251: Pictorial Press Ltd/
    Alamy Stock Photo
Page 252: Mary Evans Picture
    Library/Alamy Stock Photo
Page 254: Granger Historical
    Picture Archve/Alamy Stock
    Photo
Page 256 (right): René Steyer
    via Wikimedia Commons
    (https://creativecommons.org/
    licenses/by/3.0/legalcode)
Page 259: legna69/iStock images